ra Composers

nieres of first and last operas

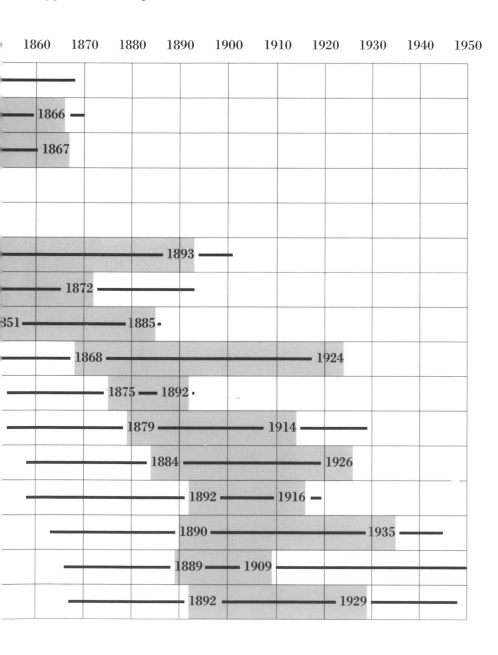

| | 1860 | 1870 | 1880 | 1890 | 1900 | 1910 | 1920 | 1930 | 1940 | 1950 |

Nineteenth-Century
ITALIAN
OPERA

Nineteenth-Century
ITALIAN OPERA

from
Rossini
to
Puccini

Danièle Pistone

---

translated by E. Thomas Glasow

AMADEUS PRESS
Reinhard G. Pauly, General Editor
Portland, Oregon

The original edition, *L'Opéra italien au XIXe siècle de Rossini à Puccini*, was published in France by Editions Champion, Paris, in 1986.

From the Translator

For their support and assistance in my efforts to update the bibliography and to create the discography of this English-language edition, I would like to thank the librarian staff of the department of music in the Buffalo and Erie County Public Library, including Judith Coon, Joyce Gianni, Helen Kahn, and—above all—music librarian Norma Jean Lamb. My thanks also extend to librarian Joyce Ciurczak and the convenient facilities of the music library, Baird Hall, of the State University of New York at Buffalo.

—E. Thomas Glasow

ISBN 0-931340-82-9

Printed in Singapore

AMADEUS PRESS
The Haseltine Building
133 S.W. Second Avenue, Suite 450
Portland, Oregon 97204, U.S.A.

Library of Congress Cataloging-in-Publication Data

Pistone, Danièle.
    [Opéra italien au XIXe siècle de Rossini à Puccini. English]
    Nineteenth-century Italian Opera from Rossini to Puccini /
by Danièle Pistone; translated by E. Thomas Glasow.
      p.   cm.
    Translated from French.
    Includes bibliographical references and index.
    ISBN 0-931340-82-9
    1. Opera—Italy—19th century. I. Title.
ML1733.P5813   1995
782.1'0945'09034—dc20   94-28692
                                   CIP
                                   MN

CONTENTS

ILLUSTRATIONS

TABLES

Leoncavallo, by Georges Villa, 1904.
In *Musica*, September 1904.

PREFACE

*A*s an extension of my research in the field of French music and after several years' university teaching,[1] which have renewed my acquaintance with the Italian language and culture, I attempt here to present the high points of Italian opera from Rossini to Puccini. I relied mainly on the study of the musical scores and correspondence of the composers and librettists themselves, as well as on contemporary press reports and publications concerned with the same subjects. In a studied effort to avoid duplication, I have omitted any information about composers or works that is readily available elsewhere.[2]

My access to necessary documents was greatly facilitated by a number of librarians and archivists, especially those of the library of the Accademia di Santa Cecilia, the Biblioteca Alessandrina, the Biblioteca Casanatense, the Biblioteca Teatrale Buccardo, and the Istituto d'Archeologia e Storia dell'Arte in Rome; the Biblioteca Braidense, the Giuseppe Verdi Conservatory, and the Museo Teatrale alla Scala in Milan; the Biblioteche Nazionali in Florence and Rome; the Biblioteca Beriana in Genoa; the Istituto di Studi Verdiani in Parma; and local libraries in Forlì, Pescia, and Reggio Emilia. Various musical pilgrimages were made as well to sites in

Bergamo, Busseto, Catania, Pesaro, and Torre del Lago and, in Paris, to the Bibliothèque Nationale and the library of Radio France. I would like to take this opportunity to express my sincere thanks to all those who allowed me the benefit of their assistance and advice.

INTRODUCTION

Since the Renaissance, the land of Michelangelo has been not only one of the principal European vanguards of the fine arts but a required setting for any cultural education. The *dramma in musica* sprang from this rich environment at the dawn of the seventeenth century, in Florence, rapidly attracting the attention of the most far-flung composers and conquering many major cities within the space of a hundred years. At the start of the Napoleonic era, on the heels of the triumphs of Pergolesi, Piccinni, and Cimarosa, Italian music still exerted the same influence: many Italian composers had established themselves abroad, and French musicians traveled to the Villa Medici to further their studies.[1]

In a country where religious music had begun to go into a genuine slump, where keyboard music could not seem to capture the public's attention, where only the rare instrumental soloist rose to international renown after the death of the diabolical Paganini, and where nothing really new appeared in the symphonic repertoire until the age of Sgambati and Martucci,[2] the nineteenth century, unlike previous decades, would see a growth in the popularity of opera in Italy almost to the exclusion of all other forms of theater.

Between 1810 and the 1920s, from Rossini's first opera to

Principal states of Italy in 1815

1. Kingdom of Piedmont-Sardinia
2. Kingdom of Lombardy-Venetia (Hapsburg)
3. Grand Duchy of Tuscany
4. Papal States
5. Kingdom of the Two Sicilies (Bourbon)

Puccini's last, Italy underwent a number of changes. Certainly the most important one occurred in 1861, on the political front, in those regions that—after the Bourbon-Hapsburg occupation in the first part of the century and the slow emergence of libertarian ideas—finally achieved their unification through the creation of the kingdom of Italy. From an artistic standpoint, neoclassicism was strongest among painters influenced by the Venetian Francesco Hayez (1791–1882), romanticism became more turbulent with Tranquillo Cremona (1837–1878), and realism starker with Lorenzo Delleani (1840–1908). Impressionists like Giovanni Segantini and Menardo Rosso were established by the end of the century, before the emergence of the Macchiaioli (Tachistes), among them Raffaello Sernesi, or the exponents of the turn-of-the-century floral style. They were succeeded by the futurists (1910) and, after the First World War, by the disciples of metaphysical painters like Giorgio de Chirico.

Stylistic developments made no less of an impact on Italian literature, from the time of Ugo Foscolo (1778–1827) to that of Giovanni Papini (1881–1956). First came the romantic age of

Facsimile of an autograph quote from *La bohème*,
Act III. In *Annuario dell'arte lirica e coreografica italiana*
(Milan: De Marchi, 1897–98), 9.

Manzoni, followed by the iconoclastic writings of the Scapigliatura, the Milanese bohemian circle that counted Arrigo Boito and Emilio Praga among its adherents. Next, the cruder style of veristic authors like Luigi Capuana and Giovanni Verga gave way to the heroic-hedonistic poetry of Gabriele D'Annunzio.

Over the course of the century, ideas of liberty and individualism prompted an acceleration of aesthetic change. Opera too underwent significant transformations, which often paralleled those of other art forms. From the period of *farsa* or *opera buffa* to that of verismo, length and form evolved considerably, as did the nature of the plots, vocal textures, and orchestral scoring. Great passion-filled dramatic works were inspired by the spirit of the Risorgimento, and the gradual rise in the popularity of operetta won acclaim for both Mascagni and Leoncavallo.

The most important of these creations, brought together in the following historical survey, are the very symbol of the evolution that shall be traced through the librettos, the music, and contemporary performance conditions.

Donizetti (1797–1848).
In *Musica*, April 1905.

Table 1. Chronology of major Italian operas. Dates are those of first performances. Composers' names and titles are followed by the name of the librettist(s) and the city of the premiere. Translations of Italian titles are given in the Index of Operas.

1810	Rossini	*La cambiale di matrimonio* (G. Rossi), Venice
1813	Rossini	*Tancredi* (G. Rossi), Venice
	Rossini	*L'italiana in Algeri* (A. Anelli), Venice
1816	Rossini	*Il barbiere di Siviglia* (C. Sterbini), Rome
	Rossini	*Otello* (F. Berio di Salsa), Naples
1817	Rossini	*La gazza ladra* (G. Gherardini), Milan
1818	Rossini	*Mosè in Egitto* (A. L. Tottola), Naples
1819	Rossini	*La donna del lago* (A. L. Tottola), Naples
1823	Rossini	*Semiramide* (G. Rossi), Venice
1827	Bellini	*Il pirata* (F. Romani), Milan
1829	Rossini	*Guillaume Tell* (de Jouy, Bis, Marrast), Paris
1830	Donizetti	*Anna Bolena* (F. Romani), Milan
1831	Bellini	*La sonnambula* (F. Romani), Milan
	Bellini	*Norma* (F. Romani), Milan
1832	Donizetti	*L'elisir d'amore* (F. Romani), Milan
1835	Bellini	*I puritani* (C. Pepoli), Paris
	Donizetti	*Lucia di Lammermoor* (S. Cammarano), Naples
1837	Mercadante	*Il giuramento* (G. Rossi), Milan
1839	Mercadante	*Il bravo* (G. Rossi), Milan
	Verdi	*Oberto* (T. Solera), Milan
1840	Donizetti	*La fille du régiment* (de Saint-Georges, Bayard), Paris
	Verdi	*Un giorno di regno* (F. Romani), Milan
	Pacini	*Saffo* (S. Cammarano), Naples
	Donizetti	*La favorite* (Royer, Vaëz), Paris
1842	Verdi	*Nabucco* (T. Solera), Milan
1843	Donizetti	*Don Pasquale* (G. Ruffini), Paris
	Verdi	*I lombardi alla prima crociata* (T. Solera), Milan
1844	Verdi	*Ernani* (F. M. Piave), Venice
	Verdi	*I due Foscari* (F. M. Piave), Rome
1845	Verdi	*Giovanna d'Arco* (T. Solera), Milan
	Verdi	*Alzira* (S. Cammarano), Naples

(continued)

1846	Verdi	*Attila* (T. Solera), Venice
1847	Verdi	*Macbeth* (F. M. Piave), Florence
	Verdi	*I masnadieri* (A. Maffei), London
1848	Verdi	*Il corsaro* (F. M. Piave), Trieste
	Donizetti	*Poliuto* (S. Cammarano), Naples
1849	Verdi	*La battaglia di Legnano* (S. Cammarano), Rome
	Verdi	*Luisa Miller* (S. Cammarano), Naples
1851	Verdi	*Rigoletto* (F. M. Piave), Venice
1853	Verdi	*Il trovatore* (S. Cammarano), Rome
	Verdi	*La traviata* (F. M. Piave), Venice
1855	Verdi	*Les vêpres siciliennes* (Scribe, Duveyrier), Paris
1856	Pedrotti	*Tutti in maschera* (M. Marcello), Verona
1857	Verdi	*Simon Boccanegra* (1st version, F. M. Piave), Venice
1857	Verdi	*Aroldo* (F. M. Piave), Rimini
1859	Verdi	*Un ballo in maschera* (A. Somma), Rome
1862	Verdi	*La forza del destino* (F. M. Piave), St. Petersburg
1867	Verdi	*Don Carlos* (Méry, du Locle), Paris
1868	Boito	*Mefistofele* (A. Boito), Milan
1871	Verdi	*Aida* (A. Ghislanzoni), Cairo
1876	Ponchielli	*La Gioconda* (A. Boito), Milan
1881	Verdi	*Simon Boccanegra* (with revisions by A. Boito), Milan
1884	Puccini	*Le villi* (F. Fontana), Milan
1887	Verdi	*Otello* (A. Boito), Milan
1889	Puccini	*Edgar* (F. Fontana), Milan
1890	Mascagni	*Cavalleria rusticana* (Menasci, Targioni-Tozzetti), Rome
1891	Mascagni	*L'amico Fritz* (P. Suardon), Rome
1892	Catalani	*La Wally* (L. Illica), Milan
	Leoncavallo	*I pagliacci* (R. Leoncavallo), Milan
1893	Puccini	*Manon Lescaut* (R. Leoncavallo, L. Illica, G. Giacosa), Turin
	Verdi	*Falstaff* (A. Boito), Milan
1895	Smareglia	*Nozze istriane* (L. Illica), Trieste
1896	Puccini	*La bohème* (Illica, Giacosa), Turin
	Giordano	*Andrea Chénier* (L. Illica), Milan
1897	Leoncavallo	*La bohème* (R. Leoncavallo), Venice
	Cilèa	*L'arlesiana* (L. Marenco), Milan

1898	Mascagni	*Iris* (L. Illica), Rome
1900	Puccini	*Tosca* (Illica, Giacosa), Rome
	Leoncavallo	*Zazà* (R. Leoncavallo), Milan
1902	Cilèa	*Adriana Lecouvreur* (A. Colautti), Milan
1903	Giordano	*Siberia* (L. Illica), Milan
1904	Puccini	*Madama Butterfly* (Illica, Giacosa), Milan
	Alfano	*Risurrezione* (C. Hanau), Turin
1906	Wolf-Ferrari	*I quattro rusteghi* (L. Sugana), Munich
1910	Puccini	*La fanciulla del West* (G. Civinini, C. Zangarini), New York
1911	Mascagni	*Isabeau* (L. Illica), Buenos Aires
1913	Montemezzi	*L'amore dei tre re* (S. Benelli), Milan
1914	Zandonai	*Francesca da Rimini* (T. Ricordi), Turin
1917	Puccini	*La rondine* (G. Adami), Monte Carlo
1918	Puccini	*Il trittico*: *Il tabarro* (G. Adami), *Suor Angelica* (G. Forzano), *Gianni Schicchi* (G. Forzano), New York
1926	Puccini	*Turandot* (G. Adami, R. Simoni), Milan

PART I: *The Librettos*

Throughout the 1800s, choosing a libretto remained the primary concern of the opera composer, though the literary text played a much less important role in Italy than it did in France. Salieri's work entitled Prima la musica, poi le parole *(First the Music, Then the Words), first produced in Vienna in 1786, is representative of the Italian approach during this period.*

CHAPTER 1

GENERAL CHARACTERISTICS

*I*n 1804, Giovanni Carpani lamented the continuing deplorable state of Italian librettos[1] and, five years later, the kingdom of Italy's department of public instruction inaugurated a libretto competition which far from achieved its intended purpose.[2] By the end of the century, however, Mascagni's contemporaries displayed much more interest in writing librettos.[3] Still later, the debate, as presented onstage in Richard Strauss's 1942 *Capriccio* (libretto by Clemens Krauss) and elsewhere, is highly indicative of the eternal conflict between words and music.[4]

Librettists

In nineteenth-century Italy, composers rarely wrote their own librettos. Albert Lortzing (*Zar und Zimmermann*, *Der Wildschütz*) and Richard Wagner especially figured as celebrated Germanic examples of composer-librettists, and Hector Berlioz did write his own texts for *Béatrice et Bénédict* (1862) and *Les Troyens* (1863), but south of the Alps the practice remained unusual for the time.

Even so, Gaetano Donizetti authored the librettos of two of his seventy-odd operas (*Il campanello di notte* and *Betly*), and there is the comparative mediocrity of Andrea Leone Tottola or Cesare

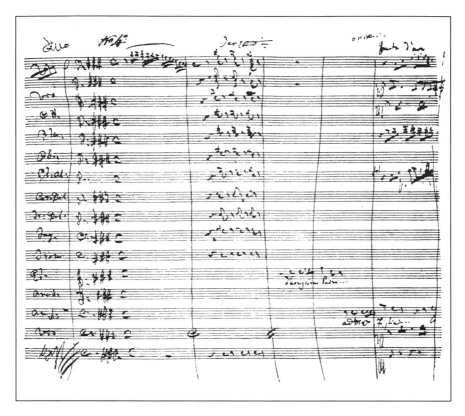

Facsimile of a page from the autograph manuscript of
Donizetti's *Il vedovo solitario* (1832). In *Annuario dell'arte lirica
e coreografica italiana* (Milan: De Marchi, 1897–98), 105.

Sterbini and the genuine merit of Felice Romani or Antonio Ghislanzoni to consider. It was not until the end of the century, however, that two composers made extraordinary marks as literary tal-
ents. Above all, there was Arrigo Boito, who wrote the text of his
Mefistofele (1868) before becoming Ponchielli's librettist for *La
Gioconda* (1876) and the brilliant inspirer of Verdi (second version
of *Simon Boccanegra*, 1881; *Otello*, 1884; *Falstaff*, 1893). Less known
but still remarkable was the talent of Ruggero Leoncavallo, who
had studied under Giosuè Carducci at the University of Bologna

and had himself written the librettos for his first operas (*I pagliacci*, *I Medici*, *Chatterton*), before collaborating on the text of *Manon Lescaut* for Puccini.[5]

Many composers nevertheless began to work more closely with their librettists, in the manner of Mozart. Thus Verdi managed to get more from Temistocle Solera—whom he tyrannized almost as much as Francesco Maria Piave—than did Donizetti before him.[6] As for Puccini, he worked quite actively with Luigi Illica and Giuseppe Giacosa; in the libretto of *Tosca*, many felicitous touches in fact came from the composer.

The working environments and concerns of the most celebrated librettists of the period differed widely indeed: Romani was active in Milan, Gaetano Rossi and Piave in Venice, Tottola and Salvatore Cammarano in Naples; and there is very little in common between Romani's classical, aristocratic talent and the themes of adventure, patriotism, and conspiracy that characterize the genius of Solera.

At the beginning of the nineteenth century, most of these writers devoted the greater part of their time to authoring librettos, as the numbers testify: Tottola produced one hundred, Rossi more than 130, Romani and Cammarano around fifty each, Piave approximately sixty, and for Ghislanzoni some eighty-five. In the last decades of the century, with the exceptions of Illica and Giacosa, writers no longer turned out as many texts, as verismo composers began to call for poetic-dramatic inspiration from friends not yet well established. Thus, Mascagni relied on his compatriot Giovanni Targioni-Tozzetti for *Cavalleria rusticana*.

Another evolutionary sign of the times was the gradually vanishing custom of resetting traditional texts. Certain Metastasian librettos had been used as often as seventy times, and some of Rossi's were also set by several different composers. Later on, if an old theme was reused (*Ernani*, *Otello*, *Nerone*), the composer normally demanded a new text, originality now prerequisite in that area as well.

Though not very many librettos were the result of a collaborative effort, there were nevertheless certain creative teams who worked in a manner similar to that of France's Meilhac and Halévy:

one planned the general outline and division into acts, the other wrote the verses. Giacosa and Illica, the librettists of several Puccini operas, are an example of one such successful pairing.

Genres

The classical era made clear distinctions between genres from the moment the parody known as *opera buffa* was born. While Pacini's first eleven operas belonged to that style, comic creations multiplied after Rossini injected new life into the genre. For proof, one need only look at the words of the irresistible "Pappatacci" trio ("eat and be quiet") in *L'italiana in Algeri*. Donizetti also set to music a large number of comic librettos which abound in funny situations, such as the one in *Il campanello di notte* in which the young rejected suitor disturbs the apothecary and his wife during their wedding night by means of various disguises and excuses— and unexpected parodies.

While a few theaters like Teatro Fondo in Naples, Teatro Valle in Rome, and the San Benedetto in Venice originally specialized in the comic repertoire, that tendency waned by mid-century. *Crispino e la comare* (1850) by brothers Luigi and Federico Ricci, *Le precauzioni* (1851) with music by Errico Petrella, and *Tutti in maschera* (1856) by Carlo Pedrotti were among the last successful examples of the *buffa* genre, for the romantic movement had brought with it a resurgence of the *opera seria*. In all Verdi's operatic canon, there are only two comic works: his second (*Un giorno di regno*) and his last (*Falstaff*). By the last decades of the nineteenth century, genres were somewhat mixed as evidenced by the character of Fra Melitone, the gruff friar in *La forza del destino*, or the farce enacted by Tonio ("My love is as hot as an oven") just prior to the tragic ending caused by the same jealous character in Leoncavallo's *Pagliacci*.

Toward the end of the century, the new operetta genre based on Parisian and Viennese molds gained a foothold as well. According to the *Gazzetta musicale di Milano* of 1 January 1893, thirty-seven of the eighty-one works that premiered in 1892 were operettas, including one *operetta mitologica* and one *operetta parodia*. Titles listed include *Cavalleria Rustico-Toscana* and *L'amico Fritto* (music by E. Ranfagni), which opened in Florence, and *Cavalleria de tarell* (in Milanese dialect, music by G. Grossi), which premiered in Buenos Aires. While librettists' names are only rarely indicated, those of composers (F. Contursi, M. Forte, C. Lombardo, L. Mantegna, L. Pierangeli, G. Scognamiglio, to name only a few) seem quite forgotten today.

The remaining breakdown of the premieres of 1892 as quoted in the same issue of the *Gazzetta musicale di Milano* is as follows: *opera seria*, twenty-seven, including *La Wally* (libretto by L. Illica, music by A. Catalani, Milan premiere), *La Tilda* (libretto by A. Graziani, music by F. Cilèa, Florence premiere), *Cristoforo Colombo* (libretto by L. Illica, music by A. Franchetti, Genoa premiere), *La mala vita* (libretto by N. Daspuro, music by U. Giordano, Rome premiere), and *I pagliacci* (libretto and music by R. Leoncavallo, Milan premiere); *scherzo*, four, (two *comici*, one *lirico*, one *musicale*); *comico*, three, *Ericleto* (by L. Bello, Caltanissetta premiere), *Oro ed amore* (by G. Falorni, Pontedera premiere), and *Le mariage galant* (by E. Missa and G. Pietrapertosa, Paris premiere); *bozzetto*, also three, including one *medioevale* and one *marinaresco*; and one each of *buffo* and *vaudeville*. The remaining five are classified as either miscellaneous (*idillio mitologico*, *leggenda indiana*, and *poema vocale e sinfonico*) or genre unspecified.

Mascagni conducted many operettas before making his mark as a composer; nor were Leoncavallo (*La jeunesse de Figaro*, 1908, and *Malbruk*, 1910) or Giordano (*Giove a Pompei*, 1921) averse to dabbling in this new genre late in their careers.

Serious opera, to which the most beautiful masterpieces of this repertoire unquestionably belong, went by a number of different labels, in Italy and elsewhere: thus *Manon Lescaut* was termed a *dramma lirico*, *Tosca* a *melodramma*, and *Adriana Lecouvreur* a *commedia-dramma*. As the *opera seria* gradually became extinct, it would appear that the genre was seeking new inspiration.

Sources of Subject Matter

Opera librettos of the time were generally based on preexisting dramas, and it is interesting to see where librettists most frequently turned for their subject matter. Tasso, Ariosto, and other classical models reigned supreme until the beginning of the nineteenth century. However, in the time of Rossini, that tendency began to change. From then on librettists tended to turn to French authors, as the figures in Table 2 indicate.

Table 2. Literary sources of librettos. Survey based on a total of 157 works: 37 by Rossini, 72 by Donizetti, 10 by Bellini, 26 by Verdi, and 12 by Puccini.

	Rossini	Donizetti	Bellini	Verdi	Puccini	Total
English	3	4	2	5	2	16
French	12	36	4	6	5	63
Germanic	1	3	0	5	2	11
Italian	6	5	1	1	2	15
Other/uncertain	15	24	3	9	1	52

Victor Hugo inspired Verdi's *Ernani* and *Rigoletto* (the latter taken from his *Le roi s'amuse*), Donizetti's *Lucrezia Borgia*, and Ponchielli's *Gioconda*, based—like Mercadante's *Giuramento*—on his *Angelo, tyran de Padoue*. Other popular French authors include Alphonse Daudet (Cilèa's *Arlesiana*); Alexandre Dumas *fils* (*La traviata*, based on *La dame aux camélias*); Erckmann-Chatrian (Mascagni's *L'amico Fritz* and *I Rantzau*); Henri Murger (*La bohème* of both Puccini and Leoncavallo); Alfred de Musset (Puccini's *Edgar* comes from *La coupe et les lèvres*); Charles Perrault (Rossini's *Cenerentola*); the Abbé Prévost (Puccini's *Manon Lescaut*); Victorien Sardou (Puccini's *Tosca* and Giordano's *Fedora*); and Alexandre Soumet (Bellini's *Norma*). Among French dramatists, Italian librettists found inspiration in Corneille (Donizetti's *Poliuto*); Racine (Rossini's *Ermione*, based on *Andromaque*); and Voltaire (Rossini's *Tancredi* and *Semiramide*, Bellini's *Zaira*, and Verdi's *Alzira*).

The influence from north of the English Channel seems to have been the result of the Anglomania that appeared in the fine arts in the eighteenth century and continued well into the nineteenth. The authors who inspired librettists most often were Lord Byron (Donizetti's *Parisina* and *Marino Faliero* and Verdi's *Due Foscari*); Sir Walter Scott (Rossini's *Donna del lago*, Bellini's *Puri-*

tani, and Donizetti's *Elisabetta, o il castello di Kenilworth* and *Lucia di Lammermoor*);[7] and William Shakespeare, with *Otello*—first set to music by Rossini, then by Verdi—Bellini's *Capuleti e i Montecchi*, and even *Macbeth* and *Falstaff* by Verdi, to name only the most celebrated borrowings.

Interest in Germanic sources of inspiration increased as the years went by. Between the time of Rossini's last opera (the Schiller-based *Guillaume Tell*) and Puccini's scores (*Le villi*, after Heine, and *La rondine*, after Willner and Reichert), the works of Verdi most clearly manifest the power of these texts: *Attila* (after Werner) and *Giovanna d'Arco*, *I masnadieri*, *Luisa Miller*, and *Don Carlo* (after Schiller). Other examples include Catalani's *Wally* (drawn from W. von Hillern), Mascagni's *Guglielmo Ratcliff* (from Heine), and Boito's *Mefistofele*, modeled on Goethe's *Faust*.

Compared to other traditional sources of inspiration, Spanish literature was minimally represented, except as the basis for Verdi's *Trovatore*, *Forza del destino*, and *Simon Boccanegra*. Though Italian authors, particularly Tasso (the springboard for Rossini's *Armida*), were often enlisted before 1800 or at the start of the nineteenth century (*Mosè in Egitto*), they dropped out of favor for a time before becoming more prevalent in the verismo era, thanks to Verga. Even so, Puccini's librettists still turned to Dante (*Gianni Schicchi*) and Gozzi (*Turandot*) for two Italian-inspired texts.

Once a textual source was chosen, the question of adaptation was far from simple. For one thing, the libretto had to be shorter than the original novel or play. The necessary compression was often achieved through a reduction in the number of characters, sometimes causing rather considerable changes in identity or personality. Thus, in *Falstaff*, Boito eliminated four Shakespearean figures: the Welsh parson Hugh Evans, his cousin Slender, Mr. Page, and his son William; Anne Page becomes Nannetta Ford in the libretto, shifting the focus of the action onto Alice's family. Another spectacular example of character reduction: of the twenty-four characters in Werner's *Attila*, only six appear in Verdi's opera of the same name. Moreover, librettists tried to highlight the key moments of a work and did not hesitate to eliminate drawn-out episodes (*La Gioconda*), or even to create brand-new scenes (the one that opens *Ernani* was Piave's own invention) or a different ending (*Lucrezia Borgia*). Arias were interpolated into all the plots as well in order to give singers a chance to display their voices, such as the Duke's "Parmi veder le lagrime" following Gilda's abduction in *Rigoletto*.[8]

Many liberties were taken by telescoping the plot or the traditional story. In *Mosè*, for example, the Ten Commandments are revealed to the prophet while he is still in Egypt. In this respect, Italian librettos hardly differ from those of Eugène Scribe.

Settings

In operatic settings, choices of time and place as well as the number of act divisions evolved in rather clear-cut trends. After the age of mythological or pastoral themes associated with the birth of opera, the vogue for historical subjects survived into the nineteenth century. Historical antiquity—introduced into the operatic repertoire at the time of Monteverdi (*L'incoronazione di Poppea*)—dropped out of favor in the eighteenth century (in spite of Handel's *Giulio Cesare* or Vivaldi's *Incoronazione di Dario*) and came back into fashion after Spontini's *Fernand Cortez* (Paris, 1809).

It is no surprise that Antiquity and the Middle Ages often served as backdrop for librettos in the romantic era, as in *Aida*, *Nabucco* (586 B.C.), *Norma* (50 B.C.), *Attila* (fifth century), *Poliuto* (857), *Macbeth* (1041), *I lombardi alla prima crociata* (1099), *Aroldo* (thirteenth century), *I vespri siciliani* (1282), and *La favorita*, *Simon Boccanegra*, and *Falstaff*, all in the fourteenth century.

The fifteenth and sixteenth centuries were the historical settings of *Beatrice di Tenda*, *I due Foscari*, *Otello*, *Il trovatore*, *Don Carlo*, *Ernani*, *Rigoletto*, *Roberto Devereux*, *Alzira*, and *Lucrezia Borgia*. The seventeenth century, on the other hand, was less frequently used (*La Gioconda*, *Iris*, *I puritani*).

In Italy and abroad, the more recent past was generally reserved for comic works, becoming more prevalent in serious opera only as the century drew to a close. *Lucia di Lammermoor*, *Un giorno di regno*, *La forza del destino*, *Un ballo in maschera*, *Manon Lescaut*, and *Andrea Chénier* all take place in the eighteenth century, while the following decades provide the setting for *La traviata*, *Cavalleria rusticana*, *I pagliacci*, *L'amico Fritz*, *La bohème*, and *Tosca*.

As shall be seen in Chapter 3, the constraints of censorship sometimes forced librettists to modify their choice of locale and time period.

Though nineteenth-century operas seldom drew on Italy's literary heritage, Italy itself nevertheless figured as the setting for many works. The popularity of Italy's most celebrated historical events (*Attila*, *La battaglia di Legnano*, *I vespri siciliani*) or the fame of several colorful personages (*I due Foscari*, *Lucrezia Borgia*, *Simon Boccanegra*) help explain this, as do the vivid Mediterranean colors of the verismo era: *Cavalleria rusticana* takes place in Sicily and *I pagliacci* in Calabria.

The popularity of Gallic subjects naturally resulted in French settings, second only to Italy in frequency of occurrence: *Gianni di Parigi* and *Maria di Rohan* by Donizetti, *La traviata*, *Andrea Chénier*, *La bohème*, and *Manon Lescaut*. It was perhaps their insatiable thirst for raw passion that transported audiences more than once to Spain (*La favorita*, *Ernani*, *Il trovatore*, *La forza del destino*, *Don Carlo*), while the British Isles remained a less popular setting[9] (*Anna Bolena*, *Lucia di Lammermoor*, *Roberto Devereux*, *Maria Stuarda*, *I puritani*, *Aroldo*, *Macbeth*, *Falstaff*). Germany (*Luisa Miller*, *Mefistofele*) and Switzerland (*La sonnambula*, *La fille du régiment*) were even less frequently used.

Occasionally more exotic locales were chosen, like Peru (*Alzira*), Japan (*Madama Butterfly*), and even Sweden, in the original conception of *Un ballo in maschera*. For this last, Verdi was subsequently forced to move the plot to Boston in order to avoid the unpleasant associations that might be stirred up by the assassination of Gustavo. Russia scarcely appears until the turn of the century, in Giordano's *Siberia* and *Fedora*.

The number of acts often faithfully adhered to the traditional Metastasian division into three. No less than twenty major nineteenth-century Italian operas are in three acts: Cilèa's *L'arlesiana*, Puccini's *Tosca*, Mascagni's *L'amico Fritz* and *Iris*, Rossini's *Otello* and *Mosè in Egitto*, Bellini's *I puritani*, Donizetti's *Lucia di Lammermoor*, *Don Pasquale*, *Poliuto*, and *Linda di Chamounix*, and Verdi's *I due Foscari*, *Attila* (with a prologue), *La battaglia di Legnano*, *Stiffelio*, *Rigoletto*, *La traviata*, *Simon Boccanegra* (also with a prologue), *Un ballo in maschera*, and *Falstaff*.

But there were departures. Of the major Italian operas of the nineteenth century, four are in one act: Donizetti's *Il campanello di notte* and *Rita*, Puccini's *Le villi*, and Mascagni's *Cavalleria rusticana*. Thirteen are in two acts: Rossini's *L'italiana in Algeri*, *Il barbiere di Siviglia*, and *La gazza ladra*, Bellini's *La sonnambula*, *Beatrice di Tenda*, and *Norma*, Donizetti's *L'elisir d'amore*, *La fille du régiment*, and *Lucrezia Borgia* (with a prologue), Verdi's *Un giorno di regno*, *Oberto*, and *Alzira*, and Leoncavallo's *I pagliacci*.

Twenty-one major operas are in four acts: Rossini's *Guillaume Tell*, Donizetti's *La favorita*, Boito's *Mefistofele* (with a prologue), Ponchielli's *La Gioconda*, Puccini's *Manon Lescaut* and *La bohème*, Giordano's *Andrea Chénier*, Leoncavallo's *Zazà*, and Verdi's *Nabucco*, *I lombardi alla prima crociata*, *Ernani*, *Giovanna d'Arco* (with a prologue), *Macbeth*, *I masnadieri*, *Il corsaro*, *Luisa Miller*, *Il trovatore*, *Aroldo*, *La forza del destino*, *Aida*, and *Otello*.

Perhaps influenced by the vast proportions of French grand opera, Verdi wrote more operas in four acts than any other composer, and, indeed, such an act division appears more often than any other in his body of work. The number five, on the other hand, was chosen by Verdi alone and only in works destined for the Paris Opéra (*Les vêpres siciliennes*, *Don Carlos*), conforming to the Meyerbeerian tradition of the "Grande Boutique," a tradition in which he felt scarcely at ease.[10]

Wagnerian dimensions did not seem to catch on in Italy, though a number of works of unusual length were created there, such as Mascagni's *Parisina* and *I Medici* by Leoncavallo, who intended his work as part of a trilogy to the glory of the Italian peninsula.

The least number of acts tend to be found in the *farsa* or the *opera buffa* (*L'elisir d'amore*, *Il campanello di notte*, *Un giorno di regno*, *Rita*) or in turn-of-the-century verismo works whose brevity may be due in part to the exigencies of the competitions for which they were written (*Cavalleria rusticana*, *I pagliacci*).[11]

Characters

The number of singing roles varied greatly in the nineteenth-century Italian repertoire. Like the number of acts, it was generally very modest in comic works (five characters in *Don Pasquale*, six in

L'elisir d'amore and *La sonnambula*) or in the shorter verismo works (four in *Iris*, five in *Cavalleria rusticana* and *L'amico Fritz*, six in *I pagliacci*). The average number fell between seven and nine during the period in question (*L'italiana in Algeri, Il barbiere di Siviglia, La fille du régiment, Lucia di Lammermoor, Nabucco, Il trovatore, Mefistofele, Aida*), while Metastasian librettos as a rule contained five or six. The number tended to increase, however, in certain great works of the second half of the century: ten in *La traviata, Un ballo in maschera, Andrea Chénier, Falstaff,* and *Tosca*; eleven in *La forza del destino* and *I vespri siciliani*; twelve in *Don Carlo* and *Manon Lescaut*; thirteen in *Rigoletto*.

In the early decades, the inclusion of royal attendants or family members of the nobility added greatly to the number of characters in serious works. The majesty of throned sovereigns still had an impact on mid-century operas: in *Nabucco* (Acts II and IV) and *I lombardi alla prima crociata* (Act II). Individuals of more humble stock were typically found in *opera buffa* or *opéra comique*, until verismo tendencies made them more ubiquitous: the Sicilian peasants of *Cavalleria rusticana*, the itinerant actors of *I pagliacci*, or even the dregs of Neapolitan society depicted in Giordano's *Mala vita*. In this respect, Italian librettos closely paralleled developments in contemporary literary styles which led from classicist, aristocratic texts to the realistic prose of Verga, at about the same time the naturalistic style of Zola or Becque was appearing in France.

Traditionally, characterization was never very deeply developed in this repertoire, though *Macbeth* (1847) represented a marked advance from the psychological point of view. Concern for propriety banished one character type until the last quarter of the century. One need only compare Rossini's setting of *Otello* with that of Verdi's to see the difference between their respective portraits of Iago. Evil, ruthless personages like Barnaba in *La Gioconda*,[12] Tonio in *I pagliacci*, and Scarpia in *Tosca* were almost inconceivable before the 1870s, even though the figures of Marcovaldo (*I lombardi alla prima crociata*) and Wurm (*Luisa Miller*) had already registered new lows in audience sympathy.

Such villains were far removed from the dignity of Norma's rival or from the heroic love of Cunizza who, in *Oberto*, wants to give Riccardo back to Leonora. Much later, the magnanimity of Zazà—who without a word sees Milio go back to the family she tries hard not to hurt—might seem an exception in a period that promoted all species of emotional excess.

As for the women, were they really always the victims of these tragedies?[13] Some are indeed frivolous, such as Lola in *Cavalleria rusticana*, Musetta in *La bohème*, Giorgetta in *Il tabarro*, and that fine example of feminine insouciance, *Zazà*'s Floriane, who sings at the Alcazar of Saint-Etienne:

> I know that I am scatterbrained;
> Like the bee I love to flutter.
> I am neither timid nor sweet
> And I live only to sing.

There are also many frail creatures who are either overwhelmed by illness (Violetta, Mimi, Manon), victimized by injustice (poor Santuzza in *Cavalleria rusticana*), or who die unjustly, as do Desdemona (*Otello*), Gilda (*Rigoletto*), Laura (*La Gioconda*), and Liù (*Turandot*). Rarely is a woman's death avenged, as in *Le villi*, whose legend is Germanic in origin.

Nevertheless, Italian operas also contain some strong-willed, formidable women: Odabella, who kills Attila, Gulnara, whom Pasha Seid does not escape (*Il corsaro*), Floria Tosca, who stabs the evil Scarpia to death, not to mention Lucrezia Borgia and Lady Macbeth. In the comic vein, feminine ruse traditionally achieves some brilliant victories, from *Un giorno di regno* to *Falstaff*, by way of the redoubtable spouse of Don Pasquale.

The *femme fatale*, the dangerous seductress, is found in Puccini, in the siren of Mainz who lures Roberto in *Le villi*, and in Tigrana, contrasted with the pure Fidelia in *Edgar*. Here as well, passions and instincts appear in unadulterated form.

Style

Italian seems to be one of the most well-adapted languages for singing, with its strong syllabic stress and its lack of nasals, diphthongs, and large consonant clusters.[14] The formal style of language, however, varied greatly over the years.

Nineteenth-century libretto texts, generally in verse, observed quite distinct conventions. Until the time of Boito, these included a seven-syllable line of verse for arias, eight-syllable lines for recitatives, and ten- or twelve-syllable lines for choruses. But many irregularities turned up. In Boito, for example, the nine-syllable verse was common, and the classic hendecasyllabic line remained the standard Italian line of verse.

Attempts to establish a dramatic prose style, in the manner essayed by French writers, met with long resistance in Italy.[15] Rhymed verse still appeared in Boito's *Nerone* (1924), though the libretto of Alfano's *Risurrezione* (1904), adapted from Tolstoy's novel by Cesare Hanau, was cast entirely in prose.

Vocabulary remained formal and codified at the start of the nineteenth century, with *amore* (love),[16] *dolor* (grief), *cor* (heart), *Dio* or *Iddio* (God), *felice* (happy), *gioia* (joy), *nemico* (enemy), *onore* (honor), *perfido* (betrayal), *sciagurato* (wretch), and *traditor* (traitor) turning up on every page. With the advent of verismo, the tone became much more familiar. This was the period when the word "mamma" replaced the traditional "madre" (mother), an unmis-

The tenor Rubini, by Dévéria.
In *Musica*, April 1905.

takable sign of the times; an example of this occurs in Turiddu's famous farewell to his mother at the end of *Cavalleria rusticana*.

Also symptomatic of change was the gradual disappearance of repeated words and syllables. That practice, still in use in *La traviata* and even in *Le villi*, is already parodied in *Falstaff* in the phrase "dalle due alle tre" (from two to three o'clock) in which the dumbfounded hero is made to repeat the time of his rendezvous with Alice, clearly intended as caricature.

Verdi presents Victor Emmanuel II with
Emilia's plebiscite requesting annexation
to Piedmont in 1859.
Drawing by E. Matania.

CHAPTER 2

PRINCIPAL THEMES

*T*he most important criterion for a good libretto is that it be dramatic, the absence of which quality would seem to explain the failure of Schubert's operas. Italian opera plots were often quite complex, as in *La forza del destino* and *Don Carlo.* Disguised identities abound—Belfiore in *Un giorno di regno,* the Duke in *Rigoletto,* Leonora in *La forza del destino*—and infant-stealing and switches at birth—*La fille du régiment, Il trovatore*—far from simplify matters. Only rarely do works of this period induce boredom.

Can it be claimed beyond a doubt that the supremacy of song made up for the otherwise indisputable flaws of a plot? The question will be addressed, but not without first emphasizing that solo narratives, such as Ferrando's in *Il trovatore* (Act I, scene 1), which had been so common to opera from the seventeenth century onward—the messenger's narrative in Monteverdi's *Orfeo,* for instance—appeared less and less in Italian opera of the nineteenth century.

In Italy, interest was sustained less by the arrangement of the plot than by the manner in which the themes were treated: love, death, religion, politics, to which were added many societal—and even supernatural—elements.

Love

Love was still, in the nineteenth century, the cornerstone of most operatic frameworks. Among the most famous works, Verdi's *Macbeth* (1847) is practically the only one whose action is spurred by other events. Outside Italy, Schoenberg's *Moses und Aron* constitutes another famous exception to this more or less general rule. Even in *Giovanna d'Arco*, Joan of Arc's feelings for Carlo VII are baldly depicted in their first-act love duet.

The concept of love changes, of course, from one period and style to another. In the age of Metastasio, it was supposed to be ruled by reason. For Violetta in Act I of *La traviata*, it is only a fleeting flame:

> *Godiam, fugace e rapido*
> *è il gaudio dell'amore;*
> *è un fior che nasce e muore,*
> *nè più si può goder!*

> Let us enjoy; love's bliss
> flies swiftly by;
> it is a flower that blossoms and dies,
> then can no longer be enjoyed!

In Act I of *La bohème*, Rodolfo and Marcello are more cynical:

> *L'amore è un caminetto che sciupa troppo,*
> *dove l'uomo è fascina*
> *e la donna l'alare;*
> *l'uno brucia in un soffio*
> *e l'altro sta a guardare.*

> Love is a little stove that consumes too much fuel,
> where the man does the burning
> and the woman the lighting;
> the one burns in an instant
> and the other stands and watches.

Despite variations in treatment, and much in the way of novels, love is usually frustrated and inevitably intensified,[1] though only rarely in these librettos are the obstacles imposed by social class. In Donizetti's *La fille du régiment*, Marie, the offspring of noble blood, is prevented from marrying the peasant Tonio; Luisa Miller is likewise separated from Rodolfo; and, in *La traviata*, Alfredo's father tears Violetta from her young lover in order to prevent his son's liaison with a woman of questionable morals from tainting his daughter's reputation. Aristocrats enjoy hardly more than an occasional fling with a commoner, as the Duke does with Gilda in *Rigoletto*.

Notwithstanding the famous example of Romeo and Juliet, family feuds are even less frequently the cause of conflict, though that is the reason Lucia of Lammermoor is prevented from marrying Edgardo of Ravenswood. Opposition sometimes takes a religious turn, as in the conflict between Giselda and Arvino in *I lombardi alla prima crociata*, or between Fenena and Ismaele in *Nabucco*. Love, however, does cause some spectacular religious conversions, like those of Fenena, Oronte (*I lombardi*), and Paolina (*Poliuto*). Age difference is hardly ever an obstacle except in comic works like *Don Pasquale*, where the only possible match for the young Norina is the equally youthful Ernesto.

Frequently, conflict assumes a political guise. The dispute between the sympathizers of Cromwell and those of the Stuarts in *I puritani* prohibits Elvira from loving Arturo Talbo, just as Norma must keep her liaison with the Roman proconsul Pollione a secret. The same cruel interdiction weighs on Elena, sister of the Austrian Duke Federigo, when she falls in love with the young Sicilian Arrigo (*I vespri siciliani*), or on the Ethiopian Aida when she falls for the Egyptian Radames.

Another sort of obstacle, the green-eyed monster jealousy, turned up more and more frequently in the hearts of spurned lovers (or those who fancied themselves as such) as the century wore on. Among the afflicted are the Count di Luna, eager to provoke Manrico (*Il trovatore*); Laura's husband, Alvise (*La Gioconda*); Otello; poor Canio in *I pagliacci*; and even Master Ford (*Falstaff*). The terrible phrase "Gelosia le fiere serpi gli avventa in petto!"[2] perfectly suits each of these characters. The notion of forgiveness occurs very rarely in this repertoire, as already mentioned in reference to *Stiffelio*, *Alzira*, and *Zazà*.

Another variation on the theme occurs in *L'amico Fritz* (1891), in which a confirmed bachelor wagers—in vain, of course—that he shall never succumb to the charms of Suzel.

Finally, in a society that placed so much importance on the concept of family, it is no surprise that parental love as well as romantic love should have been so consistently glorified. "Il mio universo è in te,"[3] confides Rigoletto to Gilda. Old Miller similarly heaps all his affection upon his daughter Luisa, while Azucena's love for Manrico is even stronger: "Il tuo sangue è sangue mio! Ogni stilla che ne versi tu la spremi dal mio cor."[4] Leonora's devotion to her father is strong in *La forza del destino*, and Turiddu has these touching parting words for his mother in *Cavalleria rusticana:* "Un bacio, mamma, addio!"[5]

Death

Concern for decorum may have been the reason tragic endings were avoided at the start of the nineteenth century. Thus the Moor and Desdemona tripped downstage hand in hand at the end of certain revivals of Rossini's *Otello*, the violent end of *Giulio Cesare* was replaced by an idyllic chorus in Handel's opera (libretto by Nicola Haym, London, 1724), and, after completing *Mireille*, Gounod changed the sad ending to a happier one.

From the 1830s on, however, love affairs in serious opera almost invariably resulted in death, even if the public was far from willing to accept such dire endings—Verdi suffered much criticism for the string of dead bodies in *La forza del destino*.[6] Many lovers are eternally united in death: Norma and Pollione, Edgardo who stabs himself in despair on hearing of Lucia's death, Luisa Miller and Rodolfo, Leonora and Manrico (*Il trovatore*), Leonora and Don Carlo (*La forza del destino*), Aida and Radames, Desdemona and Otello, Nedda and Silvio (*I pagliacci*), Andrea Chénier and Maddalena de Coigny.

In comparison to these emotion-packed final curtains, the death of an evil villain (like Scarpia in *Tosca*) or even a spectacular suicide (like that of Gioconda, who just before dying learns that Barnaba has killed her poor blind mother) seems to make less of an impact. Nevertheless, the glorification of the sort of fate in which love triumphs over all, epitomized by Romeo and Juliet or Tristan and Isolde, was in Italy treated more cautiously in opera than in the novel. Yet it makes the operas written between 1850 and 1900 genuine romantic masterpieces of redemption-through-death, since death is used in them less as a dramatic device than as one of the aspirations of human existence, in which past regrets combine with dreams of eternity.

Religion

The Church seems much more of a presence in Italian opera than in the operas of Germany and France, in which countries religion had taken a step backward in the eighteenth century.

Numerous scenes take place on holy ground, no doubt in order to emphasize the exceptional nature of the situation. Thus *Nabucco* opens inside the Temple of Solomon in Jerusalem; the librettist has even prefaced the act with a quotation from the Bible (Jeremiah 32:3): "Thus saith the Lord: Behold I will give this city into the hands of the King of Babylon; he will destroy it with fire." Much later, the Romanesque church of Sant'Andrea della Valle is presented in the first act of *Tosca*, and a scene in *Cavalleria rusticana* resounds with the singing of an Easter hymn. Many props also add a religious touch, such as the crucifix that Floria Tosca places on Scarpia's corpse. Monasteries figure as havens of peace, so indispensable to the quelling of passion, in *La favorita* and *La forza del destino*. One of the most frequent reminders is aural, the sound of church bells, present in *I vespri siciliani*, *Rigoletto*, and *Tosca*, among others.

Invocations and prayers to the Supreme Being also occur in a good number of the serious operas of the period. Among them are Desdemona's "Ave Maria"; the "Ave Maria" in Cilèa's *Tilda*; the opening scene of *Norma*, with its invocation by the High Priest Oroveso and the Druids; the prayer in the second act of *Oberto*; the "Salve Maria" (Act I, scene 1) and the hymn of praise to God that concludes *I lombardi alla prima crociata*; the Miserere in *Il trovatore* (Act IV, scene 1); the "De profundis" in *I vespri siciliani* (Act IV); Faust's prayer in the final pages of *Mefistofele*; and even the rather conventional invocations that close the first act of *Le villi*.

Nevertheless, such scenes occur more and more infrequently in later operas, and a few profane remarks even appear in librettos

written at the century's close. Roberto says to Anna in Puccini's
Villi: "Ah, dubita di Dio, ma no, dell'amor mio non dubitar."[7]
Thereafter, love prevailed over religious sentiment.

Politics and Society

It is with respect to contemporary political movements that
nineteenth-century Italian opera remained most clearly a product of
its time. Occupied by the Bourbons in the south and the Haps-
burgs in the north (see the map in the Introduction), and already
fanned by the revolutionary spirit of the Napoleonic era, the Italian peninsula fought for more than a generation to win its free-
dom and establish a unified state. It is no wonder then that libertarian themes appeared in 1826, in Mercadante's *Donna Caritea*
(libretto by P. Pola), and in Pacini's *Arabi nelle Gallie* (libretto by L.
Romanelli, 1827); the former contains the famous "Chi per la patria muore è vissuto assai."[8] Similarly, Rossini's *Mosè in Egitto* glo-
rifies the suffering of the oppressed Hebrews, *Guillaume Tell* too
contains patriotic sentiments, and *L'italiana in Algeri*'s "Pensa alla
patria" served to unite the inhabitants of the peninsula. Nor is
there any lack of such references in Bellini or Donizetti,[9] though
they were not to create any stormy repercussions until later on.

Meanwhile, patriotic fervor intensified. After the first revolutions (1820–21), the birth of "Giovine Italia" (1831), and Mazzini's
first attempts at insurrection (1833) came the success of Gioberti,
whose *Primato morale e civile degli Italiani* was so well received upon
its publication in 1843. Soon thereafter, in 1847, the daily paper *Il
Risorgimento* was founded by Cavour. Simultaneously, Verdian
opera was doing its part. In *Oberto* (libretto by Solera, 1839), the
Count expresses his emotions upon his return from exile with these
touching words: "O patria terra, alfine io ti rivedo . . . Patria diletta
. . . Di nuovo pianto / Vengo a bagnarti, o dolce suol natio."[10]

I lombardi alla prima crociata (libretto by Solera, 1843) resounds
with "Amo la patria immensamente"[11] and "Grande e libera l'Italia
sarà."[12] *Macbeth* (libretto by Piave, 1847) contains the suffering of
the exiled Scots: "Fratelli! gli oppressi / Corriamo a salvar."[13] And
the work ends with Malcolm's words: "Fu spento l'oppressor! / La
gioia eternerò / Per noi di tal vittoria."[14]

La battaglia di Legnano (libretto by Cammarano, 1849) opens with the "Viva Italia!" chorus, and even in *I vespri siciliani* (libretto by Scribe and Duveyrier, 1855), the Sicilian Procida sings at the beginning of Act II: "O patria, o cara patria."

The revolutions of 1848 (12–27 January in Sicily, 23 January and 18–22 March in Milan, 22 May in Naples) fueled even more interest in operatic patriotism. Later, when events came to a head between the end of 1859 (the beginning of the war against Austria) and November 1860 (the entry of Victor Emmanuel II into Naples), waves of sympathy were more and more flamed by the operatic stage. On 10 January 1859 the "Guerra" chorus in *Norma* unleashed violent anti-Austrian sentiment at La Scala, and at Teatro Apollo in Rome on 2 January 1861, a large patriotic demonstration erupted during a performance of *La traviata*.

After the creation of the kingdom of Italy (27 April 1861) and the annexation of Venice (1866) and the Papal States (1870), these issues naturally lost a great deal of their topicality. Focus turned instead to a number of formerly neglected social questions. This period also saw the emergence of the working proletariat (First International, 1864–72; Second International, 1889), while in Milan a "Partito operaio independante" was formed in 1882. The socialist party was organized in 1892–93, just prior to Italy's Industrial Age (1896–1913). The common people became real players in the Italian opera repertoire with Smareglia's *Nozze istriane* (libretto by Illica, 1895).

Indeed, in a country whose unification was effected within a conservative context and whose left wing only timidly came into power in 1876, it was not until *Andrea Chénier* (libretto by Illica, 1896) that the Italian stage presented a genuine tirade against the aristocracy, through the character of Gérard in the first act. The introduction of characters from the lower echelons of society sprang from two sources: one the rather traditional *opera buffa*, the other the more contemporary texts of Giovanni Verga (1840–1922), who had been active in social movements since 1860. His stories ushered in the age of verismo (1890), the first time that *opera seria* glorified the lower classes. Puccini, in his youthful works, brought the middle-class world to life (*Le villi, Edgar, La bohème, Manon Lescaut, Tosca*). Later he explored the working class (*Il ta-*

barro), though not without forays into exoticism (*Madama Butterfly*, *Turandot*),[15] as did Montemezzi (*L'amore dei tre re*).

Social concerns were much more sharply drawn in French works of the period, as seen in works inspired by Emile Zola, like Alfred Bruneau's *L'attaque du moulin* and *Messidor* or Gustave Charpentier's *Louise*.[16] In France, however, after the violent revolutions of 1789, 1830, and 1848, the people had already assumed power by 1871, under the Paris Commune, eight years before the appearance of the left wing of the government marked the actual start of the republic.

The Irrational

Love of nature or local color are not very pronounced in Italian opera of this period; responsibility for touching the audience with these romantic devices was usually left to the set designer or even the composer (the musical evocation of dawn breaking over the Eternal City, for example, at the beginning of the third act of *Tosca*). Librettos, on the other hand, frequently drew on irrational elements that could exert a special fascination on the mind of the reader or the composer. Busoni claimed that the musical expression in opera was best served by the unreal.[17]

Fantastic elements abound in most romantic opera of the period, from Meyerbeer's *Robert le diable* to Schumann's *Genoveva*. The demons and angels in *Giovanna d'Arco* and the ghost of Banquo (*Macbeth*, Act II, scene 3) also belong, along with many others, to this romantic arsenal. Even Jacopo Foscari's dungeon hallucinations, "Sorgon di terra mille e mille spettri,"[18] are not unlike certain mad scenes in which passion is pushed beyond reason, as in Act III of *Lucia di Lammermoor*, the end of the second act of *Linda di Chamounix*, Act II of *I puritani* (perhaps the most beautiful bel canto mad scene), *Anna Bolena* (final scene), and *Roberto Devereux*, when Queen Elizabeth imagines the hero being led to the scaffold.

Other remarkable elements include Doctor Dulcamara's magic potion (*L'elisir d'amore*), the somewhat mysterious and terrifying character of Azucena in *Il trovatore*, the presence of Ulrica and the gathering of enchanted herbs in *Un ballo in maschera*, gypsies like Preziosilla in *La forza del destino* or the palm readers in *La traviata*, and the witches on the heath in *Macbeth* (Acts I and III), or on Brocken Peak in *Mefistofele* (Act II).

Allusions and references to irrational elements are everywhere: Gioconda's blind mother, La Cieca, is accused of sorcery (Act I), and a sorceress is said to have been responsible for embroidering Desdemona's handkerchief (*Otello*, Boito's libretto, Act III, scene 2).

The irrational undoubtedly played a poetic function in Italian opera, helping the audience accept the complicated plots by making them frankly undecipherable at times, making utterly futile any attempts to explain the action logically. By penetrating the subconscious, it reinforced within the spectator a certain respect for the powers of the occult and other dark forces—easily done in the land where many still believed that werewolves lurked under each full moon.

I. R. TEATRO ALLA SCALA.

Dal giorno 13 al 17 del corr. Maggio avranno luogo due Recite, nelle quali agirà Madama **MALIBRAN** rappresentando il Melodramma

NORMA

La Compagnia sarà composta inoltre dalle

Siguore GARCIA RUEZ	. . . .	ADALGISA
„ RUGGERI TERESA	. . .	CLOTILDE
e dai Siguori REINA DOMENICO	. . .	POLLIONE
„ MARINI IGNAZIO	. . .	OROVESO
„ VASCHETTI GIUSEPPE	.	FLAVIO

Nell' intermezzo dei due atti vi sarà un PASSO A SETTE espressamente composto dal sig. *Egidio Priora*, eseguito dallo stesso, e dalle signore *Rabel, Ancement, Bonalumi, Braschi Amalia, Frassi Adelaide e Romagnoli*.

Con altro avviso sarà indicato precisamente il giorno della prima recita, restando fissato quello della seconda nel suenunciato giorno 17, e saranno pure indicati i prezzi d'ingresso e delle Sedie chiuse.

Dal Camerino dell' I. R. Teatro alla Scala il 3 Maggio 1834.

Facsimile of a La Scala playbill for an early production of *Norma*. In *Annuario dell'arte lirica e coreografica italiana* (Milan: De Marchi, 1897–98), 91.

CHAPTER 3

STYLISTIC EVOLUTION AND BOUNDARIES

No one will contest the great changes that occurred between *La cambiale di matrimonio* (1810) and *Falstaff* (1893), and again to *Gianni Schicchi* (1918). And yet, in the field of the libretto, which provided a basic form of packaging, a sort of predictable mold for these works, three different aesthetics seem to emerge, dominated by the century's great wave of romanticism.

The Classical Tradition

As many critics have noted, the classical spirit seemed to endure in Italy with more persistence than in other countries,[1] and, indeed, classical restraint became even more prevalent under the influence of the Greek revival at the beginning of the second half of the nineteenth century.[2] Carlo Gozzi only used pre-romantic techniques, but Foscolo and Leopardi could be considered as much eminent representatives of Italian romanticism as professed anti-romantics. Giosue Carducci (1835–1907) managed to blend the classical and revolutionary traditions into one.

Italian librettists of the early decades, up to and including Romani, were in fact advocates of classicism, and in Mercadante's *Vestale* (to an 1840 libretto by Cammarano) many vestiges of that school persist. As discussed in Chapter 1 in the sections on settings and style, the Metastasian three-act pattern lost some ground in the first part of the century, but the style remained true to other past conventions much longer, through the versified text and the choice of words. The same preference for the classical can be observed in the settings and characters invariably drawn upon by the librettists.

Romanticism

The romantic era in Italian literature may be said to have begun with Berchet in 1816 (*Lettera semi-seria di Grisostomo*), after the period of late eighteenth-century sentimental drama (F. A. Avelloni, C. Federici). Some early indications of romanticism can be felt in Rossini's *La donna del lago* (libretto by Tottola); in the dark colors of Bellini's *Bianca e Fernando* (libretto by Romani); in the artist's passion in Bellini's *Adelson e Salvini* (libretto by Tottola); in the subject of *Il pirata*; and in the last works of Donizetti, such as *La favorita*.[3] Italian opera of this period seldom reflected any interest in legends, unlike turn-of-the-century Germany, where, thanks to Herder and the Brothers Grimm, popular culture had been quick to rediscover the folkloric "voice of the people." Elements of the fantastic nevertheless existed in Italian librettos, and there was no lack of outdoor and nocturnal settings among them, particularly in stage directions having to do with scenery.[4] In any case, romanticism in Italian opera was driven more by the ubiquitous spirit of the Risorgimento and by the free expression of emotion, ever more liberal and excessive. That is what gives these works their real dramatic drive and shape.

Verismo

Italian romanticism undoubtedly took the form of a search for truth as well,[5] even for the Scapigliati. In opera, where emotional expression generally overshadows ordinary routine, it is no surprise that verismo came to the fore through displays of violent excess of passion. Librettos bound by such an aesthetic essentially proceed along this line: "I loved you, you betrayed me, so I'll kill you"—hence the catastrophic endings of *Cavalleria rusticana* and *Pagliacci*. Their texts are closer to the speech of common folk, and in cruder tones, but at the same time a healthy strain of romanticism runs through Italian operatic verismo. Federico in Cilèa's *Arlesiana*, in spite of the realistic setting of Daudet's original, is above all a romantic hero whose all-consuming passion drives him to suicide.

Thus ends the singular history of the Italian opera libretto, long faithful to classical models and yet barely removed from romanticism in the last years of the nineteenth century, and even the beginning of the twentieth.

Even if everyday elements tried to blot out one aspect of the romantic ideal—with *Falstaff* bordering on a parody of the star-crossed lovers in the semi-mechanical lyricism of Fenton and Nannetta, and with Rodolfo and Mimi in Puccini's *Bohème* seemingly beyond the realm of their counterparts Marcello and Musetta—Prunier's words in Act I of Puccini's *Rondine* (libretto by Adami) apply very well to the Italian operatic style of the period: "Nel fondo d'ogni anima c'è un diavolo romantico, è più forte di me, di noi, di tutti."[6]

The Censor

Some of the most beloved operatic subjects, because of their political actuality or sacred character, were often prime targets of censorship.[7] Prayers were the first items to undergo changes. Thus, the "Ave Maria" in *I lombardi alla prima crociata* (1843) became a "Salve Maria." *Giovanna d'Arco* was given under the title *Orietta di Lesbo* in Palermo in 1847, and *Poliuto* was refused performance in Naples. *Stiffelio*, concerning adultery on the part of a minister's wife, was especially mutilated by the censors and finally remade by Verdi into *Aroldo*.

Changes imposed by the censor on the libretto of *Attila* (text by Solera set to music by Verdi) follow.[8] The original version is on the left, the modifications on the right.

Prologue, scene 1

Gemiti, sangue, <u>stupri</u>, rovine	Gemiti, sangue, <u>morti</u>, rovine
terra <u>beata</u> tu sei per noi.	terra <u>diletta</u> tu sei per noi.

Prologue, scene 3

di <u>Vergini</u> straniere.	di <u>giovani</u> straniere.

Prologue, scene 6

turbo che <u>Dio d'un soffio</u> suscitò.	turbo che l'<u>ira d'Austro</u> suscitò.
<u>Lode al Signor—Lode al Signor!</u>	<u>E un riso il dì—L'aura è d'april.</u>

Act I, scene 2

rammenti	possenti
<u>di Giuditta che salva Israel?</u>	<u>Sono i voti d'un alma fedel.</u>

Act I, scene 3

<u>M'apparve immane un veglio</u>	<u>Donna s'appar terribile</u>
<u>che mi afferrò la</u> chioma:	<u>con la turrita</u> chioma:
<u>Di flagellar l'incarco</u>	<u>Roma son'io; l'orgoglio</u>
<u>contro ai mortali hai sol;</u>	<u>a me dinante è insano;</u>
t'arretra! <u>or chiuso è il varco;</u>	t'arretra! <u>il Campidoglio</u>
<u>questo dei numi è il suol.</u>	<u>vietato è a pie' profano.</u>
<u>Roma iniqua</u> io muovo a te.	<u>O superba</u>, io muovo a te.

Act I, scene 5

<u>Vieni, le menti visita</u>	<u>Pace, di tua bell'irride</u>
<u>o spirto creator,</u>	<u>deh spandasi il seren,</u>
<u>dalla tua fronte piovere</u>	<u>placa lo spirito turgido</u>
<u>fanne il vital tesor</u> . . .	<u>piovi la calma in sen</u> . . .

Act I, scene 6

<u>I guasti sensi illumina</u>	<u>Taccia lo spirto bellico</u>
<u>spirane amore in sen,</u>	<u>ovunque olezzi amor.</u>
<u>l'oste debella e spandasi</u>	<u>Torni a brillar sul cespide</u>, [sic]
<u>di pace il bel seren.</u>	<u>dopo tant'ire, il fior.</u>

Changes that were politically motivated occurred no less frequently. In the title of one of Bellini's early works, the name Fernando was changed to Gernando in order to avoid any comparison with Ferdinand IV, King of the Two Sicilies (1816–25). Quite often, a work was transplanted to a completely different geographical and/or historical locale in order to cover up any references that might fan public hostility. Hence the changes imposed on *Un ballo in maschera*, whose action was transferred from Stockholm to Boston.[9] But censorship existed outside Italy as well; in early twentieth-century Russia, for example, *Tosca* was relocated, not without some implausibility, to the Paris of the French Revolution, with the heroine murdering General Gallifet, one of the leaders of the anti-revolutionary party.[10]

Throughout the peninsula, each major opera capital might judge a work differently: thus, when the libretto of *Un ballo in maschera* (entitled *La vendetta in domino*) was rejected by Naples, the composer was able to refuse to accept the altered libretto proposed to him and produce the work as he envisioned it in Rome.

This last case notwithstanding, the Papal city was one of the most difficult to please. For a long time, Rome had three levels of censorship: Austria, the Vatican, and the Holy Office, or Bishopric. There, *Norma* became *La foresta d'Armensul*, and the duet "Gridendo libertà" in *I puritani* was altered to "Gridendo lealtà." The following is a list of title changes to operas by Verdi, most proposed in Rome and Naples.

Ernani	→ *Il corsaro di Venezia* (Naples)
Giovanna d'Arco	→ *Orietta di Lesbo* (Rome and Naples)
Attila	→ *Gli unni e i romani* (Palermo)
La battaglia di Legnano	→ *L'assedio di Arlem* (Rome)
Stiffelio	→ *Guglielmo Wellingrode* (Rome)
Rigoletto	→ *Viscardello* (Rome)
	→ *Clara di Perth* (Naples)
	→ *Lionella* (Naples)
La traviata	→ *Violetta* (Rome and Paris)
La forza del destino	→ *Don Alvaro* (Rome)

The same concern for social propriety forced Giordano's *Mala vita* (libretto by N. Daspuro, Rome 1892) to be revived under the title *Il voto* in Milan in 1897 and in Naples in 1902—the same city whose most sordid districts were depicted in the opera itself.

Censorship thus manifested itself as one of the most conservative forces, together with the public's lingering classical orientation. Though in sharp contrast to Mediterranean tendencies toward free expression of emotion and despite the country's spectacular political developments, censorship assured librettos would evolve only at a gradual pace.

As the century progressed, changes in the style of the music itself—less dependent upon ideological and behavioral customs—were much more noticeable to the listener.

A French production of *I pagliacci* at the Cercle de l'Union Artistique, Paris, with Mme de Nuovina as Nedda and Lubert as Canio. In *Le Théâtre* 4, 1899.

PART II: *The Music*

The focus of this section will be upon those composers whose periods of activity are featured on the endpapers of this book. A comparative summary of their compositional traits will be offered, with particular regard to the voice, the orchestra, formal structure, and musical language. The generation still active during the transitional period between Mozart and Rossini— Torchi (1760–1814), Fioravanti (1770–1837), Benincori (1779–1821)—will not be discussed; on this subject, the interested reader is advised to consult Edward Dent's The Rise of Romantic Opera, *edited by Winton Dean and published by Cambridge University Press in 1976.*

Though Part III offers many more figures of this type, a few odd statistics straight off will give an idea of the staggering number of operas created during the course of the century. According to the Gazzetta musicale di Milano *of 1858, a certain Basevi counted 641 operas written between 1842 and 1857; between January 1896 and June 1897, 118 new works were composed: 44 operettas, 38 opere serie, 1 semi-seria, 5 bozzetto, 2 vaudeville, and 27 miscellaneous or unspecified (from* Annuario dell'arte lirica e coreografica italiana, *published in Milan by De Marchi in 1897–98, pages 32–35).*

CHAPTER 4

COMPOSERS

Before turning to the major stylistic traits and innovations of the period, much less the impact of foreign styles upon Italian composers, treated in Chapter 7, let us first consider the interesting matter of the composers' backgrounds, formative years, and the number of operas they produced. This introductory chapter is concerned with the stylistic affinities that, despite inevitable exceptions, helped to ensure a sort of generic homogeneity among the works written between 1810 and the beginning of the twentieth century.

Background and Formative Years

Not all the great composers grew up in the same sort of environment. Some came from very humble backgrounds, such as Spontini, Verdi (whose father ran a small tavern in Roncole, near Parma), and Donizetti and Mascagni, whose families would dearly have preferred their sons go into the practice of law.

Several composers, however, were raised congenially among musicians: Rossini's father played the horn, and Pacini was the son of a tenor. Bellini and Puccini were the son and grandson, respectively, of choirmasters. Indeed, religious training was still a common practice and may explain in part the frequency of church-related subjects in works by artists of the period. Verdi himself, before making his first mark on the local musical scene, began his studies at a very early age with the village organist.

Not until the last decades of the century, with the rise in the number of music schools, were young artists able to acquire the sort of training that, though it may have been less in keeping with their personal taste, could be described as comprehensive. Composers born in the middle of the century, such as Boito, Puccini, and Mascagni, benefited from this sort of early education, which had the further advantage of introducing them into Milanese artistic and literary circles, where they came into contact with the Scapigliati and bohemians of the day.

In addition to the conservatories, theaters—thanks to obligatory instructional outings in large cities—provided the best school for these composers. Nor should one underestimate the impact of competitions sponsored by town councils and publishers like Sonzogno.

General cultural education varied greatly, from that of Verdi—who claimed to be an ignorant peasant[1]—to that of Boito or Leoncavallo, who were more solidly versed in literature.

Finally, the precociousness of certain composers is remarkable, especially those at the start of the century who mounted their first opera before the age of twenty: Pacini, Rossini, and later Ponchielli, among them. Later on, as the frequency and possibility of performance diminished, it took longer to make one's talent known. Still the majority of composers, including Donizetti, Mercadante, Bellini, Verdi, Pedrotti, Catalani, Puccini, Mascagni, Cilèa, and Giordano, made their debuts between the ages of twenty and thirty.

Output

The number of operas produced by each composer diminished sharply over the years, undoubtedly a sign of the growing complexity of the genre, and even of its impending decline. In the nineteenth century, we are a far cry from the hundred-odd operas of an Alessandro Scarlatti, for example. Though Pacini or Donizetti each still managed to produce around seventy scores for the stage and Mercadante around sixty operas, Rossini stopped at thirty-

Facsimile of a page from the autograph manuscript of
Mascagni's *Cavalleria rusticana*. In *Annuario dell'arte lirica
e coreografica italiana* (Milan: De Marchi, 1897–98), 5.

The tavern owned by Verdi's family in the village of
Le Roncole, near Busseto. Long thought to be Verdi's
birthplace and still a national monument, recent research by
Mary Jane Phillips-Matz (*Verdi: A Biography*, published by
Oxford in 1993) places the family here no earlier than 1833.
Photo, *Les Préludes*, 1985.

seven, Bellini at ten, and Verdi at twenty-six. Puccini wrote no
more than a dozen, and other turn-of-the-century composers
(Catalani, Cilèa) a half-dozen.

An opera's length varied generally in proportion to the number
of acts.[2] Verismo scores tended to be the shortest: an hour and a
quarter each for *Cavalleria rusticana* and *I pagliacci*, today usually
performed back-to-back in the same evening. At the other end of
the scale are works lasting over three hours, including Verdi's *Aida*,
Don Carlo, *Forza del destino*, *Luisa Miller*, *Nabucco*, *Otello*, *Trovatore*,
Ballo in maschera, and *Vespri siciliani*. The average duration is two
and a half hours, the running time of *Andrea Chénier*, *La bohème*,
Falstaff, *Lucia di Lammermoor*, *Manon Lescaut*, *Simon Boccanegra*,
Tosca, and *La traviata*.

How much credence should be given to claims of the speed at
which some of these scores were composed? In 1843 Henri Blanchard wrote in the *Revue et gazette musicale*: "Nothing becomes

outmoded more quickly in Italy than an opera; the fault lies with the composers who produce them with such deplorable facility."[3] According to Azevedo,[4] Rossini is supposed to have written *Semiramide* in forty days, practically a maximum gestation time for the composer whose famous "Aria de'risi" from *Tancredi* was thus nicknamed because it was allegedly completed in the time it takes to cook rice! Pacini was said to have composed *Saffo* in twenty-eight days. No doubt many of these works took longer to write than popular anecdotes claim. Donizetti, for example, took three to six months, not eleven days, to put the finishing touches on *Don Pasquale.*[5] As for Puccini, he generally composed in a leisurely manner. The most spontaneous-sounding passages in *La bohème* are the ones that gave the composer the most trouble; ideas came to him easily, but the organization of them required a great deal of effort.[6]

Stylistic Overview

The most genuinely new music at the beginning of the nineteenth century was that of Rossini, who kindled fresh interest in the *opera seria* at a time when audiences were focusing their attention more on the ballets performed between the acts of an opera than on the opera itself.[7] Like all innovations, those of the master of Pesaro were far from universally accepted, despite the fact that the heavier orchestration, particularly rich in brass, the dramatic accompanied recitative, the famous crescendos, and the flashy, repeated cadential figures at the end of phrases at least partially recalled Mozart and continued to echo in the music of Offenbach. The simple melodies and clear rhythms of the music of "Giove Rossini,"[8] designed to please, made an indelible mark on the Italian style. His friend Giovanni Pacini and others were clearly influenced by Rossini's music, and traces of his style remain even in Verdi. "Si vendetta" in *Rigoletto* is similar to a page in Rossini's *Otello*, and the accompaniment to Leonora's "Quel suon, quelle preci" in the *Trovatore* Miserere is reminiscent of "Qual mesto gemito" in the first-act finale of *Semiramide*.

Bellini, who achieved success with *Il pirata* (1827), seemed more influenced by Paisiello and Zingarelli, though the many strettas in his scores and the crescendo in the overture to *Il pirata* owe a great deal to Rossini.

By the same token, certain Bellinian traits also turn up in Verdi, notably in prison scenes or unconventional finales (*Otello*, end of Acts I, II, and IV), and even in a few melodies: Count Rodolfo's "Tu non sai" in the first act of *La sonnambula* virtually parallels Zaccaria's cabaletta in *Nabucco* (Act I) or Silva's cabaletta in *Ernani* (Act I).

Donizetti, who first earned public acclaim with *Anna Bolena* (1830), practiced his art with a great deal of diversity.[9] Routine formulas of near-martial flavor (beginning of the wedding scene in *Lucia di Lammermoor* or the opening bars of Act II of *L'elisir d'amore*) exist alongside very ornately wrought passages (Lucia's Mad Scene). Yet, his musical discourse sometimes achieves a beautiful intensity, as in *La favorite*, for example. For this reason, comparisons are often made between Donizetti and Verdi: between *Maria Stuarda* ("Sul viso") and *Nabucco* ("Le folgore"), or between *La favorite* ("Mon arrêt") and *Macbeth* ("Or tutti sorgete"). However, the master from Busseto towers over all others in his attention to expression, demanding more effort on the part of the soloists and an unusual degree of conviction in the choral ensembles.

The tone of Catalani's works—from *La falce* (1875) to *La Wally* (1892)—differs considerably from Verdian vigor,[10] while verismo composers like Mascagni, Leoncavallo, and Giordano unleashed the most violent passions of all. Among them, Cilèa was virtually the only one to display a more elegiac vein.

Puccini's style sprang from rich melodic foundations but was capable of subtleties worthy of Debussy and full of novel touches, reaching its zenith in *Turandot*.

In spite of the differences in individual styles, many traits were shared by the various composers whose approaches to vocal and orchestral composition are examined in the next two chapters.

CHAPTER 5

THE VOICE

*T*raditionally, the world of Italian opera was ruled by the singer, under whose tyranny composers often had to alter their original intentions by adding arias willy-nilly to satisfy them. Thus, when Henriette Clémentine Meric-Lalande refused to sing in *Lucrezia Borgia* in 1833 unless given an additional rondo, Donizetti obliged with "Era desso il mio figlio." Several composers also married famous singers: Rossini's first wife was Isabella-Angela Colbran and Verdi's second wife Giuseppina Strepponi. Bellini's passion for Giuditta Grisi and La Pasta is well known. Singers usually inspired the most vociferous displays of admiration in the opera house, sometimes resulting in out-and-out fistfights between opposing factions, as early as the Todists and Maratists in 1783—the former in support of Luisa Todi (1753–1833) and the latter for Gertrude Mara (1749–1833). As recently as 1951, fans of Callas and Tebaldi went at it in similar fashion.

Yet there is something quite unique about the ultra-montane voice with regard to the Italian language, to the common tessituras of the period, and to the style of writing adopted by composers for soloists and chorus.

From *Manifesto agli amatori della buona musica*
(Rome: Stamperia di Lino Contedini, 1822)

*La manifesta decadenza, e depravazione della Musica ormai
non lontana dalla barbaria, ed in cui sembra che facciasi a gara
per introdurre ogni sorte di stravaganze, sostituendo all'arta [sic]
il capriccio, all'armonia il rumore, alla dolcezza e soavita la dif-
ficoltà e la scompstezza del canto, sicche la Musica odierna giunta
all'orecchio si arresta, e piu non trova la via di penetrare fino al
cuore. . . .*

*I cantanti si sono convertiti in Violini ed in Flauti, le canti-
lene, bene spesso, si osservano fuori di natura, talvolta in discor-
dia col basso fondamentale. . . .*

*L'opera ridotta ad Accademia, e a Centone, e la poca atten-
zione dei Spettatori, ben compatibili se più non curano l'interesse,
e la concatenazione della Rappresentanza, contenti egualmente
d'un Dramma dei più squisiti, che di qualunque altro benchè sfor-
nito del senso comune, purchè non manchino i Cori, che spesso
non vi hanno che far nulla, purchè gl'Istromenti da fiato siano
sempre in azione e i Cantanti non risparmino scale semitonali, e
faccian sentire un diluvio di note in ogni battuta.*

The decadence and corruption manifest in today's music bor-
ders on the barbaric, in which composers seem to be competing
with each other by introducing all sorts of bizarre effects, replac-
ing art with whim, harmony with noise, sweetness and smoothness
with difficult and awkward vocal lines, so that when the music
reaches the ear, it stops, unable to find the way to the heart. . . .

Singers have turned into violinists and flutists; we notice that
melodies quite often have nothing natural about them and sometimes clash with the bass line.

Opera [is] reduced to stale, academic formulas and [to] the
lack of attention on the part of spectators, to be pitied if they no
longer pay any heed to the importance and meaning of the performance, being just as satisfied with the most exquisite drama as
with one of less merit, even one lacking in common sense, provided
that there are plenty of choristers, who usually have nothing to do
anyway, provided that the wind instruments are kept busy and
that the singers aren't stingy with their chromatic scales and pour
into their ears a flood of notes in every measure.

Italian Vocal Style

The extroverted, luminous, radiant, supple, elastic qualities of Italian-trained voices were praised by many singing teachers.[1] The language's wealth of vowels endows the voice with great clarity and a special *morbidezza* (a sort of lush sensuality). The strong, well-projected sound is more conducive to natural breathing than to the laryngeal system; the typically Italian way of putting it is "si canta coll'eco," or by modulating the breath. Italian singing is all *slancio*, or warm exuberance, and the only commonly used glottal stop is the turn-of-the-century sob.

In Italy, two schools of teaching developed simultaneously: one in Milan, characterized by particularly clear emission of tone, producing vast numbers of sopranos and tenors, and the other technique, darker ("cupa") and less airy, in Naples, where many beautiful low voices were trained. The *vlac*, or sudden burst of energy signaling the Neapolitan approach to operatic singing, fascinates to this day.[2]

Whatever the method, the art of singing made striking advances during the course of the nineteenth century. The sort of vocal bullfighting known as bel canto,[3] implying supreme agility, and adored by Hegel and Schopenhauer, in fact began to disappear during the romantic era as voices strove for more and more volume. All contemporary reports agree on this point, some of them suggesting a German influence:

> The rhythmic aspect of vocal expressivity, including runs and the thousand forms of ornamentation which throughout history have made Italian singers markedly superior to those of other nations, seems now to be less a matter of concern than in former times. Today, more importance is given to attacking and holding the note, and no aspiring diva has escaped being thus influenced by the German method.[4]

The celebrated French tenor Gustave Roger also recognized this development, which he attributed to the quest for profundity:

> The Italian school has never had much depth of thought, though at least it could write accommodatingly for the

voice. Now, it aims for seriousness without attaining it and ruins the sturdiest lungs within a few years.[5]

The latter remark truly belongs to the era of the 120-decibel grand opera voice like the *tenore di forza*, which first turns up in Verdi in *La forza del destino* (1862).

The tendency toward louder singing often went hand in hand with an exploitation of the high register, which considerably increased the difficulty of the melodies being written.[6] Take the role of Nabucco, for example, with its high notes written for a particularly thankless *filo di voce*, the high D-flat at the end of Lady Macbeth's Sleepwalking Scene, Manrico's high C in "Di quella pira" (*Il trovatore*, Act III), Radames's high B-flat at the end of "Celeste Aida," marked *morendo*, or the *pianissimo* high A-flat at the end of Desdemona's prayer in the last act of Verdi's *Otello*.

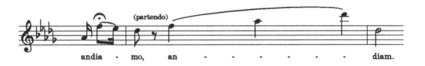

andia - mo,   an - - - - - - diam.

Example 1. Lady Macbeth's high D-flat,
Verdi, *Macbeth* (Act IV).

The situation was aggravated at the time by the gradual decline in frequency of piano rehearsals, which typically had been twelve in number in the past; the number had now dropped to five or six, or even one or two.[7]

All the changes that went along with the development of opera during the last years of the nineteenth century inevitably led to a crisis in the art of singing. In 1889, one observer deplored the neglect of bel canto and the uselessness of instruction whose incorrect methods aimed to form young artists too quickly.[8] Victor Maurel himself declared, during a conference given in Milan on 2 February 1892, "The art of singing, from the point of view of interpretation, is experiencing a state of crisis which today seems to have reached its climax."[9] It was in this period, too, that singers began to be expected to act convincingly.[10]

The soprano Eva Tetrazzini (1862–1938).
She made her debut in Florence in 1882
as Marguerite in *Faust*. She later married
conductor Cleofonte Campanini.
In *Musica*, April 1905.

Voice Categories

Operatic traditions changed perhaps a bit too rapidly during
the course of the nineteenth century. Women, for example,
banned from the operatic stage since the end of the seventeenth
century, reappeared on it by the end of the eighteenth. Indeed, it
was in 1798 in Bologna that Maria Gozzetti was allowed to tread
the boards in men's clothing.[11] This was about the same time that
witnessed the disappearance of the castratos, soon replaced by the
deeper female voices. Napoleon began in 1796 to take measures
against the continuation of their art, and Giovanni Battista Velluti
(1781–1860)—the last great Italian castrato, who had sung in works
like Rossini's *Aureliano in Palmira* (1813) and Meyerbeer's *Crociato*

in Egitto (1824)—retired from the stage in 1829. The Sistine Chapel became one of the last havens of the castrato singers, who later included Domenico Mustafa (1829–1912) and Alessandro Moreschi (1858–1922), the "Angelo di Roma," who reduced his audiences to tears whenever he sang the Jewel Song from *Faust* in the salons of Rome. Bellini's Romeo and Rossini's Tancredi and Sigismondo were all performed by women. What's more, the female contralto occupied a crucial position in Rossini's vocal distributions, one that remained virtually unique throughout the century, as shown in Table 3. There are in fact only four contralto roles in all Verdi's operas (Federica in *Luisa Miller*, Maddalena in *Rigoletto*, Ninetta in *I vespri siciliani*, and Ulrica in *Un ballo in maschera*) and a single one in Puccini (the Aunt in *Suor Angelica*).

Table 3. Vocal categories in Italian opera scores. Survey based on a total of 85 works: 37 by Rossini, 10 by Bellini, 26 by Verdi, and 12 by Puccini.

	Rossini	Bellini	Verdi	Puccini
Soloists	265	68	224	58
Sopranos	43	14	40	16
Mezzo-sopranos	34	10	20	5
Contraltos	20	0	4	1
Tenors	81	19	64	17
Baritones	6	7	30	11
Basses	81	18	66	8

The mezzo-soprano was no longer relegated to confidantes, rivals, or secondary parts as in the past. Azucena in *Il trovatore* inaugurated the great series of dramatic mezzo parts, and the role of Princess Eboli (*Don Carlo*) was soon assigned to the same type of voice. While at the start of the century it sufficed to recruit only sopranos and altos for the season, it eventually became necessary to differentiate between *soprano drammatico* (Norma), *soprano drammatico antico* (with a lesser range capability), *soprano lirico* (Mimi), and *soprano leggero*, also called *sfogato* (Norina).[12] Soon the list would also include the *soprano lirico spinto*, of which Verdi's Desdemona is a classic example.

Later, the lower male voices came into their own, first in Verdi,[13] then in Puccini. The kind of voice for which Mozart had written so many leading roles (Almaviva, Figaro, Don Giovanni, Masetto, Guglielmo, Papageno) was not very widely appreciated in Italy at the beginning of the nineteenth century. Nabucco, without being a genuine baritone part, was already conceived in the low tenor register. Later Rigoletto, Simon Boccanegra, Iago, and *Falstaff*'s title character and Ford became the most famous examples of Verdi baritone roles; all required a greatly expanded vocal range and the suavity of a tenor.

The demands on the bass also underwent considerable change. Limited in the past to *buffa* parts, the bass voice became more lyrical, and even virtuosic, in Rossini's operas. Later on, although Fra Melitone remains the *basso comico* in *La forza del destino*, the bass was often cast as a noble, serious character (Federico Barbarossa in *La battaglia di Legnano*, Philip II and the Grand Inquisitor in *Don Carlo*), including many a high priest (Oroveso in *Norma* and Padre Guardiano in *La forza del destino*). For the role of Zaccaria in *Nabucco*, Verdi composed some of his most beautiful bass solos ("Sperate o figli" in Act I; "Tu sul labbro" in Act II).

The soprano and the tenor, *prima donna*[14] and *primo uomo*, maintained their leading-role status throughout the century. Of all Verdi's works, *Nabucco* is the only one without a tenor aria. Nevertheless, high-range male voices ceased singing in falsetto around 1820[15] and adopted a technique of "vocal covering" that consisted of stretching the voice without changing the timbre in order to pass from mid-range to high, avoiding the undesirable "break" between the two registers.

From Recitative to *Canto fiorito*

There were three ways of setting a text to music in Italy, hence three types of singing: *declamato* (recitative), *spianato* (cantabile), and *fiorito* (embellished, or even melismatic). When Rossini was embarking on his career, Italian opera was generally a series of arias strung together by long stretches of *recitativo secco*. In his memoirs,

Goldoni claimed it was customary to give five arias to each of the principal characters, three to each of the secondary ones, and one to minor characters.[16]

In the eighteenth century, arias differed from each other more by their character, which is to say by their expressive content, than by their form: *aria di sentimento, aria di mezzo carattere, aria di bravura, aria d'agilita.* From a structural standpoint, the bipartite form so dear to Mozart was much less frequent in Italy than the varied reprise, the rondo, and the *aria da capo.* After 1750, from the time of Alessandro Scarlatti, Italian embellishments became more and more common in reprises or final phrases, and the idiom of Porpora (1682–1767) and Piccinni (1728–1800) abounds in all kinds of florid divisions. This sort of virtuosity is hardly absent in Rossini, and it became a solidly established fashion outside of Italy as well, as shown by the music of Boieldieu, Hérold, and Auber. Pacini was also considered the "maestro of the cabaletta" (the final, rapid, ornamented sections of arias).

Bellini, on the other hand, was partial to *canto spianato*, weaving the melody closely to the text, even though he often employed the sort of enchanting grace notes which, in another context, add so much to Chopin's compositions for the piano.

Example 2. "Casta diva," Bellini, *Norma* (Act I, scene 1).

Such a return to a simpler, more moving style had already been attempted before. Algarotti (1756) and Gluck (in his preface to *Alceste*, 1767) wanted music to be more closely linked to the text. The gradual disappearance of the castrato and the elimination of improvisational tendencies led to an important development. From 1823 on, composers like Rossini preferred to write out vocal ornaments rather than allow their music to be disfigured by the unchecked imaginations of individual interpreters. Indeed, a reduction in the amount of *fioriture* in arias is already noticeable in Donizetti and even more apparent in Verdi. Verdi's early works nevertheless make extensive use of ornamentation, as can be seen in *Ernani* (the brilliant cadenza at the end of Elvira's first-act aria), *Attila* (Odabella in the Prologue), *Macbeth* (Sleepwalking Scene), *La traviata* (Brindisi), *Il trovatore* (Leonora's first-act cabaletta, "Di tale amor"), *Don Carlo* (Eboli's Song of the Veil), and the melismas that pervade the mad scenes of the 1830s (*Lucia di Lammermoor* and *I puritani*). Such showers of notes or arpeggios were noted appreciatively by Balzac in the novella, *Massimila Doni*, and up to and including *La forza del destino*, all Verdi's cavatinas contain an unaccompanied cadenza after a dominant-seventh chord, and even more substantial ones in duets. As the composer grew older, however, his arias became less decorative. In *Falstaff*, coloratura is almost nonexistent. It does serve to convey the supernatural atmosphere of Nannetta's last-act Queen of the Fairies solo, but more often carries with it the unmistakable tone of parody. In fact, it is on the word "somaro" (jackass) that Falstaff sings one of the few ornaments in the score (Example 4). This same technique had already appeared in *I pagliacci*, when Tonio-Taddeo serenades the beautiful Nedda-Colombina, underscoring the quaint grotesqueness of the rustic players' skit.

Though vocal ornamentation tended to disappear over the course of time, the aria format maintained its preeminence, though not without some modifications. The first half of the century continued traditions like the *aria di sorbetto* (sung while spectators leisurely partook of refreshing ices in their boxes) or the *aria di baule* (literally, "suitcase aria") which singers would carry in their luggage and interpolate, at their own discretion, into whatever opera they were singing at the moment. Melodic self-borrowing was, moreover, quite common in opera of the time, and Rossini himself was not above recycling some of his most beautiful tunes; a reckoning of all such cases in his operatic works would yield a substantial number indeed!

Example 3. Lucia's Mad Scene, "Ardon gl'incensi,"
Donizetti, *Lucia di Lammermoor* (Act III, scene 2).

Example 4. Verdi, *Falstaff* (Act III, scene 2).

Indiscriminate self-borrowing gradually disappeared, however, and in the second half of the century the desire to do something new and different began to extend to the writing of arias as well. Bellini often used the A-A-B-A pattern; Donizetti frequently resorted to strophic melodies (as in "Una furtiva lagrima" in *L'elisir d'amore*). But the most common practice in the nineteenth century was to connect a sometimes vocally demanding recitative with a lyrical cavatina and a double-verse cabaletta, ornamented on the reprise. The innovative Bellini sometimes omitted the final cabaletta, which in his opinion damaged the dramatic sense of the aria. Elsewhere, as in Lady Macbeth's scene in the second act of Verdi's *Macbeth*, the cabaletta is directly linked to the recitative with no intervening slow movement. On the other hand, there is no cabaletta after Banquo's recitative and slow aria. In fact, in *Macbeth* there are only two instances of the traditional recitative-cavatina-cabaletta structure: Lady Macbeth's first scene and Macduff's in Act IV.[17] What is more, the number of arias that departed from the conventional mold was increasing during that period.

In Verdi, a wide range of formal terminology was developed for the aria, above all the cavatina and the romanza,[18] but also the *ballata*, the *canzone*, the *canzonetta*, the *notturno*, and the *preghiera*. Melodic reprises also occur frequently in his works: in *La traviata*, there are strophic arias, and as late as *Otello* there is the famous Willow Song (Example 5). In *Falstaff*, however, the arias are sketchier in form, sometimes only a tune set to couplets ("Quand'ero paggio").

But the great show-stopping tunes so beloved by fans and which composers sometimes had to keep secret until the last minute (such as "La donna è mobile" in *Rigoletto*) inevitably turn up

Giuseppe Verdi, ca. 1845,
by Ch. Geoffroy.

Example 5. Desdemona's Willow Song, "Piangea cantando,"
Verdi, *Otello* (Act IV).

in this repertoire. In verismo operas, arias are sometimes barely distinguishable from *arioso* ("Ridi, Pagliaccio" for example, at the end of the first act of *I pagliacci*), though they are much more likely to be full-blown ("Lamento di Federico" in Cilèa's *Arlesiana*).[19]

This form of lyricism, taken up even in works like Richard Strauss's *Rosenkavalier* (1911) or Stravinsky's *Rake's Progress* (1951), continued in opera south of the Alps. *Recitativo secco*, on the other hand, gradually disappeared during the first half of the nineteenth century. The declamation in Rossini's *Tancredi* and *Otello* already exhibits remarkable advances. The sort of semi-monotonic dry recitative still persisted in certain works, such as *L'elisir d'amore* (at number 12 in Donizetti's score) and even Verdi's *Giorno di regno*, but the most significant development of the period was the gradual return to a more expressive *arioso* style. Bellini was a pioneer in the close binding of word to music, and in Donizetti there are scenes that are quite surprising for the period (especially in *La favorita*). Verdi's conception of dramatic declamation in *Macbeth* (1847, Macbeth's big scene in Act I) was ahead of its time, as were indeed *Luisa Miller*'s *parlando* (1849) or Azucena's recitals in *Il trovatore*. There are also some highly affective lines in Ponchielli's *Gioconda* (1876), in the last act when the heroine returns Laura to Enzo. Among the most beautiful later examples of emotional declamatory solos are Leoncavallo's famous "Ridi, Pagliaccio" and, dating from 1887, Iago's "Credo" in Verdi's *Otello* (Example 6). The success of the "Credo" was recognized early on, and in April 1912 a critic for the Parisian magazine *Musica* wrote of it:

The role of Iago is perhaps the most difficult in the great baritone repertoire; but, on the other hand, it is fair to say

that in no other opera has there been achieved with as
much power such perfect unity between the meaning of
the word and the force given to it by the musical line.

Later, in *Falstaff* (1893), the essence of the score derives from a
type of *arioso* whose melody is rather fleet and tricky to sing, truly
anticipating twentieth-century developments.

It should not be forgotten that the close-knit relation between
word and music had already been achieved by Russian composers
—Glinka and above all Dargomyzhsky (*The Stone Guest*) even before works by The Mighty Five, including Mussorgsky's *Boris
Godunov*—nor that in *Pelléas et Mélisande* (1902), Debussy would
propose a type of declamation that remained faithful to the rigors
of French pronunciation. In Italy as well, the monotonic chant

Example 6. Beginning of Iago's "Credo,"
Verdi, *Otello* (Act II).

crept back in, permitting a softening of phrase beginnings, for example, and an emphasis on important words by intervallic jumps; this technique appeared from Puccini on, in *Manon Lescaut* and in *Tosca* (Act I, after number 13 in the score, with the Sacristan's lines), in Cilèa's *Adriana Lecouvreur* (1902), and in Montemezzi's *Amore dei tre re* (1913).

The ever-increasing need for expressiveness spurred the most spectacular development in nineteenth-century Italian opera: the tightening of the bond between the literary text and the musical phrase. This was a far cry from the age of Rossini, when the same words could be used in more than one melody. Later developments responded to the growing interest in dramatic diction—even in highlighting the accents of vernacular speech—despite a continued collective national inclination to grant highest priority to the melodic line.

The Chorus

Duets, usually expressing love, are often prized for their melodic beauty: Alfredo and Violetta in "Parigi o cara" in the last act of *La traviata*, Radames and Aida in "O terra addio" at the end of *Aida*, Rodolfo and Mimi in "O soave fanciulla" at the end of the first act of *La bohème*. The *quartetto*, in which four different characters express themselves individually—a technique already embraced by Alessandro Scarlatti—has some very famous nineteenth-century counterparts, such as the one in *Rigoletto*; in addition, there are some magnificent sextets (*Lucia di Lammermoor*, Act II). But the chorus is no less ubiquitous in Italian opera of the 1800s.

In existence since the time of Monteverdi (*L'Orfeo*) and continuing with Cesti (*Il pomo d'oro*), the chorus was later reduced in size, especially in Venetian scores, for economic reasons.[20] In France, on the other hand, Lully's operas depended on the chorus for some of their most beautiful effects (the Shiverers' Chorus in *Isis*, for example). In the eighteenth century, Gluck gave the chorus a more vital part to play in the dramatic action. It came back into fashion in Italy with Jommelli and Traetta, though it remained quite static, as in Rossini (*Mosè in Egitto*, *Guillaume Tell*) and Bellini (*Norma*) later on.

Until the 1850s, the role of the chorus assumed an ever-increasing importance in Italian opera, though this development was far from satisfying to many lovers of bel canto. Defenders of the "good school" represented by Zingarelli, Fioravanti, and Paisiello in fact deplored the spread of what they considered to be useless music.[21]

With a mighty push from Donizetti, whose choruses already announce (*Marino Faliero*), narrate (*Maria Stuarda*), and comment on the action (*Belisario*), the transformation continued most tellingly in Verdi.[22] Nineteen of his twenty-six operas open with a chorus (the exceptions are *I masnadieri*, *Rigoletto*, *Il trovatore*, *La forza del destino*, *Aida*, *Simon Boccanegra*, and *Falstaff*). What is more, fifteen of his operas end with one. The choruses of Verdi may magnificently set the mood of a scene (the drinking chorus in the first act of *Ernani*), provide the entire final reaction ("Notte d'orror" at the end of *Un ballo in maschera*), or comment on the action (following the murder of Duncan, at the end of the first act of *Macbeth*). In Solera's librettos (*Nabucco*, *I lombardi alla prima crociata*), the chorus is already placed right in the center of the action, their rhythmic vigor combined forcefully with the topicality of the patriotic message they were meant to convey to the audiences of the Risorgimento. Their impact was great, whether in the famous song of the Hebrew slaves ("Va pensiero" in Act III of *Nabucco*), the pilgrims' chorus in *I lombardi* (Act II), or the chorus of exiled Scots in the last act of *Macbeth*. This last was foreshadowed by Rossini's *Mosè in Egitto* (Act I) when the Israelites pray for their deliverance. In Verdi, the chorus even manages to become a structural element, as in *Falstaff*.

Some choral numbers, including several of Rossini's, even wound up in the repertories of village bands, for although they were written in a great variety of styles, a few were quite simple: the drinking scene of *Le comte Ory*, the chorus of young maidens in *Attila* (Act I, scene 2), the chorus of ladies-in-waiting in *Ernani* (Act I), the young peasants offering fruit and flowers to Giulietta in *Un giorno di regno* (Act I, scene 2), and the children's chorus in Verdi's *Otello* (Act II). It should be added that the majority of nineteenth-century Italian choruses are homophonic.[23]

Soon after Italy's unification and the last works of Verdi, operatic choruses lost a great deal of their former impact. While verismo works were still capable of beautiful effects (the chorus of cherubim in the prologue of Boito's *Mefistofele*, or—a genuine "choral act"—the Café Momus scene in *La bohème*), they hardly ever called for such massive textures, and choral writing remained quite understated right through Montemezzi's *Amore dei tre re*.

Obviously composers' interest in writing for the human voice never flagged during the romantic era. Their treatment of the instruments of the orchestra, as accompanists and even soloists, though not so obvious, also deserves our attention.

Tamburini, by Dantan.
In *Le Charivari*, 7 August 1838.

TOSCA

LIBRETTO DI V·SARDOU
L·ILLICA - G·GIACOSA
MUSICA DI G·PUCCINI
G·RICORDI & C·EDITORI

CHAPTER 6

THE ORCHESTRA

Orchestral music underwent radical changes in Italy during the 1860s especially, when the vogue for public concerts, following the example of those in Paris or Brussels, began to spread throughout the peninsula.

The widely held view that the Italian opera orchestra is nothing but an enormous accompanying guitar deserves to be put in perspective. It is true that composers in the first decades of the nineteenth century did not make the listener very conscious of the orchestra, and soloistic passages were less common in Bellini than in Rossini—who was sometimes dubbed "Signor Vacarmi" or "Tamburossini." Still, orchestral scoring varied rather considerably over the course of these hundred years. Special orchestral effects are far from negligible, and there are some quite beautiful symphonic passages to be found in Italian opera of the nineteenth century.

The Instruments

In Italy, strings formed the core of the opera orchestra—even more so than in other countries.[1] The growth in the size of the wind section, in opera and in other music,[2] annoyed more than a

Example 7. Opening of the overture, Bellini, *Norma*.

few opera goers on the peninsula.[3] And yet, these works relied for a long time on a "classical" wind scoring for two flutes, two oboes, two clarinets, and two bassoons, a reliance that persisted in *Norma*, *L'elisir d'amore*, *Lucia di Lammermoor*, *I puritani*, *La fille du régiment*, and *La favorita*, and even in *Nabucco*, *Rigoletto*, *La traviata*, *Il trovatore*, and *La forza del destino*. *La Gioconda* and *Cavalleria rusticana* differ from these only by the addition of a third flute. Only rarely before the 1880s and 1890s did scores call for tripled winds —three flutes, three oboes, three clarinets, and three bassoons—as in *I pagliacci* and *Tosca*. Those with minor departures from a fully tripled scoring for winds include *Le villi* (only two clarinets), Verdi's *Otello* (four bassoons), and *Andrea Chénier* and *La bohème* (four flutes and one bassoon).

The brass, on the other hand, adopted the "romantic" arrangement—four horns, two trumpets, three trombones, and tuba—outright and more rapidly (*Ernani*, *Un ballo in maschera*).

The role of these instruments began to grow even as early as in Pacini's *Saffo* and in *Don Carlo*, and such scoring remained standard in the major Italian operas of the second half of the nineteenth century, with a few variations: three trumpets in *I pagliacci*, *Manon Lescaut*, *La Wally*, and *Tosca*; four trumpets in *Don Carlo* and *La Gioconda*; five trumpets in *Le villi*.

The harp, a traditional favorite in the theater, was used frequently, and the overall increase in size of the orchestra often led composers—especially those in the latter half of the century—to score for a pair of harps (*Nabucco*, *La forza del destino*, *Mefistofele*, Verdi's *Otello*, *I pagliacci*). The organ, associated with the numerous religious scenes of Italian opera, is heard in *Luisa Miller*, *Il trovatore*, *Mefistofele*, *Otello*, and *I pagliacci*. The accordion makes an appearance in *Mefistofele* as well. The percussion section usually consisted of timpani, and even bass drum and cymbals, to which other effects were occasionally added. Bells were perhaps the most frequent addition (*Lucia di Lammermoor*, *Luisa Miller*, *Un ballo in maschera*, *La Wally*); most memorably, they signal the massacre at the end of *I vespri siciliani* and toll the death knell in *Il trovatore* (Act IV, scene 1). The glockenspiel turns up in *Mefistofele*, *La Gioconda*, and *Le villi*, *Tosca* makes use of the recently invented celesta, and *La bohème* includes a xylophone.

Outside the orchestra pit, other sounds issued from the stage itself: mandolin, guitar, and bagpipe in Verdi's *Otello* (Act II), and the lute in *Falstaff* (in fact scored for guitar). The piano shows up only in later works: in Giordano's *Fedora* it is heard on stage in the second act, as in *Zazà*.

Principal Symphonic Passages

One of the essential functions of the theater orchestra has always been to introduce the singing that follows. The overture was traditionally the most ubiquitous symphonic number in nineteenth-century Italian opera, though it went by different names. Verdi termed it a "sinfonia" in *Oberto*, *Un giorno di regno*, *Nabucco*, *Giovanna d'Arco*, *Alzira*, *Luisa Miller*, and *I vespri siciliani*. It soon competed with the term "prelude" (*Ernani*, *I due Foscari*, *Attila*, *Macbeth*, *Il corsaro*, *Rigoletto*, *Un ballo in maschera*, *La forza del des-*

tino), a semantic switch made perhaps in order to emphasize the darker hues of an orchestral introduction like *Attila*'s, which differed from the *spiritoso* and *vivace* rhythms of the overture to *Un giorno di regno* or the serene detachment of overtures written for earlier works like *Oberto*. This change in terminology is obviously analogous to the one adopted by Wagner in *Lohengrin* and *Tristan*, but it must be noted that it occurred much earlier in the Italian repertoire, for the opening of *Lucia di Lammermoor*, which dates from 1835.

During the course of the nineteenth century, instrumental preambles tended to become shorter (*I due Foscari, Il corsaro*), even disappearing altogether,[4] though not without inciting vigorous disapproval. Thus, the *Revue et gazette musicale* of 28 May 1847 reported that the abbreviated introduction to *Macbeth* was scandalous—even though Rossini (*Mosè in Egitto*), Bellini (*Beatrice di Tenda*), and Donizetti (*L'elisir d'amore*) had already done likewise. Besides, had not the introduction to Verdi's earlier *I lombardi* (1843) been one of the shortest ever, prior to *Il trovatore*'s introduction, which was all of forty-seven bars in length? Later, *Don Carlo, Simon Boccanegra, Otello, Falstaff, Manon Lescaut* (fifty bars), *Tosca* (twenty-four bars), and *Adriana Lecouvreur* (twenty-one bars) provided audiences with very brief symphonic openings, a tendency which probably grew out of the poor reputation Italian opera overtures suffered abroad, as the following criticism from 1832 indicates: "Italian composers attach but little importance to a certain noise which they call overture"![5]

Indeed, audiences of the day paid very little attention to these orchestral offerings, whose subtler musical effects were frequently drowned out by people moving about or talking. Composers nevertheless attempted to emulate the sort of close relation between the overture and the rest of the opera that Gluck had achieved so successfully in *Alceste* and *Iphigénie en Aulide*. In order to transport the listener into the mood of the work, composers usually chose to have the orchestra present the main tunes of the opera right away—for example, Verdi uses "Va pensiero" in the overture to *Nabucco*. The openings to *I masnadieri, Attila*, and *Rigoletto* are the only ones by Verdi to use no melodies from the opera itself.

Only rarely are overtures based on a single theme, like the one that opens *Luisa Miller*. Generally they present, after a slow introduction, at least two melodies, often in binary form, a pattern typical of Rossini and present in Verdi's *Aroldo*: A B (dominant)–A'B' (tonic). In *Un giorno di regno*, the initial *sinfonia* even appears in a sort of abbreviated sonata form whose middle modulating episode is nothing but a development of the secondary theme. Other introductions, like the overture to *Guillaume Tell* and the prelude to *Cavalleria rusticana*, are based on a number of melodies. In the case of *Cavalleria rusticana*, three themes closely associated with the plot are taken up: the theme of Santuzza's love for Turiddu, the tune of their duet, and Turiddu's Siciliana (Example 8).

Whatever their duration and structure, these overtures are today nevertheless often regarded as highly successful symphonic entities, as exemplified by the overture to *La forza del destino* (1862), though that celebrated orchestral passage was not conceived in the form in which we now know it until 1869 (Example 9). Among Verdi's other works, the orchestral introductions to *Giovanna d'Arco*, *Luisa Miller*, and *Alzira* are just as remarkable—and, for all its brevity, the opening of *Aida* is no less dense (Example 10).

Besides these purely symphonic moments, instrumental music also accompanied dances or ceremonial entrances. Contrary to the custom in France, ballets were rarely integrated into opera in Italy. Generally only those Italian works written for the Paris Opéra were provided with ballet interludes: *La favorite* and *Les vêpres siciliennes*, with its celebrated half-hour-long Ballet of the Four Seasons (Act III). Ballets were often added whenever an Italian score was presented at the Paris Opéra, from *Macbeth* to *Otello*. One outstanding exception to Italian custom is the Dance of the Hours in the third act of *La Gioconda*, and Amazons perform a ballet honoring the princess in the third act of Cilèa's *Adriana Lecouvreur*.

Noteworthy as well are the number of old-style dances that are introduced, even incidentally, into operas written during the last half of the century. The Duke of Mantua dances the minuet with the Countess Ceprano in the first act of *Rigoletto*, and *I pagliacci*'s traveling players enact their pantomime (Act II) to the strains of the same dance. The minuet is also taught to Manon Lescaut in Puccini's work of the same name, and the gavotte appears in the first act of Giordano's *Andrea Chénier*.

Example 8. The three themes of the prelude,
Mascagni, *Cavalleria rusticana*.

Example 9. Overture, Verdi, *La forza del destino*.

Example 10. Opening of the prelude, Verdi, *Aida*.

Martial tunes gave rise to some of the most celebrated themes in nineteenth-century opera. "Suoni la tromba" (from *I puritani*) served as the basis for the famous *Hexaméron* keyboard transcription of Bellini's melody consisting of a set of variations by Chopin, Czerny, Herz, Liszt, Pixis, and Thalberg. The Triumphal March from *Aida* is very similar, not only in its rhythm but also in its repeated intervallic patterns.

Example 11. Triumphal March, Verdi, *Aida* (Act II); compare to the march theme from *I puritani*, "Suoni la tromba," in the Appendix, "Famous Melodies."

Much less common than these essentially choreographic set pieces are the orchestral fugue in *Macbeth* (end of Act IV), the *fuga infernale* of the Walpurgis Night Scene in Boito's *Mefistofele* (Act II), and the choral fugue finale of *Falstaff* ("Tutto nel mondo è burla").

An unmistakable sign of orchestral music's coming of age was the proliferation of intermezzos in works composed toward the end of the century, whatever their duration. Act III of *I lombardi alla prima crociata* opens with a beautiful prelude containing a memorable violin solo, though that practice was relatively uncommon in the early decades. A few intermezzos of this later era have acquired genuine celebrity: those of *Cavalleria rusticana*, *I pagliacci*, *Manon Lescaut*, and the atmospheric prelude to the last act of *Tosca*. Tunes already familiar to the listener may be used in them, like the reprise of Canio's famous aria in *I pagliacci*'s intermezzo.

The Functions and Effects of Orchestration

All this makes it clear that one of the fundamental roles of orchestral music was to create the appropriate psychological atmosphere or to prolong the emotional effect of a scene. Some of these results were achieved by rather novel orchestrational techniques, bearing witness to the skill that this sort of writing required, especially toward the end of the century. Hence, at the beginning of the third act of Puccini's *Bohème*, parallel fifths in the flutes effectively depict the desolate atmosphere of the Barrière d'Enfer just before dawn.

Example 12. Opening of Act III, Puccini, *La bohème*.

There is no lack of descriptive music in this repertoire, then; musical characterization and even tone-painting on the whole are rendered quite explicitly. For example, in one spot in the second act of *Oberto*, Verdi specifies that the orchestra must express "the action of a duel." The depiction of natural phenomena was also rather popular, as evidenced by the frequent *tempeste*, or storms, in romantic scores: *Guillaume Tell*, *Aroldo*, and *Otello*.

Nevertheless it is true that the orchestra's main function was to accompany the singers. So strong was the appeal of the human voice, however, that when they were not accompanying singers, the orchestra's instruments often sought to imitate vocal timbres. This seems particularly clear in introductions to cavatinas. In "Casta diva" (*Norma*, Act I), the entire melody is exposed by a solo flute before the priestess begins to sing, and in the Mad Scene in *Lucia di Lammermoor*, the same instrument blends most artistically with the florid vocal line. Much less well known but just as lovely are the flute solos in *Alzira*. Outstanding instrumental effects are no less varied in Italian opera than in the works of a Cherubini, for example, and they often acquire quite characteristic emotional connotations. It is no accident that the violin of *L'amico Fritz*, occasionally gypsylike in tone, is so prominent in a work totally devoted to love; some poignant cello solos are inspired by the same subject, such as the one in the overture to Donizetti's *Maria di Rohan*.

Orchestras tended to become more and more flexible as the century wore on, permitting even greater differentiation of timbres. Here as well, the development in Verdi seems particularly illustrative, from the solid tonal blocks of *Oberto* and *Un giorno di regno* to the instrumental transparency of *Falstaff.* Even in works of Puccini, in which doubling might frequently be taken for granted (as much in *Manon Lescaut* as in *Tosca*), the delicacy of the orchestral texture sometimes brings Debussy to mind: in Act III of *La bohème* or the opening of *Il tabarro*, for example.

Scoring and instrumental style therefore developed extensively in Italian opera over the course of the nineteenth century, and some of these changes strongly influenced the overall structure and style of these works, as the next chapter will show.

CHAPTER 7

FORM AND LANGUAGE

Structure

The listener's overall impression of an operatic style is influenced more by formal structure and expressive mode than by orchestral details. Traditionally, an Italian opera consisted of an orchestral overture (with the occasional interlude or transitional passage), recitatives, arias, and various vocal ensembles. The eighteenth century's Piccinni was perhaps the first composer to write significant quintets and sextets, and there were some very fine pieces of this type in the nineteenth century: the trio in Act III of *I lombardi*, the fugal finale in *Falstaff*, the famous quintet in *Anna Bolena*, and many other examples already cited. One quite exceptional case is the presence of spoken narration in the intermezzo portion of *Le villi*.

The grandest climaxes, however, were provided by the great concerted finales. Ambitious even in Piccinni, from Spontini on they almost always consisted of an ensemble with chorus, most often in three-quarter time. There are such majestic moments in *Semiramide*, *Attila* (Act I), *Macbeth* (end of Act I and the Banquet Scene finale, Act II), and *Tosca* (the *Te Deum* at the close of Act I). Bellini, however, was less conventional in this respect; at the end of the first act of *Norma*, for example, there is a dramatic *terzetto* instead of the expected grand finale.

Verismo works, on the other hand, bring down the curtain in a much more spectacular manner. In *Cavalleria rusticana* and *I pagliacci*, the final orchestral bars are quite abrupt once jealousy has quenched its murderous thirst for vengeance. This was already nearly the case in *La traviata* and *Carmen*, operas whose realism often anticipated the verismo style.

In most of these works, the final bars also feature a return of the most memorable melody. It is difficult, however, to refer to this as a *leitmotiv* technique, as in Wagner. In Italian opera it is usually a matter of nonsystematic echoes, already occurring in the first part of the century in Rossini, as well as in Donizetti's *Lucia di Lammermoor* (whose love-duet theme, "Verranno a te sull'aure," reappears in the Mad Scene) and *Don Pasquale* (quartet at the end of Act II). Verdi's operas are filled with such echoic reprises: *Oberto* (the melody of the first-act love duet is taken up by the chorus of attendants in Act II), *Attila* (reminiscences of the dream), *Macbeth* (whose second-act prelude recalls "Fatal mia donna" in the preceding act), *Rigoletto* ("La maledizione"), and *La traviata* (where Alfredo's Act I "Di quel amor" returns twice in the orchestra in the last act).[1] The term *tema-cardine* (pivot theme)[2] would seem appropriate here. While the device occurs often in Verdi, it assumes no greater significance in his later works than in his earlier ones; in *Falstaff*, the mechanical repetition of Quickly's "dalle due alle tre" is even caricaturish.

Puccini willfully used a handful of musical themes as his point of departure, gradually building his work around them. Thus *Tosca*'s opening chords are better appreciated when we realize that they in fact constitute Scarpia's theme. In *La bohème*, the use of fragments from "Che gelida manina" and "Mi chiamano Mimì" (Act I) is less unusual. In verismo scores, such motivic recall is common, putting greater emphasis on the dramatic effect of certain key situations. Thus in *I pagliacci*, the melody of "Ridi, Pagliaccio" is introduced in the prologue, in the orchestral interlude, and at the end of the opera. Such repetitions were facilitated by the fact that the custom of dividing an opera into separate "numbers" had by then virtually disappeared. Indeed, at the beginning of the nineteenth century, cavatinas, choruses, finales, and so on were entities quite unto themselves. Later, more dramatic "scenes" were often added to them (as in Weber's *Euryanthe*); these scenes might be assembled with any number of theatrical devices coinciding with the characters' entrances and exits, as in spoken theater. There are more *pezzi chiusi* (closed numbers, forming separate wholes) in Donizetti than in Bellini. As for Verdi, he abandoned his strict adherence to the practice in *Don Carlo* and thereafter. And yet, operas broken into numbers made a comeback in Europe in the twentieth century, as witnessed by Hindemith's *Cardillac* (1926) and Stravinsky's *Rake's Progress* (1951). Busoni even wrote in 1921 that "opera can only be composed of numbers."[3] It is certain that this practice sparked new variety and contrast in scoring and style— the essential art of opposition. The lack of opposition causes music to go over much less well with the general public, and the Italians have always understood this, not only in regard to overall structure but also in the specific style of these works, where poison is combined with joyous libation (*Lucrezia Borgia*), where bacchanalian revelry fills our ears as Violetta is dying,[4] or where Gustavo is felled by his assassin at the climax of a dance that suddenly comes to an end (*Un ballo in maschera*).

Melody

Even more than the impact of certain structural elements— perhaps because structure is anchored in the mind with the aid of a few memorable melodic fragments—certain musical phrases are what audience members take with them as souvenirs upon leaving the opera house.[5] Among Italian composers, few indeed could be said to have resisted the temptation to write a catchy tune. Stendhal found more melody in Paisiello than in all other composers put together.[6] Stravinsky's comment on the subject was even more trenchant: "There is more substance and true invention in the aria 'La donna è mobile,' for example . . . than in the rhetoric and vociferations of *The Ring*."[7] Is this merely a prejudiced, neoclassic view, intent on crushing once and for all "le fantôme du Vieux Klingsor"?[8] Stravinsky also wrote that "Bellini inherited melody without having even so much as asked for it, as if Heaven had said to him, 'I shall give you the one thing Beethoven lacks.'"[9] The claim is a bit peremptory, perhaps, but no one would dream of denying the Italian composers' gift for *canto spianato*, or vocal embellishment.[10]

Their secret lies in the relative simplicity of line, in phrases that generally lean on the strong notes of the scale and that usually proceed in conjunct degrees, as in "Una furtiva lagrima" (*L'elisir d'amore*), Violetta's desperate "Amami Alfredo" (*La traviata*), and "Celeste Aida."

Example 13. "Celeste Aida," Verdi, *Aida* (Act I).

The use of old modal scales is less common in Italian opera than in French opera, though the typically artful reliance on major and minor is far from monotonous. As Puccini averred, "There is one area in which we Italians are superior to German composers, and that is our ability to express infinite sadness with the major scale."[11] Indeed one need only listen to the sextet in *Lucia di Lammermoor* (in D-flat major), the final scene in *Rigoletto* (in the same key), or the end of *Aida* (in B-flat major) to be convinced. Besides, chromaticism is not uncommon: in Act II of *La traviata*, for example, it is used to express Violetta's confusion and doubt; toward the end of the century, it sometimes sneaks in unexpectedly (Example 14).

Also typically *fin de siècle*, an ever-increasing concern for expressiveness—including outbursts of octave jumps—made difficult demands on the voice (Example 15). And yet, at a time when vocal writing was becoming extremely complicated and tortuous elsewhere, the generous outpourings of verismo melodies confirmed the indisputable melodic genius of the composers of the Italian school.

Example 14. Passage from the Prologue,
Leoncavallo, *I pagliacci.*

Example 15. Leoncavallo, *I pagliacci* (Act I).

Harmony

Contrary to current popular opinion, the merits of Italian opera need hardly depend on melody alone. To cite but one example, the beauty of the overture to Donizetti's *Belisario* is due to the skillful transitions between each section. Donizetti's more insistent, martial, even Germanic, rhythms tend to be criticized, but the subtlety of his use of intervals, the Neapolitan sixths (prelude to *Lucia di Lammermoor*) or augmented fifths (in the same opera, Act

II, "Ti rimprovero"), is underestimated. The augmented fifth was frequently used by Puccini as well, in the second act of *Madama Butterfly*, for example. The unexpectedness of some of Verdi's harmonies is also remarkable: the tonal suspension for thirty-two bars in *Il corsaro*, the unresolved seventh in the duet between Gilda and the Duke in Act II of *Rigoletto*, and the chordal progressions underneath the twelve strokes of midnight in *Falstaff* (Example 16).[12] Italian composers used the seventh (often created by appoggiaturas) to heighten tension, as in the accompaniment of the famous "Ridi, Pagliaccio" (Example 17).

The most novel harmonic strokes occur in works by composers who wrote in the latter part of the century. In *Le villi*, Puccini writes perfect parallel chords in Anna's romanza (at number 3 in the score, measures 3, 5, 11, and 13), and at the beginning of Verdi's *Otello*, the curious sustained organ pedal embodies musically the storm's insidious force. Earlier, in *Norma* (Example 18), Bellini managed to create a harmonic atmosphere that curiously foreshadows Wagner's *Tristan*. Not surprisingly, the German composer so admired Bellini's opera that he wrote an aria for Oroveso to replace number 8 in Act II, which he tried in vain to have sung by Lablache in 1838.[13]

Foreign Influences

During the nineteenth century, the reigning school of opera was unquestionably Italian. As the decades passed, unhappily, it altered; one of the first influences to have an effect upon it was that of the German music drama, particularly the Wagnerian variety.

Many critics looked disapprovingly upon this trend until around 1870,[14] and Italian operas bearing traces of German influence were not very well received by the public before then. There was a poor welcome for both Franco Faccio's *Profughi fiamminghi* (1863) and Verdi's *Don Carlos*, which with its Germanic-style brass writing was premiered at the Paris Opéra in 1867; Boito's *Mefistofele* was hissed in Milan in 1868. But after 1871, when *Lohengrin* was first produced in Italy, Bologna became the Wagnerian capital *par excellence*. Four years later, Boito's *Mefistofele* was in fact warmly received there. In 1883, *The Ring* was given in Venice,

Example 16. Vocal score, Verdi, *Falstaff* (Act III, scene 2),
Milan: Ricordi, 347–348.

Example 17. "Ridi, Pagliaccio," Leoncavallo, *I pagliacci* (Act I).

Example 18. Finale, Bellini, *Norma* (Act III).

Florence, Rome, Turin, Milan, and Trieste. In the last years of the nineteenth century, on the peninsula and elsewhere, the influence of Wagner began to spread. In spite of its rustic characters and the difference in setting, even *I pagliacci* (in the prologue) shows traces of it. And on 11 March 1902, La Scala premiered Franchetti's *Germania*, whose subject and style are unequivocally Teutonic.

Even while the German school was making its impact, the Paris Opéra was exerting its own influence. Rossini, Bellini, Donizetti, Verdi—all sojourned in the French capital at the height of their careers. Later, Boito and Catalani went there to study at the Paris Conservatory. Leoncavallo lived there in poverty, giving a few piano lessons, playing in cafés, and composing little songs. Thenceforth Italian musicians tried to emulate the French school.

The five-act grand opera, epitomized by Meyerbeer, also became a model for various take-offs after *Les vêpres siciliennes*[15]—in spite of Verdi's lack of sympathy for the composer of *Les Huguenots*. The choruses in *La forza del destino*, for example, bear traces of the French style: the muleteers in Act II, scene 1, and the Rataplan chorus at the end of Act III. Later, at the same time French opera

Verdi's home at Sant'Agata.
Photo, *Les Préludes*, 1985.

was being performed more and more frequently south of the Alps,[16] the vogue of Massenet, whose *Manon* was an immediate success in Italy, took hold; the first act of *Andrea Chénier* reflects this trend. Composers like Cagnoni and Marchetti seem perfectly attuned to the French spirit, and Cilèa was one of the first in Italy to own a copy of the score of Debussy's *Pelléas et Mélisande*.[17] Some orchestrations, such as those of Puccini, evoke a similar atmosphere as a necessary alternative to verismo.

But these various influences and developments had an impact on a given operatic locale only if they could reach the actual performance stage. It is therefore essential at this point to examine the customs and workings of the typical nineteenth-century Italian opera house.

PART III: *Performance*

The material aspects of producing opera—the type of theater, audience response, makeup of the company or quality of the singers—quite often influenced a composer's choice of subject, instrumentation, and even the character of the vocal writing. In order to truly appreciate the nature of this remarkable repertoire, one must understand how and under what circumstances opera houses functioned in the nineteenth century.

CHAPTER 8

ADMINISTRATION

When Rossini embarked on his career, the institution known as opera had already been in existence for a long time. It is an easy matter, therefore, to pinpoint the centers of operatic activity by first identifying the major opera houses of the period.

Opera Houses

The large number of opera theaters in operation in Italy during the romantic era testifies to the popularity of the genre, if proof be needed.[1] Nevertheless, it is amazing that in 1838, Genoa—a city of some 100,000 inhabitants—welcomed its opera fans with a total of 9500 seats.[2] By 1897 there were 450 theaters listed in the *Annuario dell'arte lirica e coreografica italiana*, including twelve in Florence, eleven in Milan, seven in Naples, six each in Turin and Rome, and three in Venice. The growing artistic involvement of cities in northern Italy during the last half of the century is notable. On the most celebrated of these stages, the major works of the period were created (Table 4).

Several buildings date from the eighteenth century: the Apollo and Argentina in Rome, Turin's Teatro Regio, La Fenice in Venice, and La Scala in Milan. But the popularity of opera and the

Table 4. Great premieres of the major Italian opera houses.

Florence	La Pergola (17th century ➔): *Macbeth*, 1847.
Milan	La Scala (1778 ➔): *La gazza ladra*, 1817; *Il pirata*, 1827; *Lucrezia Borgia*, 1833; *Norma*, 1835; *Il giuramento*, 1837; *Il bravo*, 1839; *Oberto*, 1839; *Un giorno di regno*, 1840; *Nabucco*, 1842; *I lombardi alla prima crociata*, 1843; *Giovanna d'Arco*, 1845; *Mefistofele*, 1868; *La Gioconda*, 1876; *Otello*, 1887; *La Wally*, 1892; *Falstaff*, 1893.
	La Cannobiana (1779–1894, replaced by Teatro Lirico): *L'elisir d'amore*, 1832.
	Teatro dal Verme (1872–1930): *Le villi*, 1884; *I pagliacci*, 1892.
	Teatro Lirico (1894–1938): *L'arlesiana*, 1897.
Naples	Teatro San Carlo (1737 ➔): *La donna del lago*, 1819; *Lucia di Lammermoor*, 1835; *Alzira*, 1845; *Luisa Miller*, 1849.
Rome	Teatro Argentina (1732 ➔): *Il barbiere di Siviglia*, 1816; *I due Foscari*, 1844; *La battaglia di Legnano*, 1849.
	Teatro Apollo (1795–1889): *Il trovatore*, 1853; *Un ballo in maschera*, 1859.
	Teatro Costanzi (1880–1946, subsequently Teatro dell'Opera): *Cavalleria rusticana*, 1890; *Tosca*, 1900.
Turin	Teatro Regio (1741–1936; Nuovo Regio 1973 ➔): *Manon Lescaut*, 1893; *La bohème*, 1896.
Venice	Teatro San Benedetto (1755–1868, later Teatro Rossini until 1925): *L'italiana in Algeri*, 1813.
	La Fenice (1792 ➔): *Semiramide*, 1823; *Ernani*, 1844; *Attila*, 1846; *Rigoletto*, 1851; *La traviata*, 1853; *Simon Boccanegra* (first version), 1857.

Note: Other major Italian opera houses include Bologna's Teatro Municipale, Genoa's Teatro Carlo Felice, and Palermo's Teatro Massimo.

Set design for Act III, scene 1, of Verdi's
Falstaff (Milan, 1893).

large number of fires[3] led to the construction of many new theaters in the nineteenth century: Trieste's Teatro Nuovo (1801), Genoa's Teatro Carlo Felice (1828), Teatro Municipale of Reggio Emilia (1857), Rome's Teatro Costanzi (1880), and Milan's Teatro Lirico (1894).

Regardless of when they were built, the interiors of these theaters consisted of a multi-tiered arrangement of boxes, or loges, rising above the orchestra level, or parterre, with gold and velvet fixtures creating a most appropriate atmosphere for the finest singing and the comfort of the audience.

When Busseto's Teatro Verdi opened in 1858, its two tiers of boxes and upper gallery, or balcony, could barely accommodate four hundred spectators, but this was in proportion to the modest size of its city. Elsewhere, Italians invariably displayed a preference for vast auditoriums. In Rome the Barberini theater, conceived in the seventeenth century, was designed to hold an audience of thirty thousand. In 1816, the Neapolitan San Carlo opera

Principal nineteenth-century Italian opera houses

1. La Pergola (Florence)
2. La Scala (Milan)
3. La Cannobiana (Milan)
4. Teatro Dal Verme (Milan)
5. Teatro Lirico (Milan)
6. Teatro San Carlo (Naples)
7. Teatro Argentina (Rome)
8. Teatro Apollo (Rome)
9. Teatro Costanzi (Rome)
10. Teatro Regio (Turin)
11. La Fenice (Venice)
12. Teatro Municipale (Bologna)
13. Teatro Carlo Felice (Genoa)
14. Teatro Massimo (Palermo)

house could hold 3500 spectators, and even in 1900, theaters averaging three thousand seats were not uncommon: La Scala and Dal Verme in Milan, the Costanzi in Rome, and Teatro Massimo Bellini in Catania. Palermo's Teatro Massimo could accommodate 2600 people, La Fenice 2500, and Parma's Teatro Regio 2300. Most theaters of any importance had at least fifteen hundred seats (Piacenza's Teatro Comunale, Brescia's Teatro Grande, Rimini's Teatro Vittorio Emanuele), the same capacity as the Bayreuth Festspielhaus.[4]

The large number of foreign theaters that produced Italian opera is another indication of the popularity of this music in the nineteenth century. In Paris, for example, the Salle Ventadour was almost exclusively devoted to the genre until it shut down in 1878. From 1847 to 1892, London's Covent Garden was baptized the "Royal Italian Opera House," and London saw the creation of Verdi's *Masnadieri* (1847) at Her Majesty's Theater (Haymarket). An Italian company was established in St. Petersburg in 1843, and Verdi's *Forza del destino* was given its world premiere at the Imperial Opera there in 1862. In New York, where Manuel Garcia's

Interior of Teatro Verdi in Busseto. Verdi's box is on the second level, indicated by an X. Photo, *Les Préludes*, 1985.

company had already toured during the 1825–26 season, Richmond Hill programmed thirty-five Italian operas in 1832, the year after it opened, and the Italian Opera House was opened there in 1833. In Cairo, an 850-seat theater, built to commemorate the completion of the Suez Canal, devoted its initial season to Italian works and in 1871 premiered Verdi's *Aida*.[5]

Though it is interesting to note the number of theaters outside Italy committed to performing Italian opera, the focus here will be upon the houses within Italy and how they organized their companies and prepared their performances.

Birth of the Spectacle

It was indeed against the peculiar backdrop of the various theater towns that projects were born and performances planned. Opera productions in Italy were always ruled by a three-fold authority: the theater director, an administrator who tried not to go too far over the budget; the unabashedly conservative impresario; and the *palchettisti*, or boxholders, who often subscribed from the time the theater was built.[6] These last were something like official patrons, maintained by every town even after 1866, when Italian theaters stopped being domanial property and were taken over by the local municipalities whose expense budgets were covered by the State.[7] In addition to these three authorities there was the influence exerted by the publishing houses, which, in Italy as in other European countries, became closely identified with certain composers in the second half of the century and owned the performance rights of their operas.

Contrary to the administrative policies of French companies, Italian companies were not obliged to remain in one theater. They were itinerant, and rosters could be changed every season, even from one performance to the next.

Since the creation of an opera began with the choosing of a subject, impresarios, directors, or publishers would sometimes suggest to the librettist a number of ideas or themes likely to lead to a box-office success. The librettist would then sell his idea to the composer. Donizetti, for example, paid Cammarano five hundred francs[8] for *Lucia di Lammermoor*, while *Il trovatore* cost Verdi one thousand ducats. [After Cammarano's death, Verdi paid his widow six hundred ducats rather than the agreed-upon five hundred for the unfinished libretto, then engaged another writer to finish it.] Later, Franchetti let Giordano have the libretto of *Andrea Chénier* for two thousand lire, the fee that Illica had previously asked of him. The publisher could then purchase the rights to the opera. Ricordi, without question one of the greatest Italian publishing houses of the period, acquired the rights for *Oberto* from Verdi for 1750 francs. But the fee paid by impresarios or publishers depended on how famous the composer was; Vaccai always received less than Bellini who, like Verdi after him, demanded as much as sixteen to twenty thousand francs for a new opera.[9] It should not be forgotten that there was no copyright law in Italy until 1865, a circumstance that often placed composers in a very vulnerable position.

The house of Ricordi published many works by Bellini, Donizetti, Verdi, and even Puccini. Francesco Lucca (1802–1872) learned the publishing trade with Ricordi and went into business for himself in 1825; his wife, Giovannina (1810–1894), carried on the business before selling out to Ricordi in 1888. Besides Mercadante, Ponchielli, Catalani, and Petrella, Lucca held the Italian rights to many foreign operas by Halévy, Meyerbeer, and Wagner. The house of Curci, created in 1860, focused mainly on operetta and ballet, but at the close of the nineteenth century, Sonzogno became Ricordi's formidable rival. Active in the field of literature since the end of the eighteenth century and the publisher of *Il Secolo*, a well-known Italian periodical, since 1866, the house began publishing music in 1876 under the direction of Edoardo Sonzogno (1836–1920). In 1883 it began organizing competitions for opera composers and acquired many verismo works (*Cavalleria rusticana*, *I pagliacci*, *L'amico Fritz*, *Andrea Chénier*).

These publishing enterprises flourished under the gradual acquisition of a repertoire that allowed them to rely on the profits from score rentals. Even Verdi began doing more business with the house of Ricordi rather than with traditional opera entrepreneurs.

Publishers might place a newly acquired score at the bottom of a drawer and forget it was there, but on the whole they were effective promoters of their composers' works and sometimes even became involved in hiring artists and funding production costs.[10] Rental rates of published scores were normally charged by the season.[11]

Composers had the right to recommend the singers most likely to ensure a work's success, but the responsibility of assembling the cast ordinarily rested with the impresario; the impresario often relied in turn on a theatrical agent in a way that, according to Gino Monaldi's discerning analogy, was akin to the methods of a comb-and-button merchant.[12]

From the end of the eighteenth century on, such intermediary agents would organize auditions and try to acquire the loyalty of individual artists by having them sign contracts before recommending them to impresarios in return for a fee: 5 percent in 1820, 8 percent in 1880.[13] They also took charge of the delivery of scores and the release of publicity. There were many theatrical agents in Italy, especially between 1850 and 1890, and their main stamping ground eventually moved from Bologna to Milan, where in the 1880s they invariably gathered at the Caffè dei Filarmonici, near the cathedral, in the Galleria Vittorio Emanuele.

Impresarios, also very numerous in Italy, sometimes managed to take advantage of the well-deserved fame of celebrities—thus, Domenico Barbaja (1778–1841), a former waiter whose astuteness made him a fortune, was for Rossini what Bartolomeo Merelli (1794–1879) became for Verdi. Merelli, called "l'aquila degli impresari" (the Eagle of Impresarios),[14] worked for La Scala from 1836 to 1864. All impresarios fought to eliminate theatrical agents and tended to assume their duties themselves.

Performances in those days were grouped into three main seasons: Carnival (from December 26 until Lent), spring (after Easter), and fall (from September to Advent).

Repertoire

Parts I and II of this book contain a general survey of the principal Italian operas of the nineteenth century. But it is critical to consider them in relation to the repertoire of the Italian peninsula as a whole and to see what constituted an actual season.

Table 6 makes it clear that a solid repertoire was becoming established in the second half of the nineteenth century and that all works being performed in the Italian opera houses of 1875 had premiered after 1800, with the exception of *Don Giovanni* and *Il matrimonio segreto*. Of the twenty-nine composers cited, the names that turn up most frequently are Verdi (eighteen works) and Donizetti (ten works), followed by Meyerbeer, Rossini, and Petrella (five each), Bellini and L. Ricci (four each), Cagnoni (three), and Gomes (two). Italian composers are naturally in the vast majority, with French composers represented by Auber (with *La muette de Portici*), Gounod (*Faust*), and Halévy (*La juive*). Although Wagner is still missing from this list, Germanic composers are slightly more in evidence: Mozart (*Don Giovanni*), Weber (*Der Freischütz*), Meyerbeer (with four French grand operas and *Dinorah*), and Flotow (*Martha* and *L'ombra*).

It is interesting to compare these statistics with two other compilations, one attempting to show the spread of Italian opera abroad (Table 5), the other containing the programs of a season fifteen years later in opera houses on the peninsula (Table 7).

In the *Gazzetta musicale di Milano* of 3 February 1889, A. Albertini provided a look at the world's most frequently performed operas of the year 1888 (Table 5). As with the information offered in Table 6, the original list did not claim to be exhaustive, but it is representative nonetheless.

The composers heading the list were still Verdi and Donizetti, followed by Meyerbeer—unchanged from the Italy of 1875. On the other hand, Bellini and Rossini were already losing popularity, while Bizet, Gounod, and even Auber were high on the scale on the international front. It seems Italy, with so many of its own masterpieces to choose from, sometimes left the meanest share of its performances to imported works.

Next let us consider the programs of Italian houses for the 1902–03 season, as they were published in *Musica e musicisti* of January 1903 (Table 7). Verdi was then still in first place (with thirty-five productions), this time followed by the remarkably rapid emergence of Puccini (twenty-one), with Donizetti (ten) in third place. The infrequent mention of Bellini (whose name appears five times) and particularly of Rossini (named only once) confirms their decline, while at the same time the nation was turning its back on Meyerbeer (named only twice) and opening the doors to Wagner (in eight productions here) and to Franchetti's *Germania*! Ponchielli was holding his own, though one might be surprised at the in-frequent mention of Leoncavallo and Mascagni. Gounod's *Faust* remained one of the most popular foreign operas in the country.

Such was the state of opera in Italy by the end of the nineteenth century. Though it is true that productions of operas by Verdi went into a decline later on, it should be noted that in our time the master of Busseto, along with the composer of *Madama Butterfly*, seems once again to be enjoying great popularity among opera goers not only in Italy, but the world over.

Victor Maurel (1848–1923) as Falstaff.
After singing in the premiere of the Italian
version of *Don Carlos* in Naples, this
French baritone created the roles of Iago
(1887) and Falstaff (1893). Anonymous
watercolor, Museum of the Opéra, Paris.

Table 5. Most frequently performed composers and operas of
1888, according to the *Gazzetta musicale di Milano* of 3 February
1889. Survey based on the programs of 205 theaters, worldwide.
Opera titles are followed by the number of performances; only a
composer's most popular works are listed.

Verdi (in 203 theaters): *La traviata*, 27; *Aida*, 25; *Il trovatore*, 24;
    La forza del destino, 18; *Ernani*, 14; *Un ballo in maschera*, 14

Donizetti (in 87 theaters): *Lucia di Lammermoor*, 25; *La favorita*,
    22; *Lucrezia Borgia*, 10; *Linda di Chamounix*, 7; *L'elisir
    d'amore*, 5

Meyerbeer (in 42 theaters): *Gli ugonotti*, 14; *Dinorah*, 10;
    L'africana, 10

Bizet (in 37 theaters): *Carmen*, 30

Bellini (in 34 theaters): *La sonnambula*, 16; *Norma*, 10;
    I puritani, 7

Gounod (in 33 theaters): *Faust*, 28

Auber (in 28 theaters): *Fra diavolo*, 24

Rossini (in 27 theaters): *Il barbiere di Siviglia*, 23;
    Guglielmo Tell, 4

Ponchielli (in 23 theaters): *La Gioconda*, 22

Thomas (in 21 theaters): *Mignon*, 15; *Amleto*, 6

Note: Further theater totals include Marchetti (16), Boito (12),
Gomes (12), Wagner (12), Petrella (9), Flotow (7), Cagnoni (7),
Halévy (6), Franchetti (5), Catalani (3), Pacini (1), and Puccini (1).

Table 6. List of works remaining in the repertoire of Italian
opera houses, according to the *Gazzetta musicale di Milano* of
7 February 1875. Composers' names and titles are followed by
the date of the premiere.

Mozart	*Don Giovanni*	1787
Cimarosa	*Il matrimonio segreto*	1792
Rossini	*Il barbiere di Siviglia*	1816
Rossini	*Otello*	1816
Weber	*Der Freischütz*	1821
Rossini	*Semiramide*	1823
Rossini	*Mosè* [the Paris *Moïse*, in Italian]	1827
Auber	*La muta di Portici*	
	[*La muette de Portici*]	1828
Rossini	*Guglielmo Tell*	1829
Bellini	*I Capuleti e i Montecchi*	1830
Bellini	*La sonnambula*	1831
Bellini	*Norma*	1831
Meyerbeer	*Roberto il diavolo*	1831
Ricci, L.	*Chiara di Rosembergh*	1831
Donizetti	*L'elisir d'amore*	1832
Donizetti	*Lucrezia Borgia*	1833
Donizetti	*Gemma di Vergy*	1834
Rossi	*I falsi monetari*	1834
Ricci, L.	*Chi dura, vince*	1834
Bellini	*I puritani*	1835
Halévy	*L'ebrea* [*La juive*]	1835
Donizetti	*Lucia di Lammermoor*	1835
Meyerbeer	*Gli ugonotti* [*Les Huguenots*]	1836
Mercadante	*Il giuramento*	1837
Donizetti	*La figlia del reggimento*	1840
Donizetti	*La favorita*	1840
Pacini	*Saffo*	1840
Verdi	*Nabucco*	1842
Verdi	*I lombardi*	1843
Donizetti	*Don Pasquale*	1843
Donizetti	*Maria di Rohan*	1843
Donizetti	*Linda di Chamounix*	1844
Verdi	*Ernani*	1844
Verdi	*I due Foscari*	1844
Verdi	*Giovanna d'Arco*	1845
Verdi	*Attila*	1846

Verdi	*I masnadieri*	1847
Verdi	*Macbeth*	1847
Flotow	*Marta*	1847
Cagnoni	*Don Bucefalo*	1847
Ricci, L.	*Il birraio di Preston*	1847
Donizetti	*Poliuto*	1848
Meyerbeer	*Il profeta* [*Le prophète*]	1849
Verdi	*Luisa Miller*	1849
Ricci Brothers	*Crispino e la comare*	1850
Di Giosa	*Don Checco*	1850
Verdi	*Rigoletto*	1851
Sanelli	*Il fornaretto*	1851
Petrella	*Le precauzioni*	1851
De Ferrari	*Pipelè*	1851
Verdi	*Il trovatore*	1853
Verdi	*La traviata*	1853
Petrella	*Marco Visconti*	1854
Apolloni	*L'ebreo*	1855
Verdi	*I vespri siciliani*	1855
Pedrotti	*Tutti in maschera*	1856
Verdi	*Aroldo*	1857
Petrella	*Jone*	1858
Verdi	*Un ballo in maschera*	1859
Gounod	*Faust*	1859
Meyerbeer	*Dinorah*	1859
Verdi	*La forza del destino*	1862
Petrella	*La contessa d'Amalfi*	1864
Cagnoni	*Michele Perrin*	1864
Meyerbeer	*L'africana*	1865
Verdi	*Don Carlo*	1867
Usiglio	*Le educande di Sorrento*	1868
Marchetti	*Ruy Blas*	1869
Petrella	*I promessi sposi*	1869
Gomes	*Il Guarany*	1870
Flotow	*L'ombra*	1870
Campana	*Esmeralda*	1870
Cagnoni	*Papà Martin*	1871
Verdi	*Aida*	1871
Ponchielli	*I promessi sposi*	1872
Gobatti	*I goti*	1873
Gomes	*Salvator Rosa*	1873

Table 7. Programs of Italian opera houses, winter season of
1902–03, according to *Musica e musicisti*, January 1903.

Alexandria	Teatro Zizinia: *Manon Lescaut*; *Tosca*; *Germania*; *Tristano e Isotta*; *Don Pasquale*; *Il barbiere di Siviglia*
Bari	Teatro Petruzzelli: *Aida*; *Ugonotti*; *Andrea Chénier*
Bergamo	Teatro Sociale: *Un ballo in maschera*; *Salvator Rosa*
Brescia	Teatro Grande: *Tosca*; *Iris*; *Ernani*
Cagliari	Teatro Civico: *Il Guarany*; *Faust*; *Cavalleria rusticana*; *I pagliacci*
Carrara	Politeama Verdi: *La bohème* (Puccini); *Faust*
Castelfiorentino	*Linda di Chamounix*
Catania	Teatro Bellini: *Tosca*; *Otello*; *Il trovatore*; *I puritani*; *La sonnambula*; *Norma*
Catanzaro	*Linda di Chamounix*; *La campana dell'eremitaggio*; *Le educande di Sorrento*
Crema	*Le educande di Sorrento*; *Tutti in maschera*; *Crispino e la comare*; *Napoli di carnovale*
Cremona	Teatro Ponchielli: *Tannhäuser*; *Tosca*; *Un ballo in maschera*
Cuneo	Teatro Civico: *Tosca*; *Il trovatore*; *Lucia di Lammermoor*
Fermo	*Tutti in maschera*; *I falsi monetari*
Ferrara	*Germania*; *Aida*; *I lombardi alla prima crociata*
Florence	Teatro Pergola: *Germania*; *Tosca*; *Manon Lescaut*; *L'elisir d'amore*
Ivrea	Teatro Civico: *Manon Lescaut*; *Un ballo in maschera*; *Crispino e la comare*
Lecce	*Ernani*; *La favorita*; *Un ballo in maschera*; *Ruy Blas*

Lisbon	Teatro de Sao Carlos: *Germania*; *Tosca*; *Otello*; *Aida*; *I maestri cantori* [*Die Meistersinger*]; *La Gioconda*; *Tannhäuser*; *Lohengrin*
Malta	*Guarany*; *Otello*; *Manon Lescaut*; *Tosca*
Mantua	*Tosca*; *Germania*
Messina	Teatro Vittorio Emanuele: *Germania*; *Aida*; *La Gioconda*; *Il trovatore*; *Norma*
Milan	Teatro alla Scala: *La dannazione di Faust*; *Luisa Miller*; *Un ballo in maschera*; *Asrael*; *I lituani*; *Oceana*
	Teatro Dal Verme: *Le villi*; *Ernani*; *Rigoletto*; *I due Foscari*; *Marta*
	Teatro Carcano: *Il trovatore*; *La traviata*; *Faust*; *La forza del destino*
Modena	Teatro Comunale: *Aida*; *Mefistofele*; *La favorita*
Novara	Teatro Coccia: *Germania*; *Manon Lescaut*; *Lucia di Lammermoor* or *La sonnambula*
Oneglia	*Faust*; *Ernani*; *Jone*
Oporto [Porto]	Teatro de Sao Joao: *Aida*; *Otello*; *Lohengrin*; *Tosca*; *Manon Lescaut*; *Tannhäuser*; *L'ebrea* [*La juive*]
Palermo	*Aida*; *La bohème* (Puccini); *La traviata*; *Dinorah*; *Sansone e Dalila*
Parma	Teatro Regio: *I vespri siciliani*; *La Gioconda*; *Lohengrin*; *La sonnambula*
Pesaro	Teatro Comunale Rossini: *La Gioconda*; *Faust*
Piacenza	Teatro Comunale: *Aida*
Pistoia	Teatro Manzoni: *La Gioconda*
Poggibonsi	*Fra diavolo*
Portoferraio	*Saffo*; *La traviata*; *L'elisir d'amore*
Prato	*La bohème* (Puccini)

(continued)

Reggio Emilia	Teatro Municipale: *A basso porto*; *Don Sebastiano*; *Rigoletto*
Rome	Teatro Costanzi: *Sigfrido* [*Siegfried*]; *Mefistofele*; *Rigoletto*; *La traviata*; *Aida*; *Il trovatore*; *Germania*; *Hänsel e Gretel*; *Manon Lescaut*
Saluzzo	*Fra diavolo*; *Lucia di Lammermoor*; *Rigoletto*
Sassari	Politeama: *Tosca*; *Linda di Chamounix*; *Ruy Blas*; *I puritani*
Savigliano	Teatro Sociale: *La bohème* (Puccini); *Il trovatore*; *L'elisir d'amore*
Siena	Teatro Rinnuovati: *La favorita*; *Giulietta e Romeo* (Gounod); *Marta*
Trieste	Teatro Verdi: *I maestri cantori*; *Falstaff*; *Il barbiere di Siviglia*; *Tosca*; *Germania*
Turin	Teatro Vittorio Emanuele: *Mefistofele*; *La Gioconda*; *Lohengrin*; *La traviata*; *Lucia di Lammermoor*; *Il trovatore* or *Un ballo in maschera*
	Teatro Balbo: *Il trovatore*; *Rigoletto*; *Lucia di Lammermoor*
Venice	Teatro Rossini: *Lucia di Lammermoor*; *La favorita*; *La traviata*; *Ernani*; *Rigoletto*
Verona	Teatro Filarmonico-Quaresima: *Lohengrin*
Vigevano	Teatro Colli-Tibaldi: *Ernani*

CHAPTER 9

INTERPRETERS

The gradual establishment of a standard repertoire guaranteed the fame of composers without overshadowing the importance of those still instrumental to the success of a work, and often the inspiration for it: namely, the interpreters.

The specific functions of the various technical elements required for the smooth running of a production may have evolved slowly over the course of the nineteenth century, but the importance of the "singing artist" was never in doubt.

Singers

Throughout the century, the real stars of the *cartelloni* (the playbills, and by extension the cast distributions) remained the singers, dominated by the *prime donne*, or leading sopranos. The Italian public successively lavished their adoration upon Giuditta Pasta, Giulia Grisi, Fanny Persiani, Marianna Barbieri-Nini, Angiolina Bosio, Adelina Patti, Gemma Bellincioni (the first Santuzza), and Celestina Boninsegna.[1]

On the other hand, it was rare for a mezzo-soprano—Adelaide Borghi was an exception—to achieve similar fame. Soprano Antonietta Pozzoni (the first Aida) did not begin singing in this tessitura

Adelina Patti (1843–1919).
Photo, Bergamasco, St. Petersburg,
courtesy William R. Moran.

until the age of thirty-five. Contraltos seemed to make more of a mark, particularly in the second quarter of the century, with Marietta Brambilla, Marietta Alboni, and Barbara Marchisio.

Of the male voices, basses remained least prone to celebrity, though Francesco Navarrini, the first Ludovico in Verdi's *Otello*, earned a great reputation on the peninsula. Genuine stardom naturally belonged to the tenor—Domenico Donzelli, Enrico Tamberlick, Francesco Tamagno, Alessandro Bonci, and of course, Enrico Caruso—and, toward the close of the century, to the baritone: first to Giorgio Ronconi and Enrico Delle Sedie, then to Antonio Cotogni, Mattia Battistini, and Fernando De Lucia, who became the teacher of Georges Thill.

In all voice categories, most of the singers who trod the boards of Italian opera stages—especially the men—were native-born. The most applauded foreign singers in Italy were women: the French Constance Nantier-Didiée, Belgian-born Marie Sasse, the Canadian Emma Albani, the British Clara Novello and Mary Shaw, and above all singers from Central and Eastern Europe (the German Sophie Cruvelli, Bohemian Adelina Stehle, Czech Teresa Stolz, and Moravian Teresina Singer).

The fees earned by these great singers give some idea of the special favors bestowed upon them. About 50 percent of the expense budgets of most opera houses was normally spent on singers' fees.[2] For instance, in the 1829–30 season Turin's Teatro Regio lavished seventy thousand lire on solo voices, while 21,000 lire was enough to cover instrumentalists' fees. In the same company, during the 1864–65 season, 116,575 lire was needed to pay the solo singers versus 30,190 lire for the orchestra and 14,935 lire for the chorus. Two years later, the prima donna alone demanded 35,000 lire, the first tenor only eighteen thousand, and the other vocal soloists between eight hundred and three thousand lire. As for the secondary singers and other supernumeraries, they had to be satisfied with between three hundred and sixteen hundred lire.[3]

The personal idiosyncrasies of certain stars have already been well documented elsewhere; still, we must mention here that these singers usually had little acting ability, and that the *prime donne* liked to sing well downstage so as to be heard all the better in their favorite showpieces, while other artists patiently waited their turns upstage. This ludicrous situation was no longer acceptable to composers in the last half of the century. That is why Verdi preferred to cast French baritone Victor Maurel in his last works.[4]

Working conditions for singers were particularly trying at the beginning of the nineteenth century, with artists required to give five or six performances per week. As roles became more demanding, such frequent appearances became impossible, but the decreased number of piano rehearsals continued to make the situation uncomfortable for the soloists.[5]

Choristers' lives had little in common with those of opera stars. Their numbers increased sharply over the century, as indicated by the following statistics: the fourteen-member chorus at Rome's Teatro Apollo of 1818 had grown to thirty-six voices by 1855[6]—a number equaled at Turin's Teatro Regio.[7] By the beginning of the twentieth century, chorus size had grown to one hundred at La Scala, eighty at Rome's Costanzi and Palermo's Teatro Massimo, seventy at Milan's Teatro Dal Verme and Venice's La Fenice, sixty at Parma's Teatro Regio and Florence's La Pergola, and forty in Piacenza and Padua.[8] This increase in choral force, no doubt influenced by French grand opera, put an additional strain on production managers' budgets.

At first these choral ensembles were all-male.[9] In 1832, for example, at La Pergola, Berlioz counted "a dozen young boys between the ages of fourteen and fifteen."[10] Women remained in the minority in these choruses for a long time; in Turin in 1845, there were only twelve women, as opposed to twenty-four men.[11]

On the whole, criticism of choruses was very harsh. In the romantic era, Berlioz declared that Italian opera choruses, weak even at the San Carlo, "are on the level of those at the Nouveautés[12] or the Vaudeville, one notch below the Paris Opéra-Comique."[13] Their limited musical abilities were often sorely tested; in 1843, Henri Blanchard could still write: "It is a miracle if one can find one member of the chorus who knows how to read music. The others chirp like parakeets."[14] The same author notes disparagingly— though not without some truth—that during the day they toil as masons and cobblers. In addition, nature seemed to have blessed them with few attractive physical features,[15] and they went on stage wearing whatever they wanted,[16] since for a long time theaters paid little attention to their costumes. What is more, the fees they received remained ridiculously low, amounting to pennies a day at Florence's Teatro Pagliano even at the close of the century.[17]

What a difference between the well-paid *prima donna assoluta*[18] at La Scala and the humble emaciated spinster, scraping a miserable existence from day to day as an alto chorister in some cubbyhole of a third-rate theater. For that matter, orchestra musicians of the period were hardly better off.

Instrumentalists and Conductors

In Italy as in the rest of Europe, orchestras assumed an ever-increasing importance during the course of the nineteenth century. We start, however, with Berlioz's acerbic remarks about La Pergola's orchestra in the early part of the century: "I saw in front of the stage a long, narrow pit containing the instrumentalists. This arrangement of the orchestra [*la masse harmonique*] is most unsatisfactory. It makes it impossible to produce an effect."[19] The same illustrious visitor also pointed out that in Rome's Teatro Valle there was only one cellist—a jeweler by trade.[20]

With the exception of the few privileged houses, Italian opera orchestras at the beginning of the nineteenth century were not very large. La Scala, for instance, boasted sixty-seven players as early as 1778.[21] There were an equal number in 1816, but the number reached one hundred by the turn of the century. By then, the most celebrated houses in Palermo (Teatro Massimo), Venice (La Fenice), and Florence (La Pergola) contained eighty, seventy, and sixty players, respectively. Others, like Trieste's Teatro Comunale, found it difficult to recruit any more than thirty musicians for their orchestras.[22]

The most striking facts about the makeups of these ensembles were the continued presence of the harpsichord,[23] which in some theaters in Italy persisted until 1850, and the richness of the double-bass section, which in Italian pit orchestras was invariably equal to, if not larger than, the cello section.[24] As elsewhere, the viola section tended to be understaffed,[25] and the brass sometimes seemed noisier than necessary in Italian opera scores. The Chevalier Van Elewick deplored the overpowering sax tuba in both

Genoa and Venice and further lamented "the overly shrill brass" of La Fenice.[26] For Fétis, all Italian orchestras were bad, but the most acceptable in his day was that of the San Carlo.[27]

Orchestra musicians were paid little more than members of the chorus. At Turin's Teatro Regio, salaries as late as 1894 were between three lire (for the third clarinet, third trombone, and bass drum players) and ten lire (for the first violin), amounting to a total of 48,000 lire per season.[28] Like choristers, the instrumentalists received their fee on a regular biweekly basis.

The conductor, situated behind the instrumental forces next to the first-tier boxes,[29] usually played with the large fraternity of violinists and led with his bow—at least until 1860.[30] About that time the first of the illustrious nineteenth-century *direttori d'orchestra* appeared. This was Angelo Mariani,[31] who gradually replaced the bow with a baton. The conductor soon became one of the most important musical personalities of an opera company.[32] After Mariani, the composer Franco Faccio, Leopoldo Mugnone, and Arturo Toscanini were all to capture the public's attention.

Formerly, it was the composer (whose contract provided for room and board) who had to conduct the first three performances from the keyboard.[33] Some composers, like Donizetti, continued to assume conducting duties off and on throughout the run; toward the turn of the century, Mascagni proved himself a very effective conductor.

But this development was not universally welcomed. As Verdi wrote on 25 March 1875 to Giulio Ricordi:

> When I began to scandalize the musical world with my formidable productions, we had to endure the tyranny of the *prime donne*, of rondos; now we also have to endure that of the conductors! Bad, very bad! Of the two evils, I prefer the first.

Dancers

Because ballet was rarely incorporated into the operas of the period, dance had a minor role to play in nineteenth-century Italian opera.

In the early part of the century, however, ballets were often given on the same bill as operas. Italy had some great dancers and ballet masters, such as Filippo Taglioni (1777–1871), Carlo Blasis (ca. 1795–1878), Jean Coralli, Pasquale Borri, Giuseppe Rota (whose *Cleopatra* was given at La Scala in 1857), Luigi Danesi (*Messalina*, 1877), and above all, Luigi Manzotti. In later years, when ballet rose to its height of popularity, Manzotti's *Excelsior* (1881) required 508 performers and extravagant scenery and *Amor* (1886) more than six hundred performers.

Nearly all these renowned choreographers made a name for themselves abroad, and sometimes even became expatriates. Originally from Sicily, Mazilier's real name was Giulio Mazarini. The same applied to many of the ballerinas, like Marie Taglioni (1804–1884), Carlotta Grisi (1819–1899), Fanny Cerrito (1817–1909), and Carolina Rosati (1826–1905). Indeed, Paris was the ballet capital of the world in the romantic era, from the ethereal whiteness of *La Sylphide* (1832) to the dazzling, colorful Ballets Russes in 1909.

When a major opera theater did have a corps de ballet—paid even less than orchestra musicians—such ensembles around the beginning of the twentieth century numbered as many as one hundred at La Scala and around forty at La Fenice.[34] They were given much to do in imported operas or in the spectacular, action-filled ballets of the end of the century.

Stage Designers and Directors

The subject of operatic scenery, which composers seldom concerned themselves with at the time, rarely turns up in the letters of Rossini or Bellini. Composers of that day and age focused their attention on vocal virtuosity or the emotional impact of their singers.

As years passed, however, the importance of staging gradually entered the picture; it is generally considered that the mixed reception of *Don Carlos* in Paris can be attributed to a neglect of that aspect of the production.

Stage settings in the nineteenth century were simulated by painted canvas backdrops containing the key elements of the scene, including the furniture. Paper was used in the smaller theaters, and unusual scenic devices—such as the six-foot-high bands of cardboard intended to represent the waves of the Red Sea in Rossini's *Mosè in Egitto*—would seem quite primitive to us today. Sets were frequently used for more than one opera, and it was not uncommon for totally anachronistic elements to be seen side by side.

In any case, there was a genuine evolution in nineteenth-century scenic design as well. The first decades inherited the neoclassic approach of the previous generation. A certain sobriety of line characterized the style of Gaspare Galliari (1761–1824) and Giovanni Pelego (1776–1817), active at La Scala after 1810. That did not preclude attempts at sumptuous *mises en scène* like those of Pietro Gonzaga, which reflected French customs embodied in the grand historical operas of Meyerbeer and Halévy. Some 250 extras filed onstage in *La juive*.[35]

With Alessandro Sanquirico (1777–1849), who succeeded Gonzaga at the most important opera house in Milan, these tendencies became tinged with genuinely romantic elements, as in *Il pirata* and *Norma*. The decors of Domenico Ferri (1784–1852), who began working at Bologna's Teatro Comunale in 1821, might even be called Gothic, with their many wild, dark, sylvan scenes. To these romantic elements, Carlo Ferrario (1833–1907) later added touches of already stark realism (*Mefistofele*, *La Gioconda*).

Set design for Act I of Leoncavallo's *Zazà* (Milan, 1900).

The time had come for historical accuracy (the fifteenth-century England of *Falstaff*), action (bicycles ridden on stage in Giordano's *Fedora*), and broad strokes of local color.

The traditional alternation of interior and exterior settings of scenes or acts, on the other hand, remained frequent, with the average opera calling for five or six different sets (*Giovanna d'Arco*, *Attila*, *Macbeth*, *Il trovatore*, *Un ballo in maschera*, *Simon Boccanegra*, *Falstaff*). The nine different settings in *I lombardi alla prima crociata* are an exception to this rule, as are those of *Un giorno di regno* and *Nabucco*, limited to only three.

In Verdi, settings representing a "public square" (*I lombardi*, Act I; *I due Foscari*, Act III; *Giovanna d'Arco*, Act II; *Alzira*, Act I; *Attila*, Prologue; *La battaglia di Legnano*, Acts I and IV; *Luisa Miller*, Act I; *I vespri siciliani*, Act I; *Simon Boccanegra*, Prologue; *Falstaff*, Act III) or a "country" landscape (called a "deliziosa campagna" in *Oberto*, Act I; "desolate" in *Giovanna d'Arco*, Act I; "deserted" in *Macbeth*, Act IV and *I masnadieri*, Act III) appear as frequently as interior settings, be they in a palace, church, or *osteria* (tavern): *Alzira*, Act II, scene 1; *I masnadieri*, Act I, scene 1; *Rigoletto*, Act III.

Practically all operas of this period contain a nocturnal scene, traditionally conveying fear, whether inside a cave (*I lombardi*, Act II, scene 2; *Macbeth*, Act III), in catacombs or a tomb (*Ernani*, Act III; *La battaglia di Legnano*, Act III), in a prison (*Roberto Devereux*, *Ernani*, *I due Foscari*, *Il trovatore*, *Don Carlo*, *Aida*), or in the mysterious light of the moon (*Norma*, *Un ballo in maschera*, *La forza del destino*, *Aida*, *La Gioconda*).

On an altogether different level are the more explosive moments when terror is heightened by natural phenomena: storms rage in *Macbeth*'s opening scene, in *Il corsaro* (Act III, scene 2), and in the last act of *Rigoletto*. Parties and drinking often provide contrast to dire developments, whether it be the brindisi in the Banquet Scene of *Macbeth*, the one in the opening act of *La traviata* (when the first symptoms of Violetta's fatal illness appear), or the party during which Gustavo is assassinated in *Un ballo in maschera*.[36]

Local color and even a touch of exoticism are further common means of providing contrast, as witnessed by Pasha Seid's harem in *Il corsaro* (Act II, scene 1) or by the character of Preziosilla and her song in the second act of *La forza del destino*.

Also essential to the staging are a small number of critical props, from Desdemona's handkerchief and Violetta's medallion to the usual swords and daggers.

For a long time, contracts required singers to furnish their own costumes,[37] but with the onset of the romantic era, some impresarios stocked various items of clothing which they would place at the artists' disposal[38] or rent out, whatever their condition. It was not until the last decades of the century that any special attention was given to costume designs.

As for stage direction, it was not taken very seriously in the first half of the century. Adelina Patti went so far as to send her secretary to rehearsals in her place. After 1880, stage directions became increasingly more explicit, as indicated in the scores of *Le villi* and *Adriana Lecouvreur*.

Italian opera productions were still a far cry from the wonderful collaborations between Gustav Mahler and Alfred Roller at the Vienna State Opera, from the reforms of Lugné-Poe, Gordon Craig, and Adolphe Appia,[39] from the bold starkness of Wieland Wagner's Bayreuth productions of the 1950s, or from the lavish aestheticism of Visconti. Nevertheless, the post-1970 ascendancy of the operatic stage director (like Chéreau, Lavelli, Ronconi, or Strehler) would not have been possible without the innovative developments of the nineteenth century.

CHAPTER 10

THE PUBLIC

*I*n a country whose roads throughout its southern half were ruled by fearsome outlaws until the 1870s,[1] where the illiteracy rate approached 75 percent as late as 1861, where only 8 percent of the population spoke a non-dialectical Italian,[2] and where the economy, marked by an acute depression from 1887 to 1890, barely made any headway until the last decades of the nineteenth century, what sort of public could an entertainment like opera hope to attract?

Different Categories of Spectators

By the eighteenth century, the audience composition had become quite diverse: aristocrats sat in the boxes and the general public usually stood on the orchestra level. In the romantic era, private boxes were largely the property of the *palchettisti*, who paid an annual fee, or *canone*, to cover a percentage of the theater expenses. Among the different types of boxes, those in the second level were most coveted and were generally occupied by the well-to-do. It was not long before the highest row of boxes lost its partitions to become the *loggione*, or balcony, where the working classes huddled together.[3] The *poltrone* or *poltroncini* on the *platea* (seats on the orchestra level) were not reserved, and eyewitness accounts unanimously concur that the most expensive finery and diamonds glittered against the backdrop of the velvet-lined boxes, while the more modestly attired bourgeois spectators occupied the main-floor seating.

Opera tickets in Italy cost much less than those of Parisian theaters. In mid-century, the least expensive seat at the Paris Opéra cost about the equivalent of one dollar, while it was possible to be seated in any of the leading Italian houses for one-fourth that amount. This of course meant that performances brought in less money for Italian administrators. It also accounted for some of the problems impresarios continually faced. Spectators were only too ready to make a fuss when an opera did not have the good fortune to please. At such times, theaters would echo with cries of "Al ladro!" (Stop, thief!) or "L'impresario in galera!" (To jail with the impresario!).

At the beginning of the nineteenth century, men had to pay more for seats than women, and foreigners more than native citizens. This custom persisted in some cases until 1830. Army officers enjoyed special reduced rates, and in the first few decades, it was quite common to see men in uniform in the front rows. They became easy targets, in the eyes of the patriots, during the more intense hours of the Risorgimento.

Audience Tastes and Behavior

In luxurious Italian opera houses such as La Scala, said by Stendhal to be the most beautiful theater in the world, or La Fenice, praised to the skies by Eugène d'Harcourt in 1907 and whose fascinating atmosphere at the time of the Austrian occupation was recreated in the Visconti film *Senso* (1954), those who occupied boxes could shut themselves off from the rest of the public by means of a curtain, or retire to the rear of their box to indulge in sorbets during the recitatives.[4] Games of chance (pharaoh, roulette, backgammon), legalized in Italy between 1753 and 1788 and again in the early nineteenth century, had one of their most effective promoters in the impresario Barbaja. Their subsequent suppression plunged producers into inevitable deficits, which had to be compensated through government subsidies.[5]

The behavior of opera goers differed from one city to the next. The much-dreaded La Scala audience, so disinclined to applause, was said to be "seated on its hands." Parma and Bergamo audiences were even more difficult, while Neapolitans acquired a reputation for being the most noisy. In Naples and elsewhere, there was no holding back disapproval; Reggio Emilia, on the other hand, laid down restrictions in 1834 against *clamori indecenti* (improper shouting) and allowed only discreet applause at the end of arias (1835) or "moderate signs of approval" (1858).[6]

As years passed, however, applause seemed to become less and less vociferous,[7] without any official moves to intensify it even with the claque. That institution, so effective in Parisian theaters,[8] prevailed under a different form in Italy, where only three or four *portoghesi* (what members of the claque were called at La Scala) were hired to applaud whatever they heard. Even so, there was no lack of clans or factions in Italy during this period, and the custom of the *partitaccio* (a hostile faction) persisted, guaranteeing a great amount of turmoil in the audience's reception of any given performance.

Dress rehearsals were usually open to the public, but ticket prices for premieres were set very high.[9] At such performances, eagerly attended by opera fans and dreaded by the singers, the public sometimes reacted unfavorably to works that later became great favorites. *Il barbiere di Siviglia*, *Norma*, *Il trovatore*, and later *Madama Butterfly* were all fiascos at their premieres. On the other hand, when a work made a great impression, its success often influenced the fashions and customs of the day: hats and culinary sauces "à la Verdi" appeared after the premiere of *Nabucco* (1842), and coiffures and attitudes "à la Mascagni" after *Cavalleria rusticana*.

Can the social function of Italian opera audiences ultimately be defined? Was the opera house the favorite haunt of young lovers, as Stendhal believed? Was it aristocratic entertainment for boxholders? Or pure escapism? It is certain that the proliferation of operettas in Italian theaters during the 1880s and the later influence of verismo were unmistakable signs of change. Singers tried desperately to combat the assault on their voices by the heavier orchestrations, but audience interest began to wane and theaters to empty, their former attraction lost.[10] Thus Paul Klee, while attending a performance in Florence's Teatro Verdi at the beginning of the twentieth century, noted that the theater "is in the shape of a rectangular box, as large as it is unkempt, on the level of popular opera" and that "not all the musicians were dressed in black."[11]

Theaters still attracted fans and melodies resonated all the same from the *forno* (bread oven), but the musical genre of opera was clearly on the decline.

Verdi's tomb in Casa di Riposo, Milan.
Photo, *Les Préludes*, 1985.

CONCLUSION

At the beginning of the twentieth century, Italian opera, so long so vital, was beset by opponents bent on its destruction. By 1909, the futurists were railing against the shrewd business of mass-producing sure-fire hits, placing the works of Verdi, Giordano, and Puccini on the same lowly plane as a Tosti romance. The only opera composer they looked upon favorably was Mascagni.

Noted critics and eminent musicians soon followed suit. Torrefranca made a point of vigorously disputing the popular belief that Italians were born opera composers and charged Puccini with catering to the basest instincts of the public with his neurotic lovers and suffering protagonists.[1]

Casella accused Donizetti and Verdi of having been businessmen, not composers,[2] and himself provided a model of Italian neoclassicism during a period when musical research, experimentation, and innovation were spreading throughout the peninsula.[3] And yet, very few Italian works dating from the years between the two world wars entered the international repertoire.[4]

Many Italian opera composers became expatriates, like Ferruccio Busoni, Ermanno Wolf-Ferrari, and later, Gian Carlo Menotti—who remain, paradoxically perhaps, the most distinguished representatives of the genre.

Such strong reaction and disapproval underline even more clearly the characteristics of Italian opera, whose principal aim was perhaps less the successful blend of the total spectacle (since ballet and scenery were not as important there as elsewhere) than the immediate communicability of universal melody, always close to the heart of the people who identified with Italian opera, and closer than ever in the verismo period.

It is hardly surprising, therefore, that in 1932, tired of the many novel but ineffectual innovations, a group of ten composers dared to proclaim their desire to revive the spirit of the operatic romanticism of yore:

> We must not forget the past. . . . We oppose so-called objective music, which as such can only represent sound in and of itself without the living expression of creative inspiration. . . . The Romanticism of yesterday . . . which was, moreover, the style of all our great masters . . . shall also be the Romanticism of tomorrow, if it is true that history weaves its destiny in a coherent fashion, without becoming lost or rewriting the myth of Sisyphus.
>
> —Ottorino Respighi, Giuseppe Mulé,
> Ildebrando Pizzetti, Riccardo Zandonai,
> Guido Zuffellato, Alberto Gasco, Alceo Toni,
> Riccardo Pick-Mangiagalli, Guido Guerrini,
> and Gennaro Napoli.[5]

Soon thereafter, Stravinsky declared his sympathy for the school,[6] and a "return to Verdi"[7] began to occur. Any survey of recent Italian opera seasons shows that the most beloved works among Italian audiences are those of the romantic era. One might also point to the influence of Puccini on the young Italian composer Lorenzo Ferrero and the unabashed lyricism of his music. In this age of "neo-simplicity," who can ignore the emotional directness of the great nineteenth-century opera composers? With a renewed interest in the more obscure operas of that period, our rediscoveries now extend to Donizetti, Mercadante,[8] and Rossini, and even Salieri fascinates the public since the release of Forman's film, *Amadeus*. Is this simple curiosity, nostalgic revival, or vital necessity?

Interior of Museo Donizettiano in Bergamo.
Photo, *Les Préludes*, 1985.

NOTES

Preface

1. One topic covered in the academic syllabus for the French Agrégation in 1982–83 and in 1983–84 was, in fact, "The High Points in Italian Opera from *Norma* to *Tosca*."
2. Many of these sources may be found in the Bibliography that concludes this book.

Introduction

1. This is in reference to the first recipients of the French Academy's Grand Prix de Rome for musical composition. French composers were not allowed to travel to the Villa Medici until 1803, long after authorization granted for painters, sculptors, and architects (1665), and engravers (1683). For more on this, see the article devoted to French composers in Rome, "Les Musiciens français à Rome," *R.I.M.F.* 5, no. 14 (June 1984) and Susan Lee Fogel, "Prize of Rome," *Opera News* 4 March 1972: 28–30.
2. For more on this subject, see S. Martinotti, *L'Ottocento strumentale italiano* (Bologna: Forni, 1972).

Chapter 1

1. See Folco Portinari, *Pari siamo! Io la lingua, egli ha il pugnale: Storia del melodramma ottocentesco attraverso i suoi libretti* (Turin: EDT/Musica, 1981), 18.
2. Vincenzo Terenzio, *La musica italiana nell'Ottocento* (Milan: Bramante, 1976), vol. 1, 34.
3. E. Maschino, "Il libretto moderno," in *Annuario dell'arte lirica e coreografica italiana*, ed. G. A. Lombardo (Milan: A. de Marchi, 1898), 51–58.
4. Despite the composer's refusal to take sides, the final scene's hymn to the glory of the female voice leaves no doubt as to Strauss's feelings!
5. In a somewhat different genre, that of the sacred drama, Pizzetti went on to write his own librettos beginning with his second work, *Debora e Jaele*.
6. L. Baldacci, *Tutti i libretti di Verdi* (Milan: Garzanti, 1975), ix.
7. Obertello, "Walter Scott e la musica," *Rassegna musicale* 5 (1932): 318–333; Jerome Mitchell, *The Walter Scott Operas* (Tuscaloosa: University of Alabama Press, 1977); R. Fiske, *Scotland in Music* (Cambridge University Press, 1983).
8. This device is well described by M. Descotes in "Du drame à l'opéra: Les transpositions lyriques du théâtre de Victor Hugo," *Revue d'histoire du théâtre* 34, no. 2 (1982): 103–156.
9. Works by Donizetti are the exception. On this, see William Ashbrook's article, "Donizetti's Historical Opera," *Opera* 20, no. 8 (August 1969): 665–669.
10. It is obvious, however, that the number of acts in these works could vary from one version to another; one example is *Don Carlo*, which in the revised Italian version has only four acts.
11. Puccini's *Villi* was conceived in one act for the Sonzogno competition but given in two acts in Turin on 26 December 1884.
12. The role of Barnaba is no less important in Victor Hugo; see note 8 in this chapter.
13. On this, see Catherine Clément in *L'opéra ou la défaite des femmes* (Paris: Grasset, 1979), trans. Betsy Wing, under the title *Opera, or the Undoing of Women* (Minneapolis: University of Minnesota Press, 1988).
14. See J. and B. Ott, *Les pédagogies de la voix et les techniques européennes du chant* (Issy-les-Moulineaux: Editions EAP, 1981).
15. *Gazzetta musicale di Milano* 7 November 1875, concerning Molière's *George Dandin*.

16. Let us not forget, though, that in French baroque opera, for example, Lully's librettist Quinault used the word "love" (*amour*) at least once every seven or eight lines.

Chapter 2

1. See John Allitt, *Donizetti and the Tradition of Romantic Love: A Collection of Essays on a Theme* (London: The Donizetti Society, 1975).
2. "The fierce serpents of jealousy attack his breast!" *Il trovatore* (Act I, scene 1).
3. "My universe is in you," *Rigoletto* (Act I).
4. "Your blood is my blood! Every drop you shed is like blood from my own heart," *Il trovatore* (Act II).
5. "One kiss, mother, farewell."
6. See J. Loschelder, *Das Todesproblem in Verdis Opernschaffen* (Cologne: Petrarca Haus, 1939).
7. "Ah, doubt God, but do not doubt my love."
8. "He who dies for the fatherland has lived long enough."
9. For a discussion of the patriotic elements in melodrama, see R. Monterosso, *La musica nel Risorgimento italiano* (Milan: F. Vallardi, 1948), 225–289.
10. "O land of my fathers, I see you again. . . . Dear fatherland . . . with a new teardrop, I come to plant you, O sweet native soil."
11. "I love the fatherland immensely," *I lombardi alla prima crociata* (Act I).
12. "Italy shall be great and free," *I lombardi alla prima crociata* (Act II).
13. "Brothers, let us hasten to deliver the oppressed," *Macbeth* (Act IV, scene 1).
14. "The oppressor has been crushed! The joy of such a victory shall endure with us forever!" *Macbeth* (Act IV, scene 4).
15. See A. Nicastro, "Reminiscenze e populismo nella poetica di Puccini," *Nuova rivista musicale italiana* 2, no. 6 (1968): 1092–1104.
16. As shown so well by M. Kelkel, *Naturalisme, vérisme et réalisme dans l'opéra de 1890 à 1930* (Paris: Vrin, 1984).
17. Ferruccio Busoni, "Abozzo di una nuova estetica delle musica," in *Lo sgardo lieto . . .*, ed. F. d'Amico (Milan: Il Saggiatore, 1977), 49.
18. "Thousands of spirits are rising from the ground," *I due Foscari* (Act II, scene 1).

Chapter 3

1. Consider G. Marteggiani's thesis in *Il romanticismo italiano non esiste* (Florence: Successori B. Seeber, 1908).
2. Consult A. La Penna's "La tradizione classica nella cultura italiana," in *Storia d'Italia* (Turin: Einaudi, 1973), vol. 5, no. 2.
3. Of this work, which he heard at Teatro Costanzi in Rome on 8 January 1902, Paul Klee wrote: "Perhaps it was not good to hear this opera before becoming acquainted with the other works of that master. It sounds more like Halévy or Meyerbeer than an anesthetized Rossini." P. Klee, *Journal* (Paris: Grasset, 1959), 85.
4. For example, in Verdi's *Giovanna d'Arco*, the second scene of the Prologue takes place in a forest clearing near the entrance to a cave, and Act I opens in a rocky outdoor encampment; see Chapter 9.
5. See U. Bosco, *Realismo romantico* (Caltanissetta and Rome: S. Sciascia, 1959).
6. "At the root of every soul is a romantic devil, stronger than I, than we, than everyone."
7. In France as well, political and religious subjects naturally provoked censorship; see O. Krakovitch, *La censure théâtrale de 1830 à 1850* (D.M.A. diss., Aix-Marseille, 1979). On Italian censorship, see C. Di Stefano, *La censura teatrale in Italia 1600–1962* (Bologna: Cappelli, 1964) and Robert J. Goldstein, "Political Censorship of the Opera in Europe: 1815–1914," *The Opera Journal* 21, no. 3 (1988): 12–26.
8. As quoted in an article by U. Rolandi, "Teatro e musica a Roma un secolo fa," *Strenna dei Romanisti* 9 (1948): 209.
9. The work would not be presented again in its Swedish setting until the 1952 Covent Garden revival, remounted soon thereafter in Paris and Stockholm.
10. S. Moisson-Franckhauser, *Serge Prokofiev et les courants esthétiques de son temps* (Paris: Publications orientalistes de France, 1974), 194.

Chapter 4

1. But Verdi's assertion must not be accepted at face value, contradicted as it is by the size of his personal library; see L. Magnani, "L''ignoranza musicale' di Verdi e la Biblioteca di Sant'

Agata," in *Testimonianze, studi e richerche in onore di G. M. Gatti* (Bologna: Istituto di Filologia Latina, 1973), 73–82.

2. See Chapter 1, "Settings."

3. "L'opéra actuel en Italie," *Revue et gazette musicale* 10 (1843): 202.

4. A. Azevedo, *Gioachino Rossini: Sa vie, ses oeuvres* (Paris: Heugel, 1865), 174.

5. P. Rattalino, "Il processo compositivo nel *Don Pasquale* di Donizetti," *Nuova rivista musicale italiana* 4 (1970): 51–68.

6. See A. M. Abell, *Entretiens avec de grands compositeurs sur la nature de leur inspiration et de leur création* (Paris: Editions du Dauphin, 1982), 143.

7. Not counting reworkings, Rossini left nineteen examples of *opera seria*, as opposed to eighteen comic works.

8. "Jupiter" was a nickname that Meyerbeer liked to use.

9. Léon Escudier considered him a veritable "chameleon"; see his *Mes souvenirs* (Paris: Dentu, 1863), 10.

10. The public sometimes regarded the music of the tubercular Catalani, who died before the age of forty, as "anemic."

Chapter 5

1. Ott, *Les pédagogies de la voix*, 271–292.

2. D. Bourlet, *Le Vlac, approche napolitaine du chant lyrique* (Paris: Van de Velde, 1978).

3. This term did not come into use until the second half of the nineteenth century.

4. Chevalier van Elewick, *De l'état actuel de la musique en Italie* (Paris: Heugel, 1875), 39.

5. G. Roger, *Le carnet d'un ténor* (Paris: Ollendorf, 1880), 21. From the entry of 6 April 1847.

6. Yet we know that, over the years, performers took liberties with the score which increased the original vocal discomfort even more. For example, the high E-flat sung at the end of Violetta's "Sempre libera" by Callas and Sutherland was not written by Verdi.

7. Gino Monaldi in *Memorie d'un suggeritore* (Turin: Bocca, 1902), 48.

8. L. Vivarelli, "Ancora della decadenza dell'arte del canto, delle sue cause e del modo di provedervi," *Gazzetta musicale di Milano*, 14 and 21 July 1889.

9. Victor Maurel, *Le chant rénové par la science* (Paris: Quinzard, 1892), 7.

10. Even singers who had previously exhibited little or no such ability in the past were looked to for improvement in this regard; see *Gazzetta musicale di Milano* 1 May 1842, "Varietà." Rosamonde Pisaroni was a notable exception, though she was unfortunately not very attractive.

11. Gino Monaldi, *Impresari celebri del secolo XIX* (Rocca San Casciano: Licinio Cappelli, 1918), 15.

12. Monaldi, *Memorie d'un suggeritore*, 23–24. Tenors were also classified as *drammatico*, *lirico* (Rodolfo), *leggero* (Nemorino), and *di forza* (Rodolfo).

13. See W. C. Goold, *The Verdian Baritone: A Study of Six Representative Operas* (diss., University of Kentucky, 1981).

14. The phenomenon of the modern prima donna began with Caroline Branchu (1780–1850).

15. Though *tenorino* is still found in Verdi in *Oberto* and *Un giorno di regno*.

16. As quoted in N. Bridgman, *La musique italienne* (Paris: P.U.F., 1973), 59.

17. See David R. B. Kimbell, *Verdi in the Age of Italian Romanticism* (Cambridge University Press, 1981), 363–364.

18. See Martin Chusid, "The Organization of Scenes with Arias: Verdi's Cavatinas and Romanzas," in *Atti del primo congresso internazionale di studi verdiani: Venezia 1966* (Parma: Istituto di Studi Verdiani, 1969), 59–66.

19. As for Puccini, see R. Mariani, "La melodia di Puccini," in *Puccini nel centenario della nascità* (Lucca: Tip. Lorenzetti & Natali, 1958), 23–30.

20. Part III of this book examines the problems created by these vocal ensembles during an opera season.

21. See, for example, the *Manifesto agli amatori della buona musica* (Rome: Lino Contedini, 1822), 9.

22. For certain critics of the time, such as Henri Blanchard, the novelty of Verdi's works was due above all to the ensemble numbers and the choruses; see *Revue et gazette musicale* 10 (1843): 204.

23. See W. Galluser, *Der Chor und die Oper* (Bellinzona: Buchdruckerei Leins & Vescovi, 1947).

Chapter 6

1. See Part III of this book for the number of instrumentalists hired by Italian opera houses.
2. As David Ewen reminds us, in *Ewen's Musical Masterworks: The Encyclopedia of Musical Masterpieces* (New York: Bonanza Books, 1954), 73, Beethoven's First Symphony puzzled early Viennese critics, who felt it made "too much use of wind instruments, so much so that the music sounded as if written for a military band."
3. The *Manifesto agli amatori della buona musica* (Rome: Lino Contedini, 1822), 9, expressed annoyance over the wind instruments' "always playing."
4. This development was not confined to Italy. In Félicien David's *Herculanum* (1859), the curtain rises at the very beginning. Sometimes long orchestral introductions were immediately cut, such as the one in Halévy's *La juive*.
5. "Lettre d'un enthousiaste sur l'état actuel de la musique en Italie," *Revue musicale* 6, no. 9 (1832): 66.

Chapter 7

1. Orchestral score (Milan: Ricordi), 352, 421.
2. See G. Roncaglia, "Il 'tema-cardine' nell'opera di Giuseppe Verdi," *Rivista musicale italiana* 47 (1943): 220, and Joseph Kerman, "Verdi's Use of Recurring Themes," in *Studies in Music History: Essays for Oliver Strunk* (Princeton, N.J.: Princeton University Press, 1968), 495–510.
3. Busoni, "Abozzo di una nuova estetica delle musica," 149.
4. The offstage chorus, "Largo al quadrupede," in the last act of *La traviata*.
5. Tonal relations too play a part; see the article by G. A. Marco and S. Levarie, "On Key Relations in Opera," *19th-Century Music* 3 (1979): 83–89.
6. Stendhal, *Promenades dans Rome* (Geneva: Edito Service, n.d.), 170.
7. Igor Stravinsky, *Poetics of Music in the Form of Six Lessons*. Trans. Arthur Knodel and Ingolf Dahl (Cambridge, Mass.: Harvard University Press, 1970), 81.
8. "The ghost of Old Klingsor" is Wagner, of course, or so Debussy described him in a letter of 2 October 1893 to Ernest Chausson.

9. Stravinsky, *Poetics of Music*, 55.
10. See Chapter 5, "Italian Vocal Style."
11. Abell, *Entretiens avec de grands compositeurs*, 147–148.
12. R. Vlad, "Anticipazioni nel linguaggio armonico verdiano," *Rassegna musicale* 21 (1951): 237–245.
13. Published in 1914 in volume 15 of Wagner's complete works, it was performed on the BBC in 1971.
14. For more on the subject, see A. Ziino, *Antologia della critica wagneriana in Italia* (Messina: Pelorinata Editrice, 1970).
15. See Julian Budden, "Verdi and Meyerbeer in Relation to *Les vêpres siciliennes*," *Studi verdiani* 1 (1982): 11–20, and E. Franzi, *La France dans l'oeuvre de Verdi* (Milan: Università Commerciale L. Bocconi, 1971).
16. See Part III of this book.
17. N. Zucco, *Francesco Cilea* (Oppido Mamertino: Barbara Ed., 1981), 55.

Chapter 8

1. According to J. Rosselli, *L'impresario d'opera: Arte e affari del teatro musicale italiano dell'Ottocento*. (Turin: EDT/Musica, 1985), 177, in 1871 there were a total of 940 theaters in 699 Italian communities.
2. See L. Gamberini, *La vita musicale europea del 1800: La vita musicale genovese* (Citta del Castello, 1978), vol. 1.
3. The San Carlo burned down in 1816, La Fenice in 1836. D. Choquet, in *Des incendies dans les théâtres* (Paris: Librairie Polytechnique, 1888), counted 37 theater fires, between 1 April 1887 and 1 April 1888, involving 629 deaths and 766 injuries.
4. Floor plans of several opera houses can be found in Eugène d'Harcourt's book, *La musique actuelle en Italie* (Paris: F. Durdilly/Fischbacher, 1907).
5. For a description of the Cairo theater, see Gérard de Nerval's *Le voyage en Orient* (Paris: Charpentier, 1860), vol. 1, 163.
6. In Busseto, for example, the *palchettisti* contributed two thousand lire when the theater was built; Verdi gave five times that amount. Verdi's box is visible in the photograph of the theater's interior that appears on the cover of this book; see also the photograph on page 85, where its precise location is marked with an X.
7. See E. Rosmini, *La legislazione e la giurisprudenza dei teatri*, 2 vols. (Milan: F. Marini, 1872).

8. It should be noted that the French franc was introduced in Italy during the Napoleonic era and that it was considered legal tender at a time when the most diverse currencies were in circulation throughout the peninsula. Nevertheless, the Piedmontese lira had become well established since 1814 and was more or less equivalent in value to the franc; see Rosselli, *L'impresario d'opera*, 180.
9. Rosselli, *L'impresario d'opera*, 55, 125.
10. van Elewick, *De l'état actuel de la musique en Italie*, 138.
11. At the beginning of the twentieth century, *Rigoletto* cost 2000 francs to rent and *Aida* 400; see d'Harcourt, *La musique actuelle en Italie*.
12. Monaldi, *Memorie d'un suggeritore*, 21.
13. J. Rosselli, "Agenti teatrali nel mondo dell'opera lirica italiana dell'Ottocento," *Rivista italiana di musicologia* 17, no. 1 (1982): 137–143.
14. Monaldi, *Memorie d'un suggeritore*, 95.

Chapter 9

1. See "Celebrated Singers" in the Appendix of this book for a more complete listing of nineteenth-century Italian vocalists.
2. Rosselli, *L'impresario d'opera*, 56.
3. A. Basso, *Il teatro della città: Storia del Teatro Regio di Torino* (Turin: Cassa di Risparmio, 1976), 319–322.
4. See Victor Maurel, *A propos de la mise-en-scène du drame lyrique 'Otello'* (Rome: Editrice Romana, 1888). The first part is entitled "Aperçu sur le théâtre chanté au XIXe siècle."
5. Monaldi, *Memorie d'un suggeritore*, 42, observes that there would only be five or six piano rehearsals for a production toward the end of his career, as opposed to a dozen in earlier days.
6. Kimbell, *Verdi in the Age of Italian Romanticism*, 54.
7. *Gazzetta musicale di Milano* 4 (1845): 15.
8. d'Harcourt, *La musique actuelle en Italie*.
9. Women had only very recently been admitted into the chorus of the Turin opera company; see *Gazzetta musicale di Milano* 4 (1845): 15.
10. "Lettre d'un enthousiaste sur l'état actuelle de la musique en Italie," *Revue musicale* 6, no. 9 (1832): 65–68.
11. *Gazzetta musicale di Milano* 4 (1845): 15.
12. It is known that Berlioz himself once sang in the chorus of this Parisian theater.

13. *Revue musicale* 6, no. 10 (1832): 75.
14. "L'opéra actuel en Italie," *Revue et gazette musicale* 10 (1843): 202.
15. Monaldi, *Memorie d'un suggeritore*, 122, in fact deplored their unattractiveness.
16. Radiciotti, among others, stresses this on several occasions in his writings on Italian opera. As for the dressing rooms of the great impresarios, they were apparently reserved for the solo artists.
17. d'Harcourt, *La musique actuelle en Italie*.
18. "Assoluta" was soon tacked on to the term "prima donna" to indicate the "crème de la crème" quality of certain roles.
19. *Revue musicale* 6, no. 9 (1832): 65–66.
20. *Revue musicale* 6, no. 10 (1832): 75.
21. There were then sixty-three players in the Paris Opéra orchestra.
22. C. Bottura, *Storia del Teatro Comunale di Trieste* (Trieste, 1885), 80.
23. Azevedo, *Gioachino Rossini*, 59, observes that the harpsichord was still in use at the San Mosè theater in Venice.
24. In 1850, there were five bass violins against two or three cellos at Teatro Apollo in Rome (Kimbell, *Verdi in the Age of Italian Romanticism*, 48); for an orchestra of sixty-five instruments, Monaldi also recommended using seven bass violins and five cellos (*Memorie d'un suggeritore*, 48).
25. L. Rossi, "Sullo stato attuale della musica in Torino," *Gazzetta musicale di Milano* 5 (1845): 15.
26. van Elewick, *De l'état actuel de la musique en Italie*, 14, 100.
27. "Lettera al Signor Fétis sulle orchestre d'Italia," in *Gazzetta musicale di Milano* 2 July 1843.
28. See Basso, *Il teatro della città*, passim. D'Harcourt gives the following figures: 4 francs for the musicians in the orchestra versus 1 franc 50 centimes per day for chorus members; see d'Harcourt, *La musique actuelle en Italie*.
29. van Elewick, *De l'état actuel de la musique en Italie*, 14.
30. Monaldi, *Memorie d'un suggeritore*, 135.
31. See "Celebrated Conductors" in the Appendix of this book for a list of the principal nineteenth-century Italian opera conductors.
32. Monaldi, *Memorie d'un suggeritore*, 141.
33. Azevedo, *Gioachino Rossini*, 101, observes that it was thus in 1816 in Rome for a production of *Il barbiere di Siviglia*.

34. On the other hand, there were only twelve dancers at Parma, and Bologna's Teatro Comunale had no ballet troupe at all; see d'Harcourt, *La musique actuelle en Italie*, passim.
35. See G. Marchioro, *Momenti ed aspetti della messa in scena* (Milan: Ricordi, 1960), 95–106.
36. See S. Kunze, "Fest und Ball in Verdis Opern," in *Die Couleur locale in der Oper des 19. Jahrhundert* (Regensburg: Bosse, 1976), 269–278.
37. Monaldi, *Memorie d'un suggeritore*, 171.
38. At La Pergola, for example, Lanari had a "vestiario" of some thirty characters; see M. de Angelis, *Le carte dell'impresario* (Florence: Sansoni, 1982), 72.
39. For more on this see B. Horowicz, *Le théâtre d'opéra* (Paris: Ed. de Flore, 1946).

Chapter 10

1. C. Barbagallo, ed., *1848–1948: Cento anni di vita italiana*, 2 vols. (Milan: Cavalotti Editori, 1949), vol. 1, 562.
2. A. Asor Rosa, "La cultura," in *Storia d'Italia* (Turin: Einaudi, 1975), vol. 4, no. 2, 839.
3. Not all theaters adopted this change simultaneously, however. It is significant that Teatro Carolina in Palermo had its balcony by 1830, while none appeared in Venice's La Fenice until 1878.
4. It was claimed at the beginning of the nineteenth century that three-fourths of any opera score was good only for accompanying the noise emanating from the backs of the boxes; see J. Carlez, *Pacini et l'opéra italien* (Caen: H. Delesques, 1888), 23.
5. In 1906, 136,000 francs went to Turin's Teatro Regio for sixty performances and 80,000 francs to Genoa for forty performances, while La Scala's subsidy had fallen from 300,000 francs to 60,000 francs; see d'Harcourt, *La musique actuelle en Italie*, passim.
6. According to O. Rombaldi's "Censura e regolamenti (1814–1859)," in S. Romagnoli and E. Garbero, eds., *Teatro a Reggio Emilia* (Florence: Sansoni, 1980), vol. 2, 207–212.
7. Monaldi, *Memorie d'un suggeritore*, 70.
8. See "L'Opéra de Paris au siècle romantique," *Revue internationale de musique française* 4 (January 1981). It is worth noting that, unlike the Palais Garnier, Paris's Théâtre-Italien had no claque.

9. Monaldi, *Memorie d'un suggeritore*, 55, 63.
10. See Guglielmo Barblan and A. Basso, *Aspetti e problemi*, vol. 3 of *Storia dell'opera* (Turin: U.T.E.T., 1977), 501 ff, for a discussion of the wave of change in public support of opera in the second half of the nineteenth century and the decay of opera as a social phenomenon. In 1906, the poor attendance at the theater in Piacenza and the small audience in Verona were noted; see d'Harcourt, *La musique actuelle en Italie*, passim.
11. Klee, *Journal*, 115.

Conclusion

1. *Giacomo Puccini e l'opera internazionale* (Turin: Bocca, 1912). By the following year, G. Bastianelli had denounced the lack of profundity in his country's operas in "Per un nuovo Risorgimento," *Le cronache letterarie* (Florence), 2 July 1911.
2. A. Casella, "L'avenir musical de l'Italie," *L'homme libéré* (Paris) 8 September 1913. He repeated his argument at a conference given at the Sorbonne on 7 February 1918, the text of which was published by the Rome Società italiana di musica moderna, n.d., in the Paris Bibliothèque Nationale, Vm. Pièce 25.
3. See F. Nicolodi, *Gusti e tendenze nel Novencento musicale italiano* (Florence: Sansoni, 1982).
4. Putnam's 1976 edition of Kobbé (*The New Kobbé's Complete Opera Book*, rev. and augmented ed. by the Earl of Harewood) discusses no Italian opera between Zandonai's *Francesca da Rimini* (1914) and Dallapiccola's *Prigioniero* (1949). The same observation applies to French opera: of the ninety-odd works premiered in the two major opera houses of Paris between 1919 and 1939, only Roussel's *Padmâvatî* (1923) and Milhaud's *Pauvre matelot* (1927) receive attention here. Conspicuously absent is Ravel's *Enfant et les sortilèges* (1925), first performed in Monte Carlo. On the other hand, R. Strauss, Schoenberg, Berg, Hindemith, Orff, and Kurt Weill could hardly be ignored in a book of this kind, indicating the international importance of German opera during the same period.
5. This manifesto was reprinted in several Italian papers in December 1932.
6. More specifically, for Donizetti's *Elisir d'amore*; see the interview by E. Zanetti, "Stravinsky ha detto," in *XIVe Festival Internazionale di Musica Contemporanea* (Venice, 1951).

7. See A. Schaeffner, "Il ritorno a Verdi: La fine del Purgatorio," *Rassegna musicale* 21 (1951): 225–236.
8. Mercadante's two best-known works, *Il bravo* and *Il giuramento*, have recently been recorded complete in Italy; see the Discography at the end of this book.

BIBLIOGRAPHY

Reference Works and Source Material

BIBLIOGRAPHIES

Ademollo, Alessandro. *Bibliografia della cronistoria teatrale italiana.* Milan: Ricordi, 1888.

Besterman, Theodore. *Music and Drama: A Bibliography of Bibliographies.* Totowa, N.J.: Rowman and Littlefield, 1971.

Bonamici, D. *Bibliografia delle cronistorie dei teatri d'Italia.* 2 vols. Livorno: R. Giusti, 1896–1905. Supplement in *Rivista musicale italiana* 26 (1919).

Bustico, Guido. *Il teatro musicale italiano.* Rome: Fondazione Leonardo, 1924. Annotated bibliography, 17th–20th centuries.

Chusid, Martin. *A Catalogue of Verdi's Operas.* Hackensack, N.J., 1974.

Cowden, Robert H. *Concert and Opera Singers: A Bibliography of Biographical Materials.* Westport, Conn., and London: Greenwood Press, 1985.

Giovine, A. *Bibliografia di teatri musicali italiani: Storia e Cronologia.* Bari: Laterza, 1982.

Hopkinson, Cecil A. *A Bibliography of the Works of Giacomo Puccini 1858–1924.* New York: Broude Brothers, 1968.

———. *A Bibliography of the Works of Giuseppe Verdi.* Vol. 2. New York, 1978.

Marschall, G. "L'Italie." In *Précis de musicologie.* Ed. J. Chailley. Paris: P.U.F., 1984. 339–351.

Surian, Elvidio. "Lo stato attuale degli studi verdiani. Appunti e bibliografia ragionata." *Rivista italiana di musicologia* 12, no. 21 (1977): 305–329.

———. "Musical Historiography and Histories of Italian Opera." *Current Musicology* (Columbia University) 36 (1983): 167ff.

Verti, R. "Dieci anni di studi sulle fonti per la storia materiale dell' opera italiana nell'Ottocento." *Rivista italiana di musicologia* 20 (1985): 124–163.

ANNALS, DICTIONARIES, AND ENCYCLOPEDIAS

Albinati, G. *Almanacco musicale giornaliero.* Milan: Ricordi, 1896.

Angelis, Alberto de. *L'Italia musicale di oggi: Dizionario dei musicisti.* Rome: Ausonia, 1922.

Capra, M. *Annuario generale del musicista d'Italia.* Turin: STEN, 1909.

Caputo, M. C. *Annuario generale della musica nel 1873–74.* Naples: D. de Angelis, 1875.

Carozzi, E. *Annuario teatrale italiano per l'annata 1887.* Milan: Tipografia nazionale, 1887.

Dassori, C. *Opere e operisti: Dizionario lirico 1541–1905.* Istituto Sordomuti, 1906.

Ewen, David. *Ewen's Musical Masterworks: The Encyclopedia of Musical Masterpieces.* New York: Bonanza Books, 1954.

Grout, Donald Jay. *A Short History of Opera.* 3rd ed. New York: Columbia University Press, 1988.

Gubernati, Angelo de. *Piccolo dizionario dei contemporanei italiani.* Rome: Tipografia del Senato, 1895.

Il teatro italiano: Anno 1913. Milan: F. Vallardi, 1914.

Loewenberg, A. *Annals of Opera 1597–1940.* 2 vols. Geneva: Societas Bibliographica, 1955.

Lombardo, G. A., ed. *Annuario dell'arte lirica e coreografica italiana.* Milan: A. de Marchi, 1898.

Orrey, Leslie, ed. *The Encyclopedia of Opera.* New York: Scribner's, 1976.

Osborne, Charles. *The Dictionary of the Opera.* New York: Simon and Schuster, 1983.

Regli, F. *Dizionario biografica dei più celebri poeti ed artisti melodram-matici . . . in Italia dal 1800 al 1860*. Turin: Dalmezzi, 1860.

Sadie, Stanley, ed. *The New Grove Dictionary of Music and Musicians*. 20 vols. Washington, D.C., and London: Grove's Dictionaries of Music, 1980.

————, ed. *The New Grove Dictionary of Opera*. 4 vols. New York: Grove's Dictionaries of Music, 1992.

AUTOBIOGRAPHIES AND MEMOIRS

Arditi, Luigi. *My Reminiscences*. New York: Dodd-Mead, 1896.

Berlioz, Hector. *Mémoires*. 2 vols. Paris: Garnier-Flammarion, 1969. Trans. Rachel (Scott Russell) Holmes and Eleanor Holmes, under the title *Memoirs of Hector Berlioz from 1803 to 1865, comprising his travels in Germany, Italy, Russia, and England*. Annotated and revised by Ernest Newman. New York: Dover, 1966.

Caruso, Jr., Enrico, and Andrew Farkas. *Enrico Caruso: My Father and My Family*. Portland, Ore.: Amadeus Press, 1990.

Duprez, G. *Souvenirs d'un chanteur*. Paris: Calmann-Lévy, 1880.

Ebers, J. *Seven Years of the King's Theatre*. London, 1828.

Escudier, Léon. *Mes souvenirs*. Paris: Dentu, 1863.

Espinchal, J. d'. *Journal d'émigration*. Ed. E. d'Hauterive. Paris: Perrin, 1912.

Ghislanzoni, Antonio. *In chiave di baritono*. Milan: A. Brigola, 1882.

Kelly, Michael. *Reminiscences of Michael Kelly of the King's Theatre and Theatre Royal Drury Lane*. New introduction by A. Hyatt King. New York: Da Capo Press, 1968.

Lumley, B. *Reminiscences of the Opera*. London: Hurst and Blackett, 1864.

Maurel, Victor. *Dix ans de carrière 1887–1897*. Paris, 1897.

Mendelssohn, Felix. *Italienisches Tagebuch*. Frankfurt: Societäts-Verlag, 1982. Hrsg. von E. Weisweiler.

(Merelli), B. *Cenni biografici di Donizetti e Mayr raccolti dalle memorie di un vecchio ottuogenario dilettante di musica*. Bergamo, 1875.

Michotte, E. *Souvenirs: Une soirée chez Rossini à Beau-Séjour (Passy) 1858*. Trans. Herbert Weinstock. 1968.

Monaldi, Gino. *L'Italia musicale moderna: I miei ricordi musicali*. Rome: Ausonia, 1921.

————. *Memorie d'un suggeritore*. Turin: Bocca, 1902.

Nicolo, (de). "Diario napoletano." *Archivio storico per le Provincie napoletane* 30 (1905).

Roeder, M. *Dal taccuino di un direttore d'orchestra.* Milan: G. Ottino, 1881.

Roux, O. *Memorie autobiografiche giovanili di Leoncavallo.* Florence: Bemporad, n.d.

Santley, Charles. *Student and Singer.* London: E. Arnold, 1892.

Stendhal. *Rome, Naples et Florence.* Paris: M. Lévy, 1854. Trans. Richard N. Coe, under the title *Rome, Naples and Florence.* New York: G. Braziller, 1960.

Stivender, David. *Mascagni: An Autobiography Compiled, Edited and Translated from Original Sources.* White Plains, N.Y.: Pro/Am Musical Resources, Inc., 1988.

Taine, Hippolyte. *Voyage en Italie.* 2 vols. Paris: Hachette, 1866.

Venosta, Giovanni Visconti. *Memoirs of Youth: Things Seen and Known 1847–1860.* Trans. William Prall. London: Constable, 1914.

OTHER CONTEMPORARY DOCUMENTS

"An Unpublished Donizetti Letter." *Journal of the Donizetti Society* 2 (1975): 271–274.

Arnaud, G. *Teatro, arte ed artisti: Mosaico d'aneddoti, escursioni storiche.* Milan: G. Gnocchi, 1869.

Arner, C. "L'arte lirica in Italia dal 1872 al 1897." In *Annuario dell' arte lirica e coreografica italiana.* Ed. G. A. Lombardo. Milan: A. de Marchi, 1897–98.

Bertrand, G. "Tournée musicale en Italie." *Le Ménestrel* 33 (1866): 188–189, 197–198.

Blanchard, H. "L'opéra actuel en Italie." *Revue et gazette musicale* 10 (1843): 202–204.

Bonaventura, A. *Saggio sul teatro musicale italiano.* Leghorn: R. Giusti, 1913.

Boucheron, R. "Esame allo stato attuale della musica dramatica in Italia." *Gazzetta musicale di Milano* 7 May 1842.

Colombani, A. *L'opera italiana nel secolo XIX.* Milan: Tipografia del Corriere della Sera, 1900.

Danjou, P. "Lettres d'Italie." *Revue et gazette musicale* 14 (1847) and 15 (1848).

Elewick, Chevalier van. *De l'état actuel de la musique en Italie.* Paris: Heugel, 1875. Official report addressed to the Belgian Royal Minister of the Interior.

Fétis, François-Joseph. "Examen de l'etat actuel de la musique en Italie." *Revue musicale* 1 (1827); 4 (1828); 12 (1832); 13 (1833); 15 (1835).

———. "Lettres sur la musique en Italie." *Revue et gazette musicale* 8 (1841); 9 (1842); 10 (1843).

Harcourt, Eugene d'. *La musique actuelle en Italie*. Paris: F. Durdilly/Fischbacher, 1907.

Hazlitt, W. *Notes of a Journey Through France and Italy*. London: Hunt and Clarke, 1826.

Lacombe, L. "Rossini, Beethoven et l'ecole italienne contemporaine." In *Philosophie et musique*. Paris: Fischbacher, 1896.

Larussa, A. *Sulle cagioni del decadimento degli teatri di Napoli*. Naples, 1850.

Lenoir de la Fage, J. J. "Lettres sur l'état actuel de la musique en Italie." *Revue et gazette musicale* 15 (1849); 17 (1850).

Lualdi, A. *Il rinnovamento musicale italiano*. Milan and Rome, 1931.

Monaldi, Gino. *Idealismo e realismo ossia il teatro melodrammatico italiano moderno e le sue diverse scuole*. Perugia, 1876.

"Musicisti italiani moderni giudicati da Antonio Bazzini." *Revista musicale italiana* 5 (1898): 141–148. Letter of 2 March 1876 addressed to J. Fuchs of Leipzig.

Parker, Roger. "Verdi and the *Gazzetta privilegiata di Milano*: An 'Official' View Seen in Its Cultural Background." *RMA Research Chronicle* 18 (1982): 51–65.

Petra, V. *Sulle condizioni dell'odierna musica italiana*. Naples: Stampiera di Salvatore Piscopo, 1854.

Porter, Andrew. "*Les vêpres siciliennes*: New Letters from Verdi to Scribe." *19th-Century Music* 2, no. 2 (1978): 95–109.

Puccini, Giacomo. *Letters of Giacomo Puccini*. Ed. Giuseppe Adami; trans. Ena Makin. New ed. rev. and introduced by Mosco Carner. London: Harrap, 1974.

Raffaelli, P. *Il melodramma in Italia*. Florence: G. Guidi, 1881.

Rossi, L. *Alcune parole sull'attuale condizione della musica in Italia*. Milan: Ricordi, 1871.

Sammartino, E. di. *Saggio critico sopra alcune cause di decadenza nella musica italiana alla fine del secolo XIX*. Rome: Tipografia F. Cuggiani, 1897.

Sassaroli, V. *Considerazioni sullo stato attuale dell'arte musicale in Italia e sull'importanza artistica dell'opera Aida e della messa di Verdi*. Genoa: Tipografia della Gioventu, 1876.

Schiedermair, L. "Venezianer Briefe F. S. Kandlers aus den Jahren

1818–1820." In *Riemann-Festschrift*. Leipzig: Max Hesse, 1909. 485–495.

Scudo, P. "Donizetti et l'école italienne depuis Rossini." *Revue des deux mondes* 1 July 1848.

Sonneck, O. G. T. "Zum Wiederaufschwung des italienischen Musiklebens." *Sammelbände der Internationalen Musikgesellschaft* 1 (1899–1900): 630–670.

General Historical Background

SOCIETY, LITERATURE, AND FINE ARTS

Albrecht-Carrie, R. *Italy from Napoleon to Mussolini*. New York: Columbia University Press, 1950.

Alexander, Alfred. *Giovanni Verga: A Great Writer and His World*. London: Grant and Cutler, 1972.

Barbagallo, C., ed. *1848–1948: Cento anni di vita italiana*. 2 vols. Milan: Cavalotti Editori, 1949.

Bezzola, G. "Aspetti del clima culturale italiano nel periodo donizettiano." In *Atti del primo convegno internazionale di studi donizettiani* 22–28 September 1975. Bergamo: Azienda Autonoma di Turismo, 1983. 29–42.

Blasi, J. de, ed. *L'Italia e gli Italiani del secolo XIX*. Florence: Le Monnier, 1930.

Cecchetti, Giovanni. *Giovanni Verga*. Boston: Twayne, 1978.

Comandini, A. *L'Italia nei cento anni del secolo XIX: 1801–1900, giorno per giorno illustrata*. Milan: A. Vallardi, 1900.

Fogel, Susan Lee. "Prize of Rome." *Opera News* 4 March 1972: 28–30.

Guichonnet, Paul. *L'Italie*. Paris: Presses Universitaires de France, 1969. From the collection "Que sais-je?" no. 286.

Holt, Edgar. *The Making of Italy 1815–1870*. New York: Atheneum, 1971.

L'Italie au temps de Stendhal. Paris: Hachette, 1966.

Luciani, Vincent. *A Brief History of Italian Literature*. New York: S. F. Vanni, 1967.

Maltese, C. *Storia dell'arte in Italia 1785–1940*. Turin: G. Einaudi, 1960.

Mariani, G. *Storia della Scapigliatura*. Rome: E. de Sanctis, 1965.

Milza, P. *Francais et Italiens a la fin du XIXe siècle.* 2 vols. Rome: Ecole Francaise de Rome, 1981.

Portinari, Folco. *Le parabole del reale.* Turin: Einaudi, 1976. On the nineteenth-century Italian novel.

Romano, S. *Histoire de l'Italie du Risorgimento a nos jours.* Paris: Le Seuil, 1977.

Sommario di statistiche storiche italiane 1861–1955. Rome: Istituto Centrale di Statistiche, 1958.

Wilkins, Ernest Hatch. *A History of Italian Literature.* Cambridge, Mass.: Harvard University Press, 1954.

ITALIAN OPERA

Barblan, Guglielmo, and A. Basso. *L'opera in Italia* and *Aspetti e problemi.* Vols. 1 and 3 of *Storia dell'opera.* Turin: U.T.E.T., 1977.

Calendoli, G. *Gli ultimi dei: Dalla scuola nazionale russa a Puccini.* Milan: A. Mondadori, 1979.

Dallapiccola, Luigi. "Words and Music in Nineteenth-Century Italian Opera." *Perspectives of New Music* 5 (1966): 121–133.

Degrada, F. *Il palazzo incantato: Studi sulla tradizione del melo-dramma dal barocco al romanticismo.* 2 vols. Fiesole: Discanto, 1979.

Della Corte, A. *Tre secoli di opera italiana.* Turin: Arione, 1938.

Ferrone, S., ed. *Teatro dell'Italia unita.* Milan: Il Saggiatore, 1980.

Galatopoulos, Stelios. *Italian Opera.* London: J. M. Dent, 1971.

Gatti, G. M. *Musicisti moderni d'Italia e di fuori.* Bologna: Pizzi, 1920.

Jacobs, Naomi, and James C. Robertson. *Opera in Italy.* London: Hutchinson, 1948.

Kimbell, David R. B. *Verdi in the Age of Italian Romanticism.* Cambridge University Press, 1981.

Klein, John W. "Verdi's Italian Contemporaries and Successors." *Music and Letters* 15 (1934): 37–45.

Levarie, Siegmund. "Epochs of Opera: Italy." *Opera News* 27 December 1969/3 January 1970: 32–37.

Lualdi, A. *Il rinnovamento musicale italiano.* Milan and Rome: Treves, 1931.

Miragoli, L. *Il melodramma italiano nella critica del secolo XIX.* Campobasso: Societa tipografica molisana, 1927.

Nicastro, A. *Il melodramma e gli Italiani.* Milan: Rusconi, 1982.

Nicolaisen, Jay R. *Italian Opera in Transition 1871–1893.* Ed. G. Buelow. Ann Arbor, Mich.: UMI Research Press, 1980.

Nicolodi, F., ed. *Musica italiana del primo Novecento: La generazione dell'80.* Florence: Palazzo Strozzi, 1980.

Pannain, G. "La musica operistica in Italia dal *Falstaff* ad oggi." In *Cinquant'anni di opera e balletto in Italia.* Rome: Bestetti, 1954.

———. *Ottocento musicale italiano.* Milan: Curci, 1952.

Paoli, O. de'. *La crisi musicale italiana 1900–1930.* Milan: Hoepli, 1939.

Pieri, M. *Viaggio da Verdi: Discorso di un italianista intorno all'opera romantica.* Parma: La Pilotte, 1977.

Pluta, E. "Die italienische Oper des Fin de siecle." *Opernwelt* 23 (1982); 24 (1983).

Salvetti, G. *Il grande melodramma da Rossini a Verdi.* Milan: Mondadori, 1978.

Schlitzer, Franco. *Mondo teatrale dell'Ottocento.* Naples: F. Fiorentino, 1954.

Serafin, Tullio, and A. Toni. *Stile, tradizioni e convenzioni nel melodramma italiano del Settecento e dell'Ottocento.* 2 vols. Milan: Ricordi, 1958.

Surian, Elvidio. "Musical Historiography and Histories of Italian Opera." Trans. Ruth De Ford and Dona De Sanctis. *Current Musicology* 36 (1983): 167–175.

Tedeschi, R. *Addio, fiorito asil: Il melodramma italiano da Boito al verismo.* Milan: Feltrinelli, 1978.

Terenzio, Vincenzo. *La musica italiana nell'Ottocento.* 2 vols. Milan: Bramante Editrice, 1976.

Tintori, Giampiero. *Palco di proscenio. Il melodramma: Autori, cantanti, teatri, impresari.* Milan: Feltrinelli, 1980.

Trezzini, L., and A. Curtolo. *Oltre le quinte.* Venice: Marsilio, 1983.

Van der Linden, A. "Une mission de F. J. Fétis en Italie en 1841." *Rivista musicale italiana* 53 (1951): 61–72.

Weaver, William. *The Golden Century of Italian Opera from Rossini to Puccini.* London: Thames and Hudson, 1980.

CITIES AND OPERA HOUSES

Hughes, Spike. *Great Opera Houses: A Traveller's Guide to Their History and Traditions.* London: Weidenfeld and Nicholson, 1956.

Weaver, William. "The Opera Public: Italy." *Opera News* 13 February 1988: 34–35.

Ancona

Morici, O. *I cento anni del Teatro delle Muse di Ancona 1827–1927.* Ancona: Stab. tip. Nacci, 1927.

Bari

Giovine, A. *Il Teatro Piccinni di Bari 1854–1964.* Bari: Bibl. del Archivio delle tradizioni popolari baresi, 1970.

————. *L'opera in musica in teatri di Bari: Statistica delle rappresentazioni dal 1830 al 1869.* Bari: Bibl. del Archivio delle tradizioni popolari baresi, 1969.

Bergamo

Donati-Petteni, G. *L'arte della musica in Bergamo.* Bergamo: Banca mutua popolare, 1930.

Bologna

Matz, Mary Jane. "Great Opera Houses: Bologna." *Opera News* 27 January 1968: 30–33.

Testoni, A. *Ottocento bolognese* . . . Bologna and Rocca San Casciano: L. Cappelli, 1930.

Trezzini, L. *Due secoli di vita musicale: Storia del Teatro Comunale di Bologna.* 2 vols. Bologna: Alfa, 1966.

Brescia

Valentini, A. *I musicisti bresciani e il Teatro Grande.* Brescia: Queriniana, 1894.

Zanetti, R. *Un secolo di musica a Brescia.* Milan: Ricordi, 1970.

Cesena

Raggi, A., and L. Raggi. *Il Teatro Comunale di Cesena.* Cesena: G. Vignuzzi, 1906.

Cremona

Santoro, E. *Il teatro di Cremona.* Cremona: Pizzorni, 1969–72.

Florence

Manzi, A. *Il teatri di musica in Firenze oggi.* [Florence], 1896.

Matz, Mary Jane. "Great Opera Houses: Florence." *Opera News* 23 March 1963: 29–31.

Morini, V. *La Reale Accademia degli Immobili ed il suo Teatro La Pergola 1649–1925.* Pisa: Simoncini, 1926.

Pinzauti, Leonardo. "Prospettive per uno studio sulla musica a Firenze nell'Ottocento." *Nuova rivista musicale italiana* 2 (1968).

Genoa

Frassoni, E. *Due secoli di lirica a Genova*. 2 vols. Genoa: Cassa di Risparmio, 1980.

Lucca

Catelani, P. B. *Il Teatro Comunale del Giglio di Lucca*. Pescia: Benedetti, 1941.

Messina

Donato, G. *Il Teatro Vittorio Emanuele di Messina*. Messina: La Grafica, 1979.

Scaglione, N. *La vita artistica del Teatro Vittorio Emanuele dal 12 gennaio 1852 al 28 dicembre 1908*. Messina: La Sicilia, 1921.

Milan

Cambiasi, P. *Rappresentazioni date nei reali teatri di Milano 1778–1872*. Milan: Ricordi, 1872.

Gatti, G. M. *Il Teatro alla Scala nella storia e nell'arte*. Milan: Ricordi, 1964.

Guttierez, B. *Il Teatro Carcano 1803–1914*. Milan: G. Abbiati, 1914.

Lingg, Ann M. "Great Opera Houses: La Scala." *Opera News* 3 December 1960: 22–27.

Monaldi, Gino. *Le opere di Verdi al Teatro alla Scala 1839–1893*. Milan: Ricordi, [1914].

Montale, E. *Prime alla Scala*. Milan: A. Mondadori, 1981.

Pavesi, M. *La presentazione del Teatro Carcano nell'ottocento melodrammatico milanese*. Tesi di Laurea: Universita di Milano, 1971.

Modena

Gandini, A. *Cronistoria dei teatri di Modena*. Modena: Tip. Sociale, 1873.

Naples

Cottrau, G. *Lettres d'un mélomane pour servir de document a l'histoire musicale de Naples de 1829 à 1847*. Naples: A. Morano, 1885.

Filippis, F. de, ed. *Cento anni di vita del Teatro San Carlo 1848–1948*. Naples: Teatro San Carlo, 1948.

Jellinek, George. "The San Carlo Celebrates." *The Opera Quarterly* 6, no. 2 (Winter 1988): 69–76.

Robinson, Michael Finlay. *Naples and Neapolitan Opera*. Oxford:

Clarendon Press, 1972.

Zaccaria, Michael A. "Glory of Naples." *Opera News* 30 January 1988: 30–32.

Padua

Brunelli, B. *I teatri di Padova.* Padua: A. Draghi, 1921.

Pittarello, C. A. *Spettacoli melodrammatici e coreografici rappresentati in Padova nei teatri Obizzi, Nuovo e del Prato della Valle dal 1751 al 1892.* Padua: A. Draghi, 1892.

Palermo

Freeman, J. *Opera Production in Palermo 1809–1830.* Diss., Harvard University, 1979.

Maniscalco Basile, L. *Storia del Teatro Massimo di Palermo.* Florence: Olschki, 1984.

Tiby, O. *Il Real Teatro Carolino e l'Ottocento musicale palermitano.* Florence: Olschki, 1957.

Parma

Cervetti, V., C. Del Monte, and V. Segreto. *Teatro Regio, città di Parma: Cronologia degli spettacoli lirici 1829–1979.* 3 vols. Parma: Grafiche STEP, 1979.

Corradi-Cervi, M. *Cronologia del Teatro Regio di Parma.* Parma: L. Battei, 1950.

Ferrari, P. E. *Spettacoli drammatico-musicali e coreografici in Parma dall'anno 1628 all'anno 1883.* Parma: L. Battei, 1883; Bologna: Forni, 1969.

Matz, Mary Jane. "Great Opera Houses: Parma." *Opera News* 7 December 1963: 26–29.

Pesaro

Cinelli, C. *Memorie cronistorie del Teatro di Pesaro dall'anno 1637 al 1897.* Pesaro, 1898.

Piacenza

Papi, E. *Il Teatro Municipale di Piacenza.* Piacenza: A. Bosi, 1912.

Pisa

Gentili, A. *Cinquant'anni dopo . . . . : Il Teatro Verdi nei suoi ricordi.* Pisa: F. Mariotti, 1915.

Ravenna

Ravaldini, G. *Spettacoli nei teatri e in altri luoghi di Ravenna 1555–1977*. Bologna: University Press, 1978.

Recanati

Radiciotti, G. *Teatro, musica e musicisti in Recanati*. Recanati: R. Simboli, 1904.

Reggio Emilia

Crocioni, G. *I teatri di Reggio nell'Emilia*. Reggio: Cooperativa lavoranti tipografi, 1907.
Romagnoli, S., and E. Garbero. *Teatro a Reggio Emilia*. 2 vols. Florence: Sansoni, 1980.

Rome

Attardi, F. *Roma musicale nell'Ottocento*. Padua: Zanibon, 1979.
Bellingardi, Luigi. "The Rome Opera Is a Hundred Years Old." *Opera* September 1981: 896–903.
Cametti, A. *Il Teatro di Tordinona poi di Apollo*. 2 vols. Tivoli: Arti grafiche A. Chicca, 1938.
Frajese, V. *Dal Costanzi all'Opera*. 2 vols. Rome: Edizioni Capitolini, 1977–78.
Incagliati. *Il Teatro Costanzi*. Rome: Tip. ed. Roma, 1907.
Monaldi, Gino. *I teatri di Roma negli ultimi tre secoli*. Naples: R. Ricciardi, 1928.
Rinaldi, M. *Due secoli di musica al Teatro Argentino*. 3 vols. Florence: Olschki, 1978.

Senigaglia

Radiciotti, G. *Teatro e musicisti a Senigaglia*. Tivoli: Majella, 1893; repr. Bologna: Forni, 1973.

Trieste

Bottura, C. *Storia del Teatro Comunale di Trieste*. Trieste: Schmidl, 1885.
Matz, Mary Jane. "Great Opera Houses: Trieste." *Opera News* 30 January 1965: 28–31.

Turin

Basso, Alberto. *Il Teatro della Città: Storia del Teatro Regio di Torino*. Turin: Cassa di Risparmio, 1976.

Urbino

Radiciotti, G. *Contributi alla storia del teatro e della musica in Urbino.* Pesaro: A. Nobili, 1899.

Venice

Lianovosani, L. *La Fenice: Gran Teatro di Venezia.* Milan: Mursia, 1974.

Nani Mocenigo, M. *Il teatro La Fenice: Note storiche e artistiche.* Venice and Giudecca: Ind. Poligr. Venete, 1926.

Pignati, T., ed. *Gran teatro La Fenice.* Venice: Marsilio, 1981.

Verona

L'Accademia Filarmonica di Verona e il suo teatro 1732–1982. Verona: Accademia Filarmonica di Verona, 1982.

Lenotti, T. *I teatri di Verona.* Verona: Linitipia Veronese, 1949.

Voghera

Maragliano, A. *I teatri di Voghera: Cronistoria.* Casteggia: Cerri, 1901.

Specialized Studies

ADMINISTRATION AND LEGISLATION

Petracchi, A. *Sul reggimento de' pubblici teatri.* Milan: G. Ferrario, 1821.

Rosmini, E. *La legislazione e la giurisprudenza dei teatri.* 2 vols. Milan: F. Marini, 1872.

Rossi-Gallieno, C. *Saggio di economia teatrale.* Milan: F. Rusconi, 1839.

Valle, G. *Cenni teorici-pratici sulle aziende teatrali.* Milan: Dalla società tipografica de' classici italiani, 1823.

AGENTS AND IMPRESARIOS

Angelis, M. de. *Le carte dell'impresario.* Florence: Sansoni, 1982.

Arcais, F. d'. "L'industria musicale." *Nuova antologia* 15 May 1879.

Modugno, M. "Domenico Donzelli e il suo tempo." *Nuova rivista musicale italiana* 18, no. 2 (April–June 1984): 200–216.

Monaldi, Gino. *Impresari celebri del secolo XIX.* Rocca San Casciano: Licinio Cappelli, 1918.

Rosselli, J. "Agenti teatrali nel mondo dell'opera lirica italiana dell' Ottocento." *Rivista italiana di musicologia* 17, no. 1 (1982): 134–154.

———. "Governi, appaltatori e giuochi d'azzardo nell'Italia napoleonica." *Rivista storica italiana* 93, no. 2 (1981).

——— *L'impresario d'opera: Arte e affari del teatro musicale italiano dell'Ottocento*. Turin: EDT/Musica, 1985.

———. *The Opera Industry in Italy from Cimarosa to Verdi*. Cambridge University Press, 1984.

Tintori, Giampiero. "Verdi e la storia della retribuzione del compositore italiano." *Studi verdiani* 2 (1983): 11–28.

SINGING AND SINGERS

Battaglia, F. *L'arte del canto in Romagna: I cantanti lirici romagnoli dell'Ottocento e del Novecento*. Bologna: Bongiovanni, 1979.

Bazetta de Vemenia, N. *Le cantanti italiane dell'Ottocento*. Novara: G. Volante, 1945.

Bragaglia, L. *Personaggi e interpreti del teatro di Puccini*. Rome: Trevi, 1977.

———. *Verdi e i suoi interpreti*. Rome: Bulzoni, 1979.

Brewer, Bruce. "Giovan Battista Rubini: A Performance Study." *Journal of the Donizetti Society* 4 (1980): 116–179.

Campanella, F. *Sulla decadenza del canto in Italia*. Naples: De Angelis, 1885.

Capri, A. "Rossini e l'estetica musicale della vocalità." *Rivista musicale italiana* 46 (1942): 353–373.

Celentano, L. *Intorno all'arte del cantare in Italia nel secolo decimonono*. Naples: Ghio, 1867.

Celletti, Rodolfo."Caratteri della vocalità di Verdi." In *Atti del 3° congresso internazionale di studi verdiani: Milano 1972*. Parma: Istituto di Studi Verdiani, 1974. 81–88.

———. "Il vocalismo italiano da Rossini a Donizetti." *Analecta musicologica* 5 (1968): 267–294 (Rossini) and 7 (1969): 214–247 (Bellini and Donizetti).

Chusid, Martin. "The Organization of Scenes with Arias: Verdi's Cavatinas and Romanzas." In *Atti del primo congresso internazionale di studi verdiani: Venezia 1966*. Parma: Istituto di Studi Verdiani, 1969. 59–66.

Crutchfield, Will. "Vocal Ornamentation in Verdi: The Phonographic Evidence." *19th-Century Music* 7, no. 1 (1983): 3–54.

Dalmonte, R. "La canzone nel melodramma italiano dell'Ottocento: Ricerche di metodo strutturale." *Rivista italiana di musicologia* 11 (1976): 230–313. A study of some one hundred works by twenty-nine composers of the first half of the nineteenth century.

Davenport, Marcia. "The Revival of Bel Canto." *Opera News* 11 January 1964: 8–13.

Della Corte, A. *Canto e Bel Canto.* Turin: Paravia, 1934.

———. *Vicende degli stili nel canto dal tempo di Gluck al 1900.* Turin: Paravia, 1933.

Delle Sedie, Enrico. *Esthétique du chant et de l'art lyrique.* 4 vols. Milan: Ricordi, 1885.

———. *Riflessioni sulle cause della decadenza della scuola di canto in Italia.* Paris: Dupont, 1881.

Egger, R. *Die Arienformen in den Opern Verdis.* Diss., Innsbruck, 1952.

Fasano, R. *Storia degli abbellimenti musicali.* Rome: De Sanctis, 1949.

FitzLyon, April. *Maria Malibran: Diva of the Romantic Age.* Bloomington: Indiana University Press, 1988.

Forbes, Elizabeth. *Mario and Grisi: A Biography.* London: V. Gollancz, 1985.

Galleria degli artisti lirici. Milan: G. Damiana, n.d.

Galluser, W. *Der Chor und die Oper.* Bellinzona: Buchdruckerei Leins & Vescovi, 1947.

Gora, E. *Cantarono alla Scala.* [Milan]: Teatro alla Scala/Electra Ed., [1976].

Hale, V. E. *The Tenor Arias in the Operas of Giuseppe Verdi.* Diss., University of Kentucky, 1973.

Henstock, Michael. *Fernando De Lucia: Son of Naples.* Portland, Ore.: Amadeus Press, 1990.

Heuss, A. "Verdi als melodischer Characteristiker." *Zeitschrift der intern. Musikgesellschaft, S.I.M.* 15 (1913): 63–72.

Hughes, Spike. "'Take Notice of the Words': Singers, Verdi Felt, Should Not Be Left to Their Own Devices." *Opera News* 14 February 1970: 8–13.

Kaufman, Thomas G. "A 19th-Century Tenor Colossus: Enrico Tamberlick." *The Opera Fanatic* Fall 1986: 19–27.

———. "Giulia Grisi: A Re-evaluation." *Journal of the Donizetti Society* 4 (1980): 180–226.

———. "Giuseppe and Fanny Persiani." *Journal of the Donizetti Society* 6 (1988): 122–151.

————. "Ronconi." *Journal of the Donizetti Society* 5 (1984): 169–206.

Klein, Herman. *The Reign of Patti.* New York, 1920.

Labanchi, A. G. *Gli artisti lirici e la scuola di canto in Italia.* Naples: F. Colagrande, 1902.

Laget, A. *Le chant et les chanteurs.* Paris: Heugel, 1874. On Italy, 85–88.

Lippmann, Friedrich. "Die Melodien Donizettis." *Analecta musicologica* 3 (1966): 80–113.

Machabey, A. *Le Bel Canto.* Paris: Larousse, 1948.

Mariani, R. "La melodia di Puccini." In *Puccini nel centenario della nascita.* Lucca: Lorenzetti & Natali, 1958. 23–30.

Mastrigli, L. *Il coro nel dramma musicale moderno.* Rome: Paravia, 1887.

Matz, Mary Jane. "Queen of Bel Canto." *Opera News* 30 March 1963: 26–28. On Giuditta Pasta.

————. "Rubini of Bergamo." *Opera News* 1 February 1969: 12–13.

Medicus, L. *Die Koloratur in der italienischen Oper des 19.Jahrhundert.* Zurich: Hug & Co., 1939.

Merlin, O. *Le chant des sirenes.* Paris: Julliard, 1969.

Monaldi, Gino. *Cantanti celebri 1829–1929.* Rome: Edizioni Tiber, 1929.

Ott, J., and B. Ott. *Les pédagogies de la voix et les techniques européennes du chant.* Issy-les-Moulineaux: Editions EAP, 1981.

Pahlen, Kurt. *Great Singers from the Seventeenth Century to the Present Day.* Trans. Oliver Coburn. London: W. H. Allen, 1973.

Pleasants, Henry. "A Shorter Vocabulary of Vocalism." *Stereo Review* May 1971: 69–72.

————. *The Great Singers, From the Dawn of Opera to Our Own Time.* New York: Simon and Schuster, 1966.

Ricci, V. *La tecnica del canto in rapporto con la pratica antica e le teorie moderne.* Livorno: R. Giusti, 1920.

Rogers, Francis. *Some Famous Singers of the 19th Century.* New York: H. W. Gray, 1914.

Schmitt, J. *Die männliche Stimmungcharaktere in den Opern Verdis.* Diss., Erlangen, 1940.

Scott, Michael. *The Record of Singing to 1914.* London: Duckworth, 1977.

Siegmund-Schultze, W. "Gedanken zum Verdischen Melodie-Typus." *Istituto di Studi Verdiani* 2, no. 4 (January–December 1961): 255–284.

COMPOSERS

The reader is also advised to consult the many published editions of composers' correspondence, essential for an understanding of their works, references to which can be found in *The New Grove Dictionary of Music and Musicians*, edited by Stanley Sadie (Washington, D.C., and London, 1980), in the bibliography following the article for each composer.

Bellini

Adamo, M. R., and Friedrich Lippmann. *Bellini: Biografia.* Turin: ERI/Ed. RAI, 1981.

"Bellini and Bel Canto." *Opera News* 28 February 1976. Special Issue.

Boromé, Joseph A. "Bellini and *Beatrice di Tenda.*" *Music and Letters* 42 (1961): 319–335.

Brauner, C. S. *Vincenzo Bellini and the Aesthetics of Opera Seria in the First Third of the Nineteenth Century.* 2 vols. Diss., Yale University, 1972.

Brunel, Pierre. *Vincenzo Bellini.* Paris: Fayard, 1981.

Cataldo, G. *Il teatro di Bellini: Guida critica a tutte le opere.* Bologna: Editori Bongiovanni, 1980.

Greenspan, C. J. *The Operas of Vincenzo Bellini.* Diss., University of California, Berkeley, 1977.

Lippmann, Friedrich. "Vincenzo Bellini und die italienische Opera seria seiner Zeit," *Analecta musicologica* 6 (1969).

Orrey, Leslie. *Bellini.* The Master Musician Series. London: J. M. Dent, 1969.

———. "The Literary Sources of Bellini's First Opera." *Music and Letters* 55 (1974): 24–29.

Weinstock, Herbert. *Vincenzo Bellini, His Life and His Operas.* London: Knopf, 1971.

Willier, Stephen A. "Madness, the Gothic and Bellini's *I pirata.*" *The Opera Quarterly* 6, no. 4 (Summer 1989): 7–23.

Catalani

Gatti, Carlo. *Alfredo Catalani.* Milan: Istituto d'Alta Cultura, 1946.

Klein, John W. "Alfredo Catalani: 1854–1893." *Music and Letters* 35, no. 1 (1954): 40–44.

———. "Toscanini and Alfredo Catalani: A Unique Friendship." *Music and Letters* 48, no. 3 (1967): 213–228.

Zurletti, M. *Catalani.* Turin: EDT/Musica, 1982.

Donizetti

Ashbrook, William. *Donizetti and His Operas.* Cambridge University Press, 1982.

Barblan, Guglielmo. "Donizetti in Naples." Trans. Derek Turner. *Journal of the Donizetti Society* 1 (1974): 105–119.

Bleiler, Ellen H. *Lucia di Lammermoor [by] Gaetano Donizetti: Complete Companion to the Opera.* New York: Dover, 1972.

Gossett, Philip. *Anna Bolena and the Artistic Maturity of Gaetano Donizetti.* Oxford: Clarendon Press, 1985.

Saracino, E. *Invito all'ascolto di Donizetti.* Milan: Mursia, 1984.

Steiner-Isenmann, R. *Gaetano Donizetti: Sein Leben und seine Opern.* Bern and Stuttgart: Hallweg, 1982.

Weinstock, Herbert. *Donizetti.* London: Knopf, 1964.

Zavadini, G. *Gaetano Donizetti: Vita e epistolario.* Bergamo: Centro Studi Donizettiani, 1970.

Giordano

Cellamare, Daniele. *Umberto Giordano.* Rome: Fratelli Palombi, 1967.

Morini, Mario. *Umberto Giordano.* Milan: Casa musicale Sonzogno, 1968.

Leoncavallo

Bonavia, Ferruccio. *Ruggero Leoncavallo.* London: Cassell, 1952.

Mascagni

Cellamare, Daniele. *Pietro Mascagni.* Rome: Palombi, 1965.

Donno, A. de. *Mascagni nel '900 musicale.* Rome: Edizioni Casa del Libro, 1935.

Favia-Artsay, Aida. "Did Mascagni Write *Cavalleria?*" *The Opera Quarterly* 7, no. 2 (Summer 1990): 83–89.

Klein, John W. "Pietro Mascagni and Giovanni Verga." *Music and Letters* 44 (1963): 350–357.

Mallach, Alan. "The Mascagni Tour of 1902: An Italian Composer Confronts the American Musical World." *The Opera Quarterly* 7, no. 4 (Winter 1990–91): 13–37.

Morini, Mario, ed. *Pietro Mascagni.* Milan: Casa Musicale Sonzogno di Piero Ostali, 1964.

Pasi, Mario. *Mascagni.* Trans. Harvey Sachs with John W. Freeman, under the title *Mascagni in North America.* New York: Treves Publishing, 1989.

Mercadante

Mooney, A. G. *An Assessment of Mercadante's Contribution to the Development of Italian Opera*. M.Mus. diss., Edinburgh, 1970.

Notardini, B. *Mercadante*. Rome: Ricordi, 1948.

Pacini

Black, John N. "The Eruption of Vesuvius in Pacini's *L'ultimo giorno di Pompei*." *Journal of the Donizetti Society* 6 (1988): 93–104.

Carlez, J. *Pacini et l'opéra italien*. Caen: H. Delesques, 1888.

Commons, Jeremy. "Giovanni Pacini and *Maria Tudor*." *Journal of the Donizetti Society* 6 (1988): 57–92.

Ponchielli

Klein, John W. "Ponchielli, A Forlorn Figure." *The Chesterian* Spring 1960: 116–122.

Matz, Mary Jane. "Ponchielli's Promise." *Opera News* 31 March 1962: 24–27.

Ponchielli 1834–1886: Saggi e ricerche nel 150° anniversario della nascita. Casalmorano: Casa Rurale ed Artigiana, 1984.

Weaver, William. "Ponchielli of Cremona." *Opera News* 10 April 1976: 8–11.

Puccini

Appleton, William S. "Puccini: The Stop and Go of Talent." *Opera News* 29 December 1973/5 January 1974: 12–16.

Ashbrook, William. *The Operas of Puccini*. Ithaca, N.Y.: Cornell University Press, 1985.

Carner, Mosco. *Giacomo Puccini: A Critical Biography*. New York: Holmes and Meier, 1988.

Del Fiorentino, Dante. *Immortal Bohemian: An Intimate Memoir of Giacomo Puccini*. New York: Prentice-Hall, 1952.

Di Gaetani, John Louis. *Puccini the Thinker: The Composer's Intellectual and Dramatic Development*. New York: Peter Lang, 1987.

Marek, George R. *Puccini, A Biography*. New York: Simon and Schuster, 1951.

Marggraf, W. *Giacomo Puccini*. Leipzig: Reclam, 1977.

Opera News July 1974. Special Puccini Issue.

Severgnini, S. *Invito all'ascolto di Giacomo Puccini*. Milan: Mursia, 1984.

Specht, R. *Giacomo Puccini*. Trans. Catherine Alison Phillips. London and Toronto: J. M. Dent and Sons, 1933.

The Opera Quarterly Autumn 1984. Special Puccini Issue.

Zappa, Paul J. "Puccini on Trial." *Opera News* 17 December 1977: 28–30.

Rossini

Appleton, William S. "Rossini: The Stop and Go of Talent." *Opera News* 8 December 1973: 18–23.

Derwent, G. H. J. *Rossini and Some Forgotten Nightingales.* London, 1934.

Edwards, Henry Sutherland. *Rossini and His School.* London: Sampson Low, Marston and Co., 1881. Condensed version of *Rossini's Life* (London, 1869).

Gossett, Philip. "Rossini in Naples: Some Major Works Recovered." *The Musical Quarterly* 54 (1968): 316–340.

———. "Rossini, Seriously." *Opera News* 22 December 1990: 20–23.

———. *The Operas of Rossini: Problems of Textual Criticism in Nineteenth-Century Opera.* Diss., Princeton University, 1970.

Meyerowitz, Jan. "How Seriously Can We Take Rossini's Serious Operas?" *High Fidelity* November 1968: 61–65.

Porter, Andrew. "A Lost Opera By Rossini." *Music and Letters* 45 (1964): 39–44.

Radiciotti, G. *Gioachino Rossini: Vita documentata, opere ed influenza sull'arte.* 3 vols. Tivoli: Artigrafiche majella di Aldo Chicca, 1927–29.

Rizzo, Francis. "Rossini's Tragic Mask." *Opera News* October 1971: 10–11. On *Semiramide.*

Rognoni, Luigi. *Gioacchino Rossini.* Turin: Einaudi, 1968.

Stendhal. *Life of Rossini.* Trans. Richard N. Coe. New York: Criterion Books, 1957.

Till, Nicholas. *Rossini: His Life and Times.* New York: Hippocrene Books, 1983.

Toye, Francis. *Rossini: A Study in Tragi-Comedy.* London, 1963.

———. "The Serious Rossini." *Opera News* 9 March 1963: 8–12.

Smareglia

Levi, V. "Un grande operista italiano: Antonio Smareglia 1854–1929." *Rivista musicale italiana* 36 (1929): 600–615.

Perpich, E. *Antonio Smareglia.* Tesi di Laurea: Universita di Trieste, 1960.

Verdi

Abbiati, Franco. *Giuseppe Verdi.* 4 vols. Milan: Ricordi, 1959.

Appleton, William S. "Verdi: The Stop and Go of Talent." *Opera News* 22 December 1973: 10–13.

Bourgeois, Jacques. *Giuseppe Verdi.* Paris: Julliard, 1978.

Budden, Julian. *The Operas of Verdi.* 3 vols. London: Cassell, 1973–81.

Gál, Hans. *Giuseppe Verdi und die Oper.* Frankfurt: Fischer Taschenbuch Verlag, 1982.

Gatti, Carlo. *Verdi: The Man and His Music.* Trans. Elisabeth Abbott. London: V. Gollancz, 1955.

High Fidelity October 1963. Special Verdi Issue.

Mendelsohn, Gerald A. "Verdi the Man and Verdi the Dramatist." *19th-Century Music* 2, nos. 2 and 3 (1978–79): 110–142; 214–230.

Oberdorfer, A., ed. *Verdi: Autobiographie a travers la correspondance.* Trans. from the Italian by S. Zavriew. Paris: Lattes, 1984.

Opera 2, no. 2 (1951). Special Verdi Issue.

Osborne, Charles. *The Complete Operas of Verdi.* New York: Knopf, 1977.

Parker, Roger. *Studies in Early Verdi 1832–1844: New Information and Perspectives on the Milanese Musical Milieu and the Operas from Oberto to Ernani.* New York: Garland Publishing, 1989.

Phillips-Matz, Mary Jane. *Verdi: A Biography.* New York: Oxford University Press, 1993.

Tintori, Giampiero. *Invito all'ascolto di Verdi.* Milan: Mursia, 1984.

Toye, Francis. *Giuseppe Verdi, His Life and Works.* London, 1931.

Walker, Frank. *The Man Verdi.* New York: Knopf, 1962.

———. "Verdian Forgeries." *Music Review* 20, no. 1 (1959): 28–37.

Weaver, William. *Verdi.* Paris: Van de Velde, 1979.

Weaver, William, and Martin Chusid, eds. *The Verdi Companion.* New York: Norton, 1988.

Weiss, Piero. "Verdi and the Fusion of Genres." *Journal of the American Musicological Society* 35 (1982): 138–156.

French sources and sojourns

Blanco, G. *Bellini a Parigi.* Catania: C. Tringale, 1977.

Caswell, A. "Vocal Embellishment in Rossini's Paris Operas: French Style or Italian?" *Bollettino del Centro rossiniano di studi* 1 (1975): 5 and 2 (1975): 5.

Cella, F. "Indagini sulle fonti francesi dei libretti di Gaetano Donizetti." *Vita e Pensiero* 4 (1921): 343–590.

Escudier, Leon. "Donizetti en France." In *Mes souvenirs.* Paris: Dentu, 1863. 41–51.

Goury, J. "Verdi et la France." In *Atti del 2° congresso internazionale di studi verdiani.* Parma: Istituto di Studi Verdiani, 1969. 565–572.

Lortal, L. *Les debuts de Rossini a Paris de 1817 a 1820.* Diss., Sorbonne, 1979.

Messenger, Michael. "Donizetti 1840: 3 'French' Operas and Their Italian Counterparts." *Journal of the Donizetti Society* 2 (1975): 99–116.

Nicastro, A. "Il teatro francese nell'evoluzione del melodramma verdiano." In *Atti del 3° congresso internazionale di studi verdiani: Milano 1972.* Parma: Istituto di Studi Verdiani, 1974. 838–849.

Pougin, A. "Donizetti en France," *Le Menestrel* 58 (1897): 267–268, 275–276, 283–284.

Prud'homme, J.-G. "Rossini and His Works in France." *The Musical Quarterly* 17 (1931): 110–137.

Various influences

Aycock, R. E. "Shakespeare, Boito and Verdi." *The Musical Quarterly* 58 (1972): 588–604.

Dean, Winton. "Some Echoes of Donizetti in Verdi's Operas." In *Atti del 3° congresso internazionale di studi verdiani: Milano 1972.* Parma: Istituto di Studi Verdiani, 1974. 122–147.

Klein, John W. "Verdi's *Otello* and Rossini's." *Music and Letters* 45 (1964): 130–140.

Leukel, J. "Puccini et Bizet." *Revue musicale de Suisse romande* 35, no. 2 (May 1982): 61–66.

Lippmann, Friedrich. "Verdi e Bellini." In *Atti del primo congresso internazionale di studi verdiani: Venezia 1966.* Parma: Istituto di Studi Verdiani, 1969. 184–196.

———. "Verdi und Donizetti." In *Opernstudien: Anna Amalie Abert zum 65. Geburtstag.* Tutzing: Schneider, 1975. 153–173.

Tartak, Marvin. "The Two *Barbieri.*" *Music and Letters* 50, no. 4 (1969): 453–469.

Wagner and the Italians

"Colloquium Verdi-Wagner." *Analecta musicolgica* 11 (1972). From a meeting held in Rome, 6–9 October 1969.

Jung, V. *Die Rezeption der Kunst Richard Wagners in Italien.* Regensburg: Bosse, 1974.

Manera, G., and G. Pugliese. *Wagner in Italia.* Venice: Marsilio, 1982.

Monaldi, Gino. *Verdi e Wagner.* Rome: G. Cinelli, 1887.

Panizzardi, M. *Wagner in Italia.* Genoa: Progresso, 1923.

Pattalino, P. "Gli inizi della critica wagneriana in Italia." *Musica d'oggi, New Series* 5, no. 1 (January–February 1962): 2–12.

Ziino, A. *Antologia della critica wagneriana in Italia.* Messina: Pelorinato Editrice, 1970.

BALLET

Bonaccorsi, A. "Danza e melodie di danza nell'opera di Verdi." *Rassegna musicale* 21 (1951): 246–251.

Gatti, Carlo, ed. *Cinquant'anni di opera e balletto in Italia.* Rome: Bestetti, 1954.

Monaldi, Gino. *Le regine della danza nel secolo XIX.* Turin: Fratelli Bocca, 1910.

Porter, Andrew. "Verdi's Ballets." *Opera News* 8 April 1972: 8–11.

Rossi, L. *Il ballo alla Scala.* [Milan]: Ed. della Scala, 1970.

Searle, Humphrey. "Ballet Music in Opera During the Nineteenth Century." Chap. 2 in *Ballet Music, An Introduction.* New York: Dover, 1973.

SETS AND STAGE DIRECTION

Adami, G. *Un secolo di scenografia alla Scala.* Milan: Bestetti, 1945.

Angelis, Alberto de. *Scenografi italiani di ieri e oggi.* Rome: Cremonese, 1938.

Bablet, D. *Le décor de théâtre de 1870 à 1914.* Paris: C.N.R.S., 1975.

Black, John N. "Cammarano's Notes for the Staging of *Lucia di Lammermoor.*" *Journal of the Donizetti Society* 4 (1980): 29–44.

Bordowitz, Harvey. "Verdi's *Disposizioni Sceniche*: The Stage Manuals for Some Verdi Operas." M.A. thesis, Brooklyn College, 1976. Copy in archives of the American Institute for Verdi Studies.

Coe, Doug. "The Original Production Book For *Otello:* An Introduction." *19th-Century Music* 2, no. 2 (1978): 148–158.

Cohen, H. Robert. "A Survey of French Sources for the Staging of Verdi's Operas." *Studi Verdiani* 3 (1985): 11–44.

Della Corte, A. "I problemi della scenografia e l'ottocento." In

Tempi e aspetti della scenografia. Turin: Edizioni Radio Italiana, 1954.

Ferrario, Carlo. *500 bozzetti scenografici.* Milan: Hoepli, 1926.

Ferrero, M. V. *La scenografia dalle origini al 1936.* Turin: Cassa di Risparmio, 1980.

Gonzaga, P. *La musique des yeux ou l'optique theatrale.* St. Petersburg: A. Pluchart, 1807.

Gori, G. *Scenografia: La tradizione e la rivoluzione contemporanea.* Rome: Casa editrice Alberto Stock, 1926.

Lucchini, A. M. *L'attività dei scenografi per il Teatro alla Scala tra il 1832 e il 1859.* Tesi di Laurea: Universita di Milano, 1977.

Mancini, F. *Scenografia italiana dal Rinascimento all'età romantica.* Milan: Fabbri, 1966.

———. "Scenografia romantica," *Critica d'arte* 15, nos. 96 and 98 (1968): 45–60; 65–80.

Marchioro, G. *Momenti ed aspetti della messa in scena.* Milan: Ricordi, 1960. 95–106.

Mariani, V. *Scenografia italiana.* Florence: Rinascimento del Libro, 1930.

Maurel, Victor. *A propos de la mise-en-scène du drame lyrique 'Otello.'* Rome: Editrice Romana, 1888.

McCorquodale, Charles P. "Operatic Stage Design 1800–1840." *Journal of the Donizetti Society* 1 (1974): 121–128.

Murano, M. T. "La scenografia delle cinque prime assolute di Verdi alla Fenice di Venezia." In *Atti del primo congresso internazionale di studi verdiani: Venezia 1966.* Parma: Istituto di Studi Verdiani, 1969.

Pigozzi, M. *La scenografia a Reggio nell'Ottocento.* Vol. 2 of *Teatro a Reggio Emilia.* Ed. S. Romagnoli and G. Garbero. Florence: Sansoni, 1980. 169–183.

Rava, F. E., ed. *Scenografia del Museo Teatrale alla Scala dal XVI al XIX secolo.* Venice: N. Pozzo, 1965. Exhibit catalogue.

Ricci, C. *La scenografia italiana.* Milan: Treves, 1930.

Silke, L. "Bibliographie der italienischen Literatur zur Scenographie des Musiktheaters." *Analecta musicologica* 17 (1976): 296–309.

Stoddard, Richard. *Stage Scenery, Machinery and Lighting: A Guide to Information Sources.* Detroit: Gale Research Company, 1977.

Torrefranca, Fausto. *La scenografia e l'opera in musica sino al romanticismo.* Turin: G. Fedetto, (1927).

DISCOGRAPHIES

Bauer, R. *Historical Records 1898–1909*. London: Sidywick & Jackson, 1972. Verdi recordings of 469 singers.

Bescoby-Chambers, J. *The Archives of Sound*. Aylesbury: Hazell Watson, [1964].

Blyth, Alan. "The Gramophone Collection: 'Madama Butterfly.'" *Gramophone* May 1991: 1993–1994.

Bontinck-Kuffel, I. *Opern auf Schallplatten 1900–1962: Ein historischer Katalog*. Vienna: Universal Edition, [1974].

Celletti, R. *Il teatro d'opera in disco*. Milan: Rizzoli, 1976.

Gammond, P. *The Illustrated Encyclopedia of Recorded Opera*. New York: Harmony Books, 1979.

Green, London. "*Rigoletto* on Records: Singers in Search of Characters." *The Opera Journal* 16, no. 1 (1983): 16–29.

Harris, K. *Opera Recordings: A Critical Guide*. New York: Drake, 1973.

Luten, C. J. "Sound and Fury: CD Reissues of the Verismo Repertory." *Opera News* November 1990: 30–40.

———. "Verdi Redivivus: The Best CD Versions of the Composer's Operas." *Opera News* September 1989: 46–49.

Mordden, Ethan. "Verismo Opera: A History and Discography." *Ovation* September 1985: 23–28.

Parsons, Charles H. *Opera Discography*. Vols. 10–12 of the *Mellen Opera Reference Index*. Lewiston, N.Y.: Edwin Mellen Press, 1990.

Steane, J. B. *The Grand Tradition: Seventy Years of Singing on Record*. 2nd ed. Portland, Ore.: Amadeus Press, 1993.

PUBLISHING FIRMS

Adami, G. *Giulio Ricordi e i suoi musicisti*. Milan and Rome: Trevisini, 1933.

Caselli, A. *Catalogo delle opere liriche pubblicate in Italia*. Florence: Olschki, 1969.

Heinsheimer, Hans. "Great Publishing Houses: Sonzogno." *Opera News* 10 December 1988: 20–22.

Lisio, G. "Sul l'epistolario di Casa Lucca." *Rendiconti del Reale Istituto Lombardo di Scienze e Lettere, Ser. 2* 41 (1908): 317ff.

Pasquinelli, A. *Francesco e Giovannina Lucca: Editori musicali a Milano 1825–1888*. Tesi di Laurea: Università di Milano, 1981.

Rattalino, P. "Editori di musica nell'Italia dell'Ottocento." In *Terzo programma*. Turin: ERI, 1965.

Sartori, C. *Dizionario degli editori musicali italiani*. Florence: Olschki, 1958.

Schlitzer, Franco. *Mondo teatrale dell'Ottocento*. Naples: F. Fiorentino, 1954. On G. Lucca, 183–214.

Vergani, O. *Piccolo viaggio in un archivio*. Milan: Ricordi, 1953.

MUSICAL STYLE

Balthazar, Scott. "Analytic Contexts and Mediated Influences: The Rossinian *Convenienze* and Verdi's Middle and Late Duets." *The Journal of Musicological Research* 10, nos. 1–2 (1990): 19–45.

———. *Evolving Conventions in Italian Serious Opera: Scene Structure in the Works of Rossini, Bellini, Donizetti, and Verdi, 1810–1850*. Diss., University of Pennsylvania, 1985.

———. "Music, Poetry and Action in *Ottocento* Opera: The Principle of Concurrent Articulations." *The Opera Journal* 22, no. 2 (1989): 13–34.

———. "Rossini and the Development of the Mid-Century Lyric Form." *Journal of the American Musicological Society* 41 (Spring 1988): 102–125.

———. "The *Primo Ottocento* Duet and the Transformation of the Rossinian Code." *The Journal of Musicology* 7, no. 4 (1989): 471–497.

Berio, Luciano. "Berio on Verdi." *Opera News* 6 December 1975: 10–13.

Bruni, M. "Funzionalita drammatica dell'accordo di quarta e sesta nello stile di Verdi." In *Atti del primo congresso internazionale di studi verdiani: Venezia 1966*. Parma: Istituto di Studi Verdiani, 1969. 36–39.

Crocker, Richard. *A History of Musical Style*. New York: McGraw-Hill, 1966.

Dallapiccola, Luigi. "Reflections on Three Verdi Operas." *19th-Century Music* 7 (1983): 55–62. On *Rigoletto*, *Simon Boccanegra*, and *Falstaff*.

Gossett, Philip. "Gioachino Rossini and the Conventions of Composition." *Acta musicologica* 42 (1970): 48–58.

Johnson, Harriet. "What Verdi Wrote: You Can't Always Tell From the Printed Score." *Opera News* 5 April 1975: 27–29.

Kerman, Joseph. "Verdi's Use of Recurring Themes." In *Studies in Music History: Essays for Oliver Strunk*. Princeton, N.J.: Princeton University Press, 1968. 495–510.

Lawton, David. "On the 'Bacio' Theme in *Otello*." *19th-Century Music* 1, no. 3 (1978): 211–220.

———. *Tonality and Drama in Verdi's Early Operas*. 2 vols. Diss., University of California, Berkeley, 1972.

Levarie, Siegmund. "Key Relations in Verdi's *Un ballo in maschera*." *19th-Century Music* 2 (1978): 143–147.

Martin, George. "Verdi's Imitation of Shakespeare, *La forza del destino*." *The Opera Quarterly* 3, no. 1 (1985): 19–29.

Parker, Roger. "Levels of Motivic Definition in Verdi's *Ernani*." *19th-Century Music* 6, no. 2 (1982): 141–150.

Parker, Roger, and Matthew Brown. "Motivic and Tonal Interaction in Verdi's *Un ballo in maschera*." *Journal of the American Musicological Society* 36 (1983): 243–265.

Pizzetti, Ildebrando. "Contrappunto e armonia nell'opera di Verdi," *Rassegna musicale* 21 (1951): 189–200.

Saussine, H. de. "L'harmonie bellinienne." *Rivista musicale italiana* 27 (1920): 477–482.

———. "Sur Bellini, harmoniste." *Rivista musicale italiana* 15 (May 1935): 63–64.

Schmiedel, P. S. *Die Entwicklung der Harmonik in Opernschaffen Giuseppe Verdis: eine Tonsystemstudie*. Diss., Leipzig, 1953.

Stravinsky, Igor. *Poetics of Music in the Form of Six Lessons*. Trans. Arthur Knodel and Ingolf Dahl. Cambridge, Mass.: Harvard University Press, 1970.

Vlad, R. "Anticipazioni nel linguaggio armonico verdiano." *Rassegna musicale* 21 (1951): 237–245.

LIBRETTOS

Alberici, S. "Appunti sulla librettistica rossiniana." *Bollettino del Centro Rossiniano di Studi* 1–3 (1978): 45–60.

Albertini, C. "A proposito dell'estetica del libretto musicale." *Gazzetta musicale di Milano* 52 (1893): 529–530.

Ashbrook, William. "The Two Faces of Boito." *Opera News* 10 April 1976: 12–15.

Baldacci, L. "I libretti di Verdi." In *Il melodramma italiano dell'Ottocento*. Turin: Einaudi, 1977. 113–124.

————. *Libretti d'opera e altri saggi.* Florence: Vallecchi, 1974.

Barblan, Guglielmo. "L'opera di Verdi e il dramma romantico." *Rivista musicale italiana* 45 (1941).

Baroni, M. "Il libretto d'opera a Bologna nell'epoca di Stendhal." *Archiginnasio* 61–63 (1971–73): 616–622.

Black, John. "Cammarano's Libretti for Donizetti." *Studi Donizettiani* 3 (1978): 115–129.

————. "Code of Instructions for the Censorship of Theatrical Works, Naples 1849." *Journal of the Donizetti Society* 5 (1984): 147–150.

————. *The Italian Romantic Libretto: A Study of Salvatore Cammarano.* Edinburgh: The University Press, 1984.

Bocchelli, R. "Verdi e Shakespeare." *Rassegna musicale* 21 (1951): 201–203.

Branca, E. *Felice Romani ed i piu riputati maestri di musica del suo tempo.* Turin: Loescher, 1882.

Bustico, Guido. "Saggio di una bibliografia musicale dei libretti musicali di Felice Romani." *Rivista musicale italiana* 14 (1907): 229–284. 291 titles, set to music between 1813 and 1891.

Commons, Jeremy. "Giuseppe Bardari." *Journal of the Donizetti Society* 3 (1977): 84–96. On the librettist of *Maria Stuarda.*

Della Corte, A. *La 'poesia per musica' e il libretto: Introduzione a una storia dell'opera.* Turin: Gheroni, 1950.

Di Stefano, C. *La censura teatrale in Italia 1600–1962.* Bologna: Cappelli, 1964.

Eisotti, V. *Schiller e il melodramma di Verdi.* Florence: La Nuova Editrice, 1975.

Fellner, Rudolph. "The Act Puccini Never Wrote: An Uncomposed Episode for *La boheme* Is Published for the First Time in English." *Opera News* 4 February 1967: 24–27.

Filoni, F. Macbeth, Otello *e* The Merry Wives of Windsor *nei libretti verdiani.* Ph.D. diss., Macerata, 1980.

Frame, Florence K. "*Madama Butterfly:* The Dramatists." *Opera News* 3 April 1976: 20–22.

Franceschetti, G. C. "La fortuna di Hugo nel melodramma italiano dell'Ottocento." *Contributi dell'Istituto di Filologia, French Series* 2 (Milan, 1961): 168–251.

Garlington, S. *Sources for the Study of the Nineteenth-Century Italian Opera in the Syracuse University Libraries: An Annotated Libretto List.* Syracuse, N.Y.: Syracuse University Libraries, 1976.

Gazzaniga, A. "La germinazione nel linguaggio di Donizetti."

Nuova rivista musicale italiana 18, no. 3 (1984): 420–433.

Goffo, M. *Les sources françaises des livrets de Puccini.* Diss., Toulouse, 1979.

Jeuland-Maynaud, M. "Legitimité de la librettologie." *Revue des études italiennes* 22, nos. 1–2 (1976): 60–101. On Verdi.

Kunath, M. *Die Oper als literarische Form.* Diss., Leipzig, 1925.

Lavagetto, M. *Quei piu modesti romanzi: Il libretto nel melodramma di Verdi: Tecniche costruttive, funzioni, poetica di un genere letterario minore.* Milan: Garzandi, 1979.

Levi, P. "Victor Hugo nel melodramma italiano." In *Paesaggi e figure musicali.* Milan: Fratelli Treves, 1902.

Link, K. D. *Literarische Perspektiven des Opernlibrettos. Studien zur italienischen Oper von 1850 bis 1920.* Bonn: Bouvier Verlag, 1975. Analyzes thirteen works, from *Rigoletto* to *Turandot.*

Lippmann, Friedrich. "Der italienische Vers und der musikalische Rythmus." *Analecta musicologica* 12 (1973); 14 (1974); 15 (1975).

———. "Zum Verhältnis von Libretto und Musik in der italienischen Opera Seria der ersten Hälfte des 19. Jahrhunderts." In *Bericht über den internationalen musikwissenschaftlichen Kongress: Bonn 1970.* Kassel: Bärenreiter, 1972.

Lollis, C. de. *Saggi sulla forma poetica italiana nell'ottocento.* Bari: Laterza, 1929.

Loschelder, J. *Das Todesproblem in Verdis Opernschaffen.* Cologne: Petrarca Haus, 1939.

Matz, Mary Jane. "Well-Versed Librettist." *Opera News* 16 March 1963: 12–13. On Francesco Maria Piave.

Moschino, E. "Il 'libretto' moderno." In *Annuario dell'arte lirica e coreografica italiana.* Milan: De Marchi, 1897–98.

Müller, R. *Das Opernlibretto in 19. Jahrhundert.* Winterthur: H. Schellenberg, 1965.

Peraldi, M. P. *Le thème de la folie dans l'opéra italien de Rossini à Verdi.* Diss., Toulouse, 1975.

Phillips-Matz, Mary Jane. "Public Sinners." *Opera News* November 1988: 24–26. On Verdi's censorship problems with *Stiffelio.*

Pogliaghi, L. *Luigi Illica.* Tesi di Laurea: Universita di Milano, 1975.

Porter, Andrew. "Don't Blame Scribe!" *Opera News* 12 April 1975: 26–27. New light on the genesis of *I vespri siciliani.*

Portinari, Folco. "Melodramma e prosa." In *Teatro dell'Italia unita.* Milan: Il Saggiatore, 1980. 199–215.

———. *Pari siamo! Io la lingua, egli ha il pugnale: Storia del melo-*

dramma ottocentesco attraverso i suoi libretti. Turin: EDT/Musica, 1981.

————. "Pari siamo: Sulla struttura del libretto romantico." In *Il melodramma italiano dell'Ottocento.* Turin: Einaudi, 1977. 545–566.

Rinaldi, M. *Felice Romani: Dal melodramma classico al melodramma romantico.* Rome: De Sanctis, [1965].

Rolandi, U. *Il libretto per musica attraverso i tempi.* Rome: Ed. dell' Ateneo, 1951.

Ross, P. *Studien zum Verhältnis von Libretto und Komposition in den Opern Verdis.* Diss., Bern, 1979; Bern: Gnägi Druck, 1980.

Salvetti, G. "La Scapigliatura milanese e il libretto d'opera." In *Il melodramma italiano dell'Ottocento.* Turin: Einaudi, 1977. 567–604.

Silva, P. "Il libretto musicale italiano negli ultimi cinquant'anni." *Bollettino della Reale Universita italiana per stranieri* November 1938: 321–327.

Smith, Patrick J. *The Tenth Muse: A Historical Study of the Opera Libretto.* London: Gollancz, 1971.

Sororu Zerbio, A. *Schiller e i libretti di Verdi.* Tesi di Laurea and Milan: Istituto Universita di Lingue Moderne, 1978.

Springer, Morris. "Hugo and the Librettists." *Opera News* 7 December 1968: 22–23.

"Tavola rotunda: libretti d'opera." In *Teatro dell'Italia unita.* Milan: Il Saggiatore, 1980. 290–319.

"Tavola rotunda: parola e musica." In *Teatro dell'Italia unita.* Milan: Il Saggiatore, 1980. 320–343.

Valleux, P. *Le personnage du tyran dans les livrets d'opera de Verdi.* Diss., Sorbonne, 1982.

Van, G. de. "Le travail du livret." *Verdi, L'Arc* 81 (1981): 14–35.

Walker, F. "The Librettist of *Don Pasquale.*" *The Monthly Musical Record* 88 (1958): 219–223.

Weckerlin, J. B. "La censure theatrale a Rome." In *Nouveaux Musiciana.* Paris: Garnier, 1917. 249–253.

Weiss, Piero. "'Sacred Bronzes': Paralipomena to an Essay by Dallapiccola." *19th-Century Music* 9, no. 1 (Summer 1985): 42–49. On the language of Risorgimento librettists.

ORCHESTRA

Berl, P. *Die Opern Giuseppe Verdis in ihrer Instrumentation.* Diss., Vienna, 1931.

Carse, Adam. "Orchestras in Vienna, in Italy and in Other Countries." Chap. 6 of *The Orchestra From Beethoven to Berlioz.* Cambridge: W. Heffer and Sons, 1948.

Collinson, M. *Orchestration for the Theater.* London: The Bodley Head, 1949.

Gossett, Philip. "The Overtures of Rossini." *19th-Century Music* 3 (1979–80): 3–31.

Harwood, Gregory W. "Verdi's Reform of the Italian Opera Orchestra." *19th-Century Music* 10, no. 2 (Fall 1986): 108–134.

Karr, Gary. "*Aida*'s First Maestro." *Opera News* 18 December 1976: 32–33.

Matz, Mary Jane. "The Man With the Baton." *Opera News* 12 January 1963: 8–12.

Monaldi, Gino. "Orchestre e direttori del secolo XIX." *Rivista musicale italiana* 16 (1909): 123–142, 531–549.

Travis, F. I. *Verdi's Orchestration.* Zurich: Juris Verlag, 1956.

Tyler, Linda. "Striking Up the *Banda*: Verdi's Use of the Stage Band in His Middle-Period Operas." *The Opera Journal* 23, no. 1 (1990): 2–22.

Vaughan, Dennis. "Puccini's Orchestration." *Proceedings of the Royal Musical Association* 87 (1960–61): 1–14.

POLITICAL INFLUENCES

Bosworth, R. J. B. "Verdi and the *Risorgimento*." *The Italian Quarterly* 14 (1970): 3–27.

Clément, Catherine. *L'opera ou la defaite des femmes.* Paris: Grasset, 1979. Trans. Betsy Wing, under the title *Opera, or the Undoing of Women.* Minneapolis: University of Minnesota Press, 1988.

Donakowski, C. L. "God and People: Manifestations of the *Risorgimento* through Music." In *A Muse for the Masses.* Chicago and London: University of Chicago Press, 1977. 236–250.

Goldstein, Robert J. "Political Censorship of the Opera in Europe: 1815–1914." *Opera Journal* 21, no. 3 (1988): 12–26.

Greenfield, K. R. *Economics and Liberalism in the Risorgimento: A Study of Nationalism in Lombardy 1814–1848.* Baltimore, 1934.

Harrison, Michael H. "Composers as Political Artists: Verdi,

Wagner and the Legacy of Politics in the Nineteenth Century." *The Opera Quarterly* 2, no. 1 (Spring 1984): 95–103.

Monterosso, R. *La musica nel Risorgimento italiano*. Milan: F. Vallardi, 1948. 225–289.

Monti, A., and A. Schinelli. *L'espressione musicale del Risorgimento italiano*. 2 vols. Milan: Ricordi, n.d.

Nordio, M. "Verdi, voce della patria, incitamento e conforto per gli Italiani irredenti." *Atti del primo congresso internazionale di studi verdiani: Venezia 1966*. Parma: Istituto di Studi Verdiani, 1969. 417–421.

Raynor, Henry. *A Social History of Music: Music and Society*. New York: Taplinger Publishing, 1978.

Rindo, J. M. *A Structural Analysis of Giuseppe Verdi's Early Operas and Their Influences on the Italian Risorgimento*. Diss., University of Oregon, 1984.

Rubsamen, W. H. "Music and Politics in the *Risorgimento*." *The Italian Quarterly* 5 (1961): 100–120.

Tavelle, N. *Verdi et la politique*. Diss., Aix-Marseille, 1981.

ROMANTICISM

Allitt, John. *Donizetti and the Tradition of Romantic Love: A Collection of Essays on a Theme*. London: The Donizetti Society, 1975.

Ashbrook, William. "When Romance Reigned: Donizetti's Music Exemplifies the Mood of the *Primo Ottocento*." *Opera News* 15 January 1977: 24–25.

Avitabile, Grazia. *The Controversy on Romanticism in Italy, First Phase 1816–1823*. New York, 1959.

Bosco, U. *Realismo romantico*. Caltanissetta and Rome: S. Sciascia, 1959.

Dent, Edward J. *The Rise of Romantic Opera*. Ed. Winton Dean. Cambridge University Press, 1976.

Einstein, Alfred. *Music in the Romantic Era*. New York: Norton, 1947.

Fubini, M. *Romanticismo italiano*. Bari: Laterza, 1971.

Marteggiani, G. *Il romanticismo italiano non esiste*. Florence: Successori B. Seeber, 1908.

Oliver, A. R. "Romanticism and Opera." *Symposium* 23 (1969): 325–332.

Puppo, M. *Il romanticismo*. Rome: Edizioni Studium, 1975.

Tomlinson, Gary. "Italian Romanticism and Italian Opera, An

Essay in Their Affinities." *19th-Century Music* 10, no. 1 (1986): 43–60.

Torrefranca, Fausto. *Le origini italiane del romanticismo musicale.* Turin: Fratelli Bocca, 1930.

VERISMO

Boyer, R. D. *Realism in European Theatre and Drama 1870–1920.* Westport, Conn., and London: Greenwood Press, 1979.

Dahlhaus, C. *Realism in Nineteenth-Century Music.* Trans. M. Whittall. Cambridge University Press, 1985.

Kelkel, M. *Naturalisme, verisme et realisme dans l'opera de 1890 a 1930.* Paris: Vrin, 1984.

Mancini, R. "Le verisme existe-t-il?" *L'Avant-Scene Opera* 50 (1982): 4–13.

Mariani, R. *Verismo in musica e altri studi.* Florence: Olschki, 1976. Collection of articles.

Marzot, G. *Battaglie veriste dell'Ottocento.* Messina: G. Principato, 1941.

Raphael, Robert. "What Ever Happened to Verismo?" *Opera News* 9 March 1968: 26–29.

Rinaldi, M. *Musica e verismo: Critica e estetica d'una tendenza musicale.* Edizioni Fratelli De Santis, 1932.

Salinari, C. *Preludio e fine del realismo in Italia.* Naples: Italgrafica, 1967.

Sansone, Matteo. "The Verismo of Ruggero Leoncavallo: A Source Study of *Pagliacci.*" *Music and Letters* 70 (1989): 342–362.

Schuller, K. G. *Verismo: Opera and the Verists.* Diss., University of Washington, 1960. Analysis of *Tosca.*

Schrader, S. *Realism in Late Nineteenth-Century Opera: A Comparative View.* Diss., Northwestern University, 1983.

Verga, Giovanni. *Cavalleria rusticana and Other Stories.* Trans. D. H. Lawrence. Westport, Conn.: Greenwood Press, 1975.

Voss, E. "Verismo in der Oper." *Die Musikforschung* 31, no. 3 (1978): 303–313.

Wright, P. D. *The Musico-Dramatic Technique of the Italian Verists.* Diss., University of Rochester, Eastman School of Music, 1965.

TRANSCRIPTIONS

Dorgan, P. P. *Franz Liszt and His Verdi Opera Transcriptions.* Diss., Ohio State University, 1982.

Suttoni, C. R. *Piano and Opera: A Study of the Piano Fantasies Written on Opera Themes in the Romantic Era.* 2 vols. Diss., New York University, 1973.

Vitale, V. "Thalberg e Liszt: L'opera in salotto e in concerto." In *Il melodramma italiano nell'Ottocento.* Turin: Einaudi, 1977. 631–642.

DISCOGRAPHY

The following is a selective listing of currently available complete CD recordings of the nineteenth-century Italian operas mentioned in this book. In the case of frequently recorded titles, an effort has been made to offer a balanced selection of recommended studio recordings, live performances, and historical reissues. The more obscure works are typically represented by a single recording which may or may not represent the last word in interpretation and/or technology.

Apolloni, Giuseppe

L'ebreo. Massimo De Bernart, conductor; Simone Alaimo Fernanda Costa, Dino Di Domenico, Armando Caforio, Paola Bidinelli, Francesco Piccoli; Francesco Cilea Chorus of Reggio Calabria; San Remo Symphony Orchestra. Live performance, October 1989. Bongiovanni GB 2089/90 2 [DDD]; two discs.

Bellini, Vincenzo

Beatrice di Tenda. Vittorio Gui, conductor; Leyla Gencer, Juan Oncina, Mario Zanasi, Antigone Sgourda; Chorus and Orchestra of Teatro La Fenice, Venice. Live performance, 1964. Nuova Era 23333/34 [ADD]; two discs.

I Capuleti e i Montecchi. Claudio Abbado, conductor; Margherita Rinaldi, Giacomo Aragall, Luciano Pavarotti, Nicola Zaccaria; Chorus and Orchestra of Teatro Comunale, Bologna. Live performance, 1966. Melodram MEL 27001; two discs.

I Capuleti e i Montecchi. Riccardo Muti, conductor; Edita Gruberova, Agnes Baltsa, Dano Raffanti, Gwynne Howell, John Tomlinson; Chorus and Orchestra of the Royal Opera House, Covent Garden. EMI CDCB 47387 [DDD]; two discs.

Norma. Richard Bonynge, conductor; Joan Sutherland, Monserrat Caballé, Luciano Pavarotti, Samuel Ramey; Chorus and Orchestra of the Welsh National Opera. London 414 476 2; three discs.

Norma. Carlo Felice Cillario, conductor; Monserrat Caballé, Fiorenza Cossotto, Placido Domingo, Ruggero Raimondi; Ambrosian Opera Chorus; London Philharmonic Orchestra. Studio recording 1972. RCA 65022 RG [ADD]; three discs.

Norma. Tullio Serafin, conductor; Maria Callas, Ebe Stignani, Mario Filippeschi, Nicola Rossi-Lemeni; Chorus and Orchestra of La Scala, Milan. Studio recording, 1954. EMI CDS 7 47304 8 [AAD]; three discs.

Norma. Tullio Serafin, conductor; Maria Callas, Christa Ludwig, Franco Corelli, Nicola Zaccaria; Chorus and Orchestra of La Scala, Milan. Studio recording, 1960. EMI CMS 7 63000 2 [ADD]; three discs.

Il pirata. Ghiglia, conductor; Monserrat Caballé, Flaviano Labò, Piero Cappuccilli; Chorus and Orchestra of the Maggio Musicale Fiorentino. Live performance, Florence 1967. Melodram MEL 27015; two discs.

Il pirata. Nicola Rescigno, conductor; Maria Callas, Pier Miranda Ferraro, Costantino Ego, Glade Peterson, Regina Sarfaty; American Opera Society Chorus and Orchestra. Live concert performance in Carnegie Hall, January 1959. Hunt 531; two discs.

I puritani. Richard Bonynge, conductor; Joan Sutherland, Luciano Pavarotti, Piero Cappuccilli, Nicolai Ghiaurov; Chorus of the Royal Opera House, Covent Garden; London Symphony Orchestra. London 417 588 2 [DDD]; three discs.

I puritani. Riccardo Muti, conductor; Monserrat Caballé, Alfredo Kraus, Matteo Manuguerra, Julia Hamari, Agostino Ferrin; Ambrosian Opera Chorus; Philharmonia Orchestra. EMI CMS 7 69663 2; three discs.

I puritani. Tullio Serafin, conductor; Maria Callas, Giuseppe di
  Stefano, Rolando Panerai, Nicola Rossi-Lemeni; Chorus and
  Orchestra of La Scala, Milan. Studio recording, 1953. EMI
  CDS 7 47308 8 [monaural]; two discs.
La sonnambula. Richard Bonynge, conductor; Joan Sutherland, Lu-
  ciano Pavarotti, Nicolai Ghiaurov; National Philharmonic Or-
  chestra. London 417 424 2 [DDD]; two discs.
La sonnambula. Antonino Votto, conductor; Maria Callas, Nicola
  Monti, Nicola Zaccaria, Fiorenza Cossotto, Eugenia Ratti;
  Chorus and Orchestra of La Scala, Milan. Studio recording,
  March 1957. EMI CDS 7 47378 8 [ADD]; two discs.
La sonnambula. Antonino Votto, conductor; Maria Callas, Nicola
  Monti, Nicola Zaccaria, Fiorenza Cossotto, Mariella Angio-
  letti; Chorus and Orchestra of La Scala, Milan. Live perform-
  ance in Cologne, 4 July 1957. Verona 2704/5 [AAD]; two discs.
La straniera. Anton Guadagno, conductor; Monserrat Caballé,
  Amadeo Zambon, Vicente Sardinero, Bianca Maria Casoni;
  Chorus and Orchestra of the American Opera Society. Live
  performance, 26 March 1969. Legato Classics LCD 134 2
  [AAD]; two discs.
Zaira. Paolo Olmi, conductor; Katia Ricciarelli, Simone Alaimo,
  Ramon Vargas, Alexandra Papadjakou; Chorus and Orchestra
  of Teatro Massimo Bellini, Catania. Live performance, 1990.
  Nuova Era 6982 83 [DDD]; two discs.

Boito, Arrigo

Mefistofele. Giuseppe Patané, conductor; Samuel Ramey, Eva Mar-
  ton, Placido Domingo, Sergio Tedesco; Hungaroton Opera
  Chorus; Hungarian State Orchestra. Sony S2K 44 983 [DDD];
  two discs.
Mefistofele. Julius Rudel, conductor; Norman Treigle, Monserrat
  Caballé, Placido Domingo, Thomas Allen; Ambrosian Opera
  Chorus; Chorus of Boys from the Wadsworth School Choir;
  London Symphony Orchestra. EMI CDS 7 49522 2 [ADD];
  two discs.

Catalani, Alfredo

Loreley. Napoleone Annovazzi, conductor; Martha Colalillo, Maria
  Luisa Garbato, Pierre Visconti, Alessandro Cassis, Gabriele
  Monici; Chorus and Orchestra of Teatro del Giglio, Lucca.

Live performance, September 1982. Bongiovanni GB 2015/16
2 [ADD]; two discs.

La Wally. Fausto Cleva, conductor; Renata Tebaldi, Mario del
Monaco, Piero Cappuccilli, Justino Diaz; Coro Lirico di Torino; Orchestre National de l'Opera de Monte Carlo. London 425 417 2 [ADD]; two discs.

La Wally. Pinchas Steinberg, conductor; Eva Marton, Francisco
Araiza, Alan Titus; Munich Radio Orchestra. Eurodisc 690732
RC [DDD]; two discs.

Cilèa, Francesco

Adriana Lecouvreur. Richard Bonynge, conductor; Joan Sutherland, Carlo Bergonzi, Francesco Ellero d'Artegna, Cleopatra
Ciurca, Leo Nucci, Michel Sénéchal; Chorus and Orchestra
of the Welsh National Opera. London 425 815 2; two discs.

Adriana Lecouvreur. James Levine, conductor; Renata Scotto,
Elena Obraztsova, Placido Domingo, Sherrill Milnes; Ambrosian Opera Chorus; Philharmonia Orchestra. CBS M2K
79310 [ADD]; two discs.

Adriana Lecouvreur. Mario Rossi, conductor; Magda Olivero,
Giulietta Simionato, Franco Corelli, Ettore Bastianini; Chorus
and Orchestra of Teatro San Carlo, Naples. Live performance,
1959. Melodram MEL 27009; two discs.

Donizetti, Gaetano

Anna Bolena. Richard Bonynge, conductor; Joan Sutherland, Susanne Mentzer, Jerry Hadley, Samuel Ramey; Chorus and Orchestra of the Welsh National Opera. London 421 096 2
[DDD]; three discs.

Anna Bolena. Gianandrea Gavazzeni, conductor; Maria Callas,
Giulietta Simionato, Nicola Rossi-Lemeni, Gianni Raimondi;
Chorus and Orchestra of La Scala, Milan. Live performance,
14 April 1957. Melodram MEL 26010; two discs.

L'assedio di Calais. David Parry, conductor; Christian du Plessis,
Della Jones, Nuccia Focile, Rico Serbo, Russell Smythe, Norman Bailey; Geoffrey Mitchell Choir; Philharmonia Orchestra. Opera Rara OR 9 [DDD]; two discs.

Belisario. Gianandrea Gavazzeni, conductor; Leyla Gencer, Mirna
Pecile, Umberto Grilli, Giuseppe Taddei, Nicola Zaccaria;
Chorus and Orchestra of Teatro La Fenice, Venice. Live per-

formance, May 1969. Melodram MEL 27051 [AAD]; two discs.

Betly. Bruno Rigacci, conductor; Domenico Trimarchi; Bongiovanni GB 2091/2; two discs.

Il campanello. Gary Bertini, conductor; Agnes Baltsa, Enzo Dara, Bianca Maria Casoni, Angelo Romero, Carlo Gaifa; Vienna State Opera Chorus; Vienna Symphony Orchestra. CBS MK 38450 [ADD]; one disc.

Don Pasquale. Gabriele Ferro, conductor; Gabriel Bacquier, Barbara Hendricks, Luca Canonici, Gino Quilico; Choeurs et Orchestre de l'Opera de Lyon. Erato 2292 45487 2 [DDD]; two discs.

Don Pasquale. Heinz Wallberg, conductor; Evgeny Nesterenko, Lucia Popp, Francisco Araiza, Bernd Weikl; Bavarian Radio Chorus; Munich Radio Orchestra. Eurodisc 77902 RG [ADD]; two discs.

L'elisir d'amore. Richard Bonynge, conductor; Joan Sutherland, Luciano Pavarotti, Dominic Cossa, Spiro Malas; Ambrosian Opera Chorus; English Chamber Orchestra. London 414 461 2 [ADD]; two discs.

L'elisir d'amore. Gabriele Ferro, conductor; Barbara Bonney, Gösta Winbergh, Bernd Weikl, Rolando Panerai; Chorus and Orchestra of the Maggio Musicale Fiorentino. Deutsche Grammophon 423 076 2 [DDD]; two discs.

L'elisir d'amore. James Levine, conductor; Kathleen Battle, Luciano Pavarotti, Dawn Upshaw, Leo Nucci, Enzo Dara; Metropolitan Opera Chorus and Orchestra. Deutsche Grammophon 429744 2; two discs.

La favorita. Richard Bonynge, conductor; Fiorenza Cossotto, Luciano Pavarotti, Gabriel Bacquier, Nicolai Ghiaurov; Chorus and Orchestra of Teatro Comunale, Bologna. London 430 038 2 [ADD]; three discs.

La figlia del reggimento. Bruno Campanella, conductor; Luciana Serra, William Matteuzzi, Enzo Dara, Monica Tagliasacchi; Chorus and Orchestra of Teatro Comunale, Bologna. Live performance, February 1989. Nuova Era 6791/92 [DDD]; two discs.

La fille du regiment. Richard Bonynge, conductor; Joan Sutherland, Luciano Pavarotti, Monica Sinclair, Spiro Malas, Jules Bruyère, Edith Coates; Chorus and Orchestra of the Royal Opera House, Covent Garden. London 414 520 2 [ADD]; two discs.

La fille du regiment. Bruno Campanella, conductor; June Anderson, Alfredo Kraus, Michel Trempont, Helia T'Hezan; Chorus and Orchestra of the Paris Opera. Live performance, May 1986. EMI CMS 7 63128 2 [DDD]; two discs.

Gianni di Parigi. Carlo Felice Cillario, conductor; Luciana Serra, Giuseppe Morino, Angelo Romero, Enrico Fissore, Elena Zilio; Chorus and Orchestra of RAI, Milan. Live performance, September 1988. Nuova Era 6752/53 [DDD]; two discs.

Imelda de'Lambertazzi. Marc Andreae, conductor; Floriana Sovilla, Diego D'Auria, Fausto Tenzi, Andrea Martin, Gastone Sarti; Italian Swiss Radio-Television Chorus and Orchestra. Live concert performance, February 1988. Nuova Era 6778/79; two discs.

Linda di Chamounix. Gianandrea Gavazzeni, conductor; Margherita Rinaldi, Alfredo Kraus, Renato Bruson, Elena Zilio, Enzo Dara, Carlo Cava. Live performance, 1975. Legato Classics LCD 121 2 [AAD]; two discs.

Lucia di Lammermoor. Richard Bonynge, conductor; Joan Sutherland, Luciano Pavarotti, Sherrill Milnes, Nicolai Ghiaurov, Huguette Tourangeau; Chorus and Orchestra of the Royal Opera House, Covent Garden. London 410 193 2 [ADD]; three discs.

Lucia di Lammermoor. Herbert von Karajan, conductor; Maria Callas, Giuseppe di Stefano, Rolando Panerai, Nicola Zaccaria; Chorus of La Scala, Milan; RIAS Orchestra. Live performance in Berlin, 29 September 1955. EMI CMS 7 63631 2 [ADD]; two discs. Also on Verona 2709/10; two discs.

Lucia di Lammermoor. Jesus Lopez Cobos, conductor; Monserrat Caballé, José Carreras, Claes H. Ahnsjö, Vicente Sardinero, Samuel Ramey, Ann Murray; Ambrosian Opera Chorus; New Philharmonia Orchestra. Philips 426 563 2; two discs.

Lucia di Lammermoor. Sir John Pritchard, conductor; Joan Sutherland, Renato Cioni, Robert Merrill, Cesare Siepi; Chorus and Orchestra of the Accademia di Santa Cecilia, Rome. London 411 622 2 [ADD]; two discs.

Lucia di Lammermoor. Tullio Serafin, conductor; Maria Callas, Giuseppe di Stefano, Tito Gobbi, Raffaele Arie, Valiano Natali, Anna Maria Canali; Chorus and Orchestra of the Maggio Musicale Fiorentino. Studio recording, 1953. EMI CMS 7 69980 2 [ADD]; two discs.

Lucrezia Borgia. Richard Bonynge, conductor; Joan Sutherland,

Marilyn Horne, Giacomo Aragall, Ingvar Wixell; London Opera Chorus; National Philharmonic Orchestra. London 421 497 2 [ADD]; two discs.

Lucrezia Borgia. Jonel Perlea, conductor; Monserrat Caballé, Alfredo Kraus, Shirley Verrett, Ezio Flagello; RCA Italiana Opera Chorus and Orchestra. RCA 66422 RG [ADD]; two discs.

Maria di Rohan. Massimo de Bernart, conductor; Mariana Nicolesco, Giuseppe Morino, Paolo Coni, Francesca Franci; Coro Filarmonico Slovacco di Bratislava; Orchestra Internazionale d'Italia Opera. Live performance, August 1988. Nuova Era 6732/33 [DDD]; two discs.

Maria Stuarda. Richard Bonynge, conductor; Joan Sutherland, Luciano Pavarotti, Huguette Tourangeau, Roger Soyer, James Morris; Chorus and Orchestra of Teatro Comunale, Bologna. London 425 410 2 [ADD]; two discs.

Maria Stuarda. Giuseppe Patanè, conductor; Edita Gruberova, Agnes Baltsa, Francisco Araiza, Francesco Ellero d'Artegna, Simone Alaimo; Bavarian Radio Chorus; Munich Radio Orchestra. Philips 426 233 2 [DDD]; two discs.

Marino Faliero. Adolfo Camozzo, conductor; Agostino Ferrin, Carlo Meliciani, Angelo Mori, Margherita Roberti, Lina Rossi, Virgilio Carbonari, Gianfranco Manganotti; Chorus and Orchestra of Teatro Donizetti, Bergamo. Live performance, October 1966. Melodram MEL 27030; two discs.

Parisina. Bruno Rigacci, conductor; Giulio Fioravanti, Renato Cioni; Chorus and Orchestra of Teatro Comunale, Bologna. Live performance, September 1964. Giuseppe Di Stefano GDS 21020; two discs.

Poliuto. Oleg Caetani, conductor; Jose Carreras, Katia Ricciarelli, Juan Pons, Laszlo Polgar; Chor der Wiener Singakademie; Wiener Symphoniker. Live performance, 1986. CBS M2K 44821 [DDD]; two discs.

Poliuto. Antonino Votto, conductor; Franco Corelli, Maria Callas, Ettore Bastianini, Nicola Zaccaria; Chorus and Orchestra of La Scala, Milan. Live performance, 7 December 1960. Melodram MEL 26006; two discs.

Roberto Devereux. Mario Rossi, conductor; Ruggero Bondino, Leyla Gencer, Anna Maria Rota, Piero Cappuccilli; Chorus and Orchestra of Teatro San Carlo, Naples. Live performance, 1967. Hunt HPCD 545; two discs.

Roberto Devereux. Julius Rudel, conductor; Placido Domingo, Beverly Sills, Suzanne Marsee, Louis Quilico; Chorus and Orchestra of the New York City Opera. Live performance, October 1970. Giuseppe Di Stefano GDS 21029 [AAD]; two discs.

Giordano, Umberto

Andrea Chénier. Riccardo Chailly, conductor; Luciano Pavarotti, Monserrat Caballé, Leo Nucci, Astrid Varnay, Christa Ludwig, Tom Krause; Chorus of the Welsh National Opera; National Philharmonic Orchestra. London 410 117 2; two discs.
Andrea Chénier. Oliviero de Fabritiis, conductor; Beniamino Gigli, Maria Caniglia, Gino Bechi, Giulietta Simionato, Vittoria Palombini, Italo Tajo, Giuseppe Taddei; Chorus and Orchestra of La Scala, Milan. Recorded 1941. EMI CHS 7 69996 2 [ADD]; two discs.
Andrea Chénier. Gianandrea Gavazzeni, conductor; Mario del Monaco, Renata Tebaldi, Ettore Bastianini, Fiorenza Cossotto, Fernando Corena; Chorus and Orchestra of the Accademia di Santa Cecilia, Rome. London 425 407 2 [ADD]; two discs.
Andrea Chénier. James Levine, conductor; Placido Domingo, Renata Scotto, Sherrill Milnes; John Alldis Choir; National Philharmonic Orchestra. RCA 20462 RG [ADD]; two discs.
Fedora. Giuseppe Patané, conductor; Eva Marton, José Carreras, Veronika Kinces, János Martin, József Gregor; Hungarian Radio and Television Symphony Orchestra and Chorus. CBS M2K 42181 [DDD]; two discs.

Leoncavallo, Ruggero

La bohème. Heinz Wallberg, conductor; Lucia Popp, Alexandrina Milcheva, Franco Bonisolli, Alan Titus, Bernd Weikl; Bavarian Radio Chorus; Munich Radio Orchestra. Orfeo 023822; two discs.
I pagliacci. Renato Cellini, conductor; Jussi Bjoerling, Victoria de los Angeles, Leonard Warren, Robert Merrill; Columbus Boy Choir; Robert Shaw Chorale; RCA Victor Orchestra. Recorded 1953. EMI CDC 7 49503; one disc.
I pagliacci. Herbert von Karajan, conductor; Carlo Bergonzi, Joan Carlyle, Giuseppe Taddei, Rolando Panerai; Chorus and Or-

chestra of La Scala, Milan. Coupled with *Cavalleria rusticana*. Deutsche Grammophon 419257; three discs.

I pagliacci. Giuseppe Patané, conductor; Luciano Pavarotti, Mirella Freni, Ingvar Wixell; National Philharmonic Orchestra. Coupled with *Cavalleria rusticana*. London 414 590 2 [ADD]; two discs.

I pagliacci. Tullio Serafin, conductor; Maria Callas, Giuseppe di Stefano, Tito Gobbi, Nicola Monti, Rolando Panerai; Chorus and Orchestra of La Scala, Milan. Coupled with *Cavalleria rusticana*. EMI CDS 7 47981 [ADD]; three discs.

Zazà. Alfredo Silipigni, conductor; Clara Petrella, Giuseppe Campora, Tito Turtura; Chorus and Orchestra of RAI, Turin. Live broadcast performance, 1969. Nuova Era 2316/7 [ADD]; two discs.

Mascagni, Pietro

L'amico Fritz. Gianandrea Gavazzeni, conductor; Mirella Freni, Luciano Pavarotti, Laura Didier Gambardella, Vicente Sardinero, Benito Di Bella; Chorus and Orchestra of the Royal Opera House, Covent Garden. Studio recording. EMI CDS 7 47905 8 [ADD]; two discs.

Cavalleria rusticana. Renato Cellini, conductor; Zinka Milanov, Jussi Bjoerling, Robert Merrill, Carol Smith, Margaret Roggero; Robert Shaw Chorale; RCA Victor Orchestra. Studio recording, 1953. RCA Victor Opera Series 65102 RG; one disc.

Cavalleria rusticana. Gianandrea Gavazzeni, conductor; Julia Varady, Luciano Pavarotti, Piero Cappuccilli; National Philharmonic Orchestra. Coupled with *I pagliacci*. London 414 590 2 [ADD]; two discs.

Cavalleria rusticana. Herbert von Karajan, conductor; Fiorenza Cossotto, Carlo Bergonzi, Giangiacomo Guelfi; Chorus and Orchestra of La Scala, Milan. Coupled with *I pagliacci*. Deutsche Grammophon 419257; three discs.

Cavalleria rusticana. Pietro Mascagni, conductor; Lina Bruna Rasa, Beniamino Gigli, Gino Bechi, Giulietta Simionato; Chorus and Orchestra of La Scala, Milan. Recorded 1942, with arias from other Mascagni operas sung by Gigli as filler on the second disc. EMI CDH 7 69987; two discs.

Cavalleria rusticana. Tullio Serafin, conductor; Maria Callas, Giuseppe di Stefano, Rolando Panerai, Anna Maria Canali, Ebe

Ticozzi; Chorus and Orchestra of La Scala, Milan. Coupled with *I pagliacci*. EMI CDS 7 47981 [ADD]; three discs.

Cavalleria rusticana. Giuseppe Sinopoli, conductor; Agnes Baltsa, Placido Domingo, Juan Pons, Vera Baniewicz, Susanne Mentzer; Chorus of the Royal Opera House, Covent Garden; Philharmonia Orchestra. Deutsche Grammophon 429 568 2 [DDD]; one disc.

Guglielmo Ratcliff. Armando La Rosa Parodi, conductor; Pier Miranda Ferraro; Giovanni Ciminelli, Renata Mattioli, Miti Truccato Pace, Ferruccio Mazzoli; Chorus and Orchestra of RAI, Rome. Live broadcast performance, 1963. Nuova Era 2336/37 [ADD]; two discs.

Iris. Giuseppe Patané, conductor; Ilona Tokody, Placido Domingo, Juan Pons, Bonaldo Giaiotti, Gabriella Ferroni; Bavarian Radio Chorus; Munich Radio Orchestra. Studio recording. CBS M2K 45526 [DDD]; two discs.

Mercadante, Saverio

Il bravo. Bruno Aprea, conductor; Dino Di Domenico, Adelisa Tabiadon, Janet Perry, Sergio Bertocchi, Stefano Antonucci; Coro Filarmonico Slovacco di Bratislava; Orchestra Internazionale d'Italia. Nuova Era 6971/73 [DDD]; three discs.

Il giuramento. Maurizio Arena, conductor; Lajos Miller, Benedetta Pecchioli, Teresa Zylis-Gara, Michele Molese; Orchestre Lyrique et Choeurs de Radio France. Live concert performance, October 1975. RPC Rudolfe Productions RPC 32417/18; two discs.

La vestale. Vjekoslav Sutej, conductor; Dunja Vejzovik, Paola Romano, Gianfranco Cecchele, Franco Sioli, Filka Dimitrova; Chorus and Orchestra of Teatro Nazionale Croato, Spalato. Live performance, April 1987. Bongiovanni 2065/66 2 [DDD]; two discs.

Pacini, Giovanni

Saffo. Franco Capuana, conductor; Leyla Gencer, Louis Quilico, Tito del Bianco, Franca Mattiucci; Chorus and Orchestra of Teatro San Carlo, Naples. Live performance, April 1967. Hunt CD 541; two discs.

Ponchielli, Amilcare

La Gioconda. Giuseppe Patane, conductor; Eva Marton, Giorgio Lamberti, Livia Budai, Anne Gjevang, Sherrill Milnes, Samuel Ramey; Hungaroton Opera Chorus; Hungarian State Orchestra. Studio recording, 1987. CBS M3K 44556 [DDD]; three discs.

La Gioconda. Antonino Votto, conductor; Maria Callas, Fiorenza Cossotto, Irene Companeez, Pier Miranda Ferraro, Piero Cappuccilli, Ivo Vinco; Chorus and Orchestra of La Scala, Milan. Studio recording, 1959. EMI Angel 49518; three discs.

Puccini, Giacomo

La bohème. Sir Thomas Beecham, conductor; Victoria de los Angeles, Jussi Bjoerling, Lucine Amara, Robert Merrill, John Reardon, Giorgio Tozzi, Fernando Corena; RCA Victor Chorus and Orchestra; Columbus Boychoir. EMI CDS 7 47235 8 [ADD]; two discs.

La bohème. Leonard Bernstein, conductor; Angelina Réaux, Barbara Daniels, Jerry Hadley, Thomas Hampson, James Busterud, Paul Plishka; Chorus and Orchestra of the Accademia Nazionale di Santa Cecilia. Deutsche Grammophon 423 601 2 [DDD]; two discs.

La bohème. Gianluigi Gelmetti, conductor; Daniela Dessì, Giuseppe Sabbatini, Paolo Gavanelli, Carlo Colombara; Chorus and Orchestra of Teatro Comunale, Bologna. Live performance of the 1988 Ricordi critical edition. EMI CDS 7 54124 2 [DDD]; two discs.

La bohème. Herbert von Karajan, conductor; Mirella Freni, Luciano Pavarotti, Rolando Panerai, Nicolai Ghiaurov; Berlin Philharmonic. London 421 049 2 [ADD]; two discs.

La bohème. Erich Leinsdorf, conductor; Anna Moffo, Richard Tucker, Mary Costa, Robert Merrill, Giorgio Tozzi, Philip Maero; Rome Opera Chorus and Orchestra. RCA Victor Opera Series 39692 RG [ADD]; two discs.

La bohème. Tullio Serafin, conductor; Renata Tebaldi, Carlo Bergonzi, Gianna D'Angelo, Ettore Bastianini, Cesare Siepi; Chorus and Orchestra of the Accademia di Santa Cecilia, Rome. London 425 534 2 [ADD]; two discs.

La bohème. Sir Georg Solti, conductor; Monserrat Caballé, Placido Domingo, Judith Blegen, Vicente Sardinero, Ruggero Raimondi; John Alldis Choir; London Philharmonic Orchestra. RCA RCD 20371 [ADD]; two discs.

La bohème. Arturo Toscanini, conductor; Licia Albanese, Jan Peerce, Francesco Valentino, Anne McKnight, Nicola Moscona, Salvatore Baccaloni; NBC Symphony Orchestra. Live NBC broadcast performances, 3 and 10 February 1946. RCA 60288 2 RG "Arturo Toscanini Collection" Vol. 55 [monaural]; two discs.

La bohème. Antonino Votto, conductor; Maria Callas, Giuseppe di Stefano, Anna Moffo, Rolando Panerai, Nicola Zaccaria; Chorus and Orchestra of La Scala, Milan. Studio recording, 1956. EMI Angel 47475; two discs.

Edgar. Eve Queler, conductor; Renata Scotto, Carlo Bergonzi, Gwendolyn Killebrew, Vicente Sardinero; New York City Opera Children's Chorus; Schola Cantorum and Opera Orchestra of New York. CBS M2K 79213 [ADD]; two discs.

La fanciulla del West. Franco Capuana, conductor; Renata Tebaldi, Mario Del Monaco, Cornell MacNeil, Giorgio Tozzi; Chorus and Orchestra of the Accademia di Santa Cecilia, Rome. London 421 595 2 [ADD]; two discs.

La fanciulla del West. Zubin Mehta, conductor; Carol Neblett, Placido Domingo, Sherrill Milnes, Robert Lloyd; Chorus and Orchestra of the Royal Opera House, Covent Garden. Deutsche Grammophon 419 640 2; two discs.

Gianni Schicchi. See *Il trittico*

Madama Butterfly. Sir John Barbirolli, conductor; Renata Scotto, Carlo Bergonzi, Anna di Stasio, Rolando Panerai; Chorus and Orchestra of the Rome Opera House. EMI CMS 7 69654 2 [ADD]; two discs.

Madama Butterfly. Oliviero de Fabritiis, conductor; Toti dal Monte, Beniamino Gigli, Mario Basiola, Vittoria Palombini; Chorus and Orchestra of the Rome Opera. Recorded 1939. EMI Angel CHS 7 69990 2; two discs.

Madama Butterfly. Erich Leinsdorf, conductor; Leontyne Price, Richard Tucker, Rosalind Elias, Philip Maero, Piero de Palma; RCA Italiana Opera Chorus and Orchestra. RCA 61602 RG [ADD]; two discs.

Madama Butterfly. Tullio Serafin, conductor; Renata Tebaldi, Carlo Bergonzi, Fiorenza Cossotto, Enzo Sordello; Chorus and Orchestra of the Accademia di Santa Cecilia, Rome. Studio recording, 1958. London 425 531 2 [ADD]; two discs.

Madama Butterfly. Giuseppe Sinopoli, conductor; Mirella Freni, Teresa Berganza, José Carreras, Anthony Laciura, Juan Pons; Ambrosian Opera Chorus; Philharmonia Orchestra. Deutsche Grammophon 423 567 2 [DDD]; three discs.

Manon Lescaut. Riccardo Chailly, conductor; Kiri Te Kanawa, José Carreras, Paolo Coni, Italo Tajo, William Matteuzzi; Chorus and Orchestra of Teatro Comunale, Bologna. London 421 426 2; two discs.

Manon Lescaut. Jonel Perlea, conductor; Licia Albanese, Jussi Bjoerling, Robert Merrill; Rome Opera Chorus and Orchestra. Studio recording, 1954. RCA Victor Opera Series 605732 RG [ADD]; two discs.

Manon Lescaut. Giuseppe Sinopoli, conductor; Mirella Freni, Placido Domingo, Renato Bruson, Kurt Rydl; Chorus and Orchestra of the Royal Opera House, Covent Garden. Deutsche Grammophon 413 893 2 [DDD]; two discs.

La rondine. Lorin Maazel, conductor; Kiri Te Kanawa, Placido Domingo, Mariana Nicolesco, David Rendall, Leo Nucci; Ambrosian Opera Chorus; London Symphony Orchestra. CBS M2K 37852 [DDD]; two discs.

La rondine. Francesco Molinari-Pradelli, conductor; Anna Moffo, Daniele Barioni, Mario Sereni, Graziella Sciutti, Piero de Palma; RCA Italiana Opera Chorus and Orchestra. RCA Victor Opera Series 602592 RG [ADD]; two discs.

Suor Angelica. See *Il trittico*

Il tabarro. See *Il trittico*

Tosca. Herbert von Karajan, conductor; Leontyne Price, Giuseppe di Stefano, Giuseppe Taddei, Carlo Cava, Piero de Palma; Vienna State Opera Chorus; Vienna Philharmonic. London 4616 70 [ADD]; two discs.

Tosca. Erich Leinsdorf, conductor; Zinka Milanov, Jussi Bjoerling, Leonard Warren, Fernando Corena; Rome Opera Chorus and Orchestra. RCA Victor Opera Series 45142 RG [ADD]; two discs.

Tosca. Victor de Sabata, conductor; Maria Callas, Giuseppe di Stefano, Tito Gobbi, Franco Calabrese, Melchiorre Luise; Chorus and Orchestra of La Scala, Milan. Studio recording, 1953. EMI CDS 7 47175 8 [AAD]; two discs.

Tosca. Sir Georg Solti, conductor; Kiri Te Kanawa, Giacomo Aragall, Leo Nucci, Spiro Malas, Piero de Palma; Welsh National Opera Chorus; National Philharmonic Orchestra. London 414 597 2 [ADD]; two discs.

Il trittico. Lamberto Gardelli, conductor; Renata Tebaldi, Mario del Monaco, Robert Merrill (*Il tabarro*); Renata Tebaldi, Giulietta Simionato (*Suor Angelica*); Fernando Corena, Renata Tebaldi (*Gianni Schicchi*); Chorus and Orchestra of the Maggio Musicale Fiorentino. London 411 655 2 [ADD]; three discs.

Il trittico. Lorin Maazel, conductor; Renata Scotto, Placido Domingo, Ingvar Wixell; Ambrosian Opera Chorus; New Philharmonia (*Il tabarro*); Renata Scotto, Marilyn Horne, Ileana Cotrubas; Ambrosian Opera Chorus; New Philharmonia (*Suor Angelica*); Tito Gobbi, Ileana Cotrubas, Placido Domingo; London Symphony (*Gianni Schicchi*). CBS M3K 79312 [ADD]; three discs.

Il trittico. Giuseppe Patanè, conductor; Ilona Tokody, Giorgio Lamberti, Siegmund Nimsgern (*Il tabarro*); Lucia Popp, Marjana Lipovsek; Munich Choir Boys (*Suor Angelica*); Rolando Panerai, Helen Donath, Peter Seiffert, Vera Baniewicz (*Gianni Schicchi*); Chorus of the Bavarian Radio; Munich Radio Orchestra. Eurodisc 690432 RC [DDD]; three discs.

Turandot. Erich Leinsdorf, conductor; Birgit Nilsson, Renata Tebaldi, Jussi Bjoerling, Giorgio Tozzi, Mario Sereni, Piero de Palma; Rome Opera Chorus and Orchestra. RCA 59322 RC [ADD]; two discs.

Turandot. Zubin Mehta, conductor; Joan Sutherland, Monserrat Caballé, Luciano Pavarotti, Nicolai Ghiaurov, Tom Krause, Peter Pears; John Alldis Choir; London Philharmonic Orchestra. London 414 274 2; two discs.

Turandot. Franco Molinari-Pradelli, conductor; Birgit Nilsson, Franco Corelli, Renata Scotto, Bonaldo Giaiotti, Piero de Palma; Chorus and Orchestra of the Rome Opera. Recorded in the Rome Opera House, 1965. EMI CDMB 69327 [ADD]; two discs.

Le villi. Lorin Maazel, conductor; Renata Scotto, Placido Domingo, Leo Nucci, Tito Gobbi; Ambrosian Opera Chorus; National Philharmonic Orchestra. CBS MK 76890 [ADD]; one disc.

Ricci Brothers

Crispino e la comare. Paolo Carignani, conductor; Roberto Coviello, Daniela Lojarro, Serena Lazzarini, Simone Alaimo; Antonio Marani; Enrico Cossutta; Riccardo Ristori; Francesco Cilèa

Chorus of Reggio Calabria; San Remo Symphony Orchestra. Live performance, November 1989. Bongiovanni GB 2095/96 2 [DDD]; two discs.

Rossini, Gioachino

Armida. Tullio Serafin, conductor; Maria Callas, Francesco Albanese, Mario Filippeschi, Alessandro Ziliani, Gianni Raimondi; Chorus and Orchestra of the Maggio Musicale Fiorentino. Live performance, 26 April 1952. Melodram 26024 [AAD]; two discs.

L'assedio di Corinto. Thomas Schippers, conductor; Beverly Sills, Marilyn Horne, Franco Bonisolli, Justino Diaz, Piero De Palma; Chorus and Orchestra of La Scala, Milan. Live performance, 11 April 1969. Melodram MEL 27043; two discs.

Aureliano in Palmira. Giacomo Zani, conductor. Luciana Serra, Helga Müller Molinari, Anna Maria Pizzoli, Paolo Barbacini; Orchestra del Teatro dell'Opera Giocosa. Ars Nova ACDAN 3164; two discs.

Il barbiere di Siviglia. Claudio Abbado, conductor; Hermann Prey, Teresa Berganza, Luigi Alva, Enzo Dara, Paolo Montarsolo; Ambrosian Opera Chorus; London Symphony Orchestra. Deutsche Grammophon 415 695 2 [ADD]; two discs.

Il barbiere di Siviglia. Alceo Galliera, conductor; Tito Gobbi, Maria Callas, Luigi Alva, Nicola Zaccaria, Fritz Ollendorf; Philharmonia Chorus and Orchestra. Studio recording, 1957. EMI CDCB 47634; two discs.

Il barbiere di Siviglia. Erich Leinsdorf, conductor; Robert Merrill, Roberta Peters, Cesare Valletti, Giorgio Tozzi, Fernando Corena; Chorus and Orchestra of the Metropolitan Opera. RCA Victor Opera Series 65052 RG [ADD]; three discs.

Il barbiere di Siviglia. Sir Neville Marriner, conductor; Thomas Allen, Agnes Baltsa, Francisco Araiza, Domenico Trimarchi, Robert Lloyd; Ambrosian Opera Chorus; Academy of St.-Martin-in-the-Fields. Philips 411 058-2 [DDD]; three discs.

Il barbiere di Siviglia. Giuseppe Patanè, conductor; Leo Nucci, Cecilia Bartoli, William Matteuzzi, Enrico Fissore, Paata Burchuladze; Chorus and Orchestra of Teatro Comunale, Bologna. London 425 520 2 [DDD]; three discs.

Bianca e Falliero. Donato Renzetti, conductor; Katia Ricciarelli, Marilyn Horne, Chris Merritt, Giorgio Surjan, Ambrogio

Riva; Chorus and Orchestra of the Pesaro Festival. Live performance, 1986, including arias and duets from *Tancredi*. Legato Classics LCD 138 3 [ADD]; three discs.

La Cenerentola. Claudio Abbado, conductor; Teresa Berganza, Luigi Alva, Renato Capecchi, Paolo Montarsolo; Scottish Opera Chorus; London Symphony Orchestra. Deutsche Grammophon 415 698 2 [DDD]; three discs.

La Cenerentola. Sir Neville Marriner, conductor; Agnes Baltsa, Francisco Araiza, Simone Alaimo, Ruggero Raimondi; Ambrosian Opera Chorus; Academy of St.-Martin-in-the-Fields. Philips 420 468 2 [DDD]; three discs.

Ciro in Babilonia. Carlo Rizzi, conductor; Ernesto Palacio, Caterina Calvi, Daniela Dessì, Oriana Ferraris, Stefano Antonucci, Enrico Cossutta; Francesco Cilèa Chorus of Reggio Calabria; Orchestra Sinfonico di San Remo. Live performance, October 1988. Hunt AK 105; two discs.

Le comte Ory. John Eliot Gardiner, conductor; John Aler, Sumi Jo, Diana Montague, Raquel Pierotti, Gilles Cachemaille, Gino Quilico; Orchestre et Choeur de l'Opéra de Lyon. Studio recording, 1988. Philips 422 406 2 [DDD]; two discs.

La donna del lago. Maurizio Pollini, conductor. Katia Ricciarelli, Lucia Valentini Terrani, Dalmacio Gonzales, Dano Raffanti, Samuel Ramey; Prague Philharmonic Chorus; Chamber Orchestra of Europe. CBS M2K 39311 [DDD]; two discs.

Ermione. Claudio Scimone, conductor; Cecilia Gasdia, Margarita Zimmermann, Ernesto Palacio, Chris Merritt, William Matteuzzi, Simone Alaimo, Mario Bolognesi; Prague Philharmonic Chorus; Orchestre Philharmonique de Monte Carlo. Erato ECD 75336; two discs.

La gazza ladra. Gianluigi Gelmetti, conductor; Katia Ricciarelli, Bernadette Manca di Nissa, Luciana d'Intino, William Matteuzzi, Ferruccio Furlanetto, Samuel Ramey, Roberto Coviello, Oslavio di Credico, Pierre Lefèbre, Francesco Musinu; Prague Philharmonic Choir; Orchestra of RAI, Turin. Live performance, Pesaro 1989. Sony Classical S3K 45 850 [DDD]; three discs.

Guglielmo Tell. Riccardo Muti, conductor; Giorgio Zancanaro, Cheryl Studer, Chris Merritt, Amelia Felle, Luciana D'Intino, Luigi Roni, Giorgio Surjan; Chorus and Orchestra of La Scala, Milan. Live performance, 7 December 1988. Philips 422 391 2 [DDD]; four discs.

Guillaume Tell. Lamberto Gardelli, conductor. Gabriel Bacquier, Monserrat Caballé, Mady Mesplé, Jocelyne Taillon, Nicolai Gedda, Louis Hendrikx, Kolos Kovacs, Gwynne Howell; Ambrosian Opera Chorus; Royal Philharmonic Orchestra. Studio recording. EMI CMS 7 69951 2 [ADD]; four discs.

L'inganno felice. Carlo Franci, conductor; Emilia Cundari, Ferdinando Jacopucci, Giorgio Tadeo, Paolo Montarsolo, Sergio Pezzetti; Chorus of RAI, Naples; Alessandro Scarlatti Orchestra. Radio broadcast performance, 1963. AS 1001; one disc.

L'italiana in Algeri. Claudio Abbado, conductor; Agnes Baltsa, Patrizia Pace, Anna Gonda, Frank Lopardo, Ruggero Raimondi, Enzo Dara, Alessandro Corbelli; Vienna State Opera Chorus; Vienna Philharmonic. Deutsche Grammophon 427331 2 [DDD]; two discs.

L'italiana in Algeri. Gabriele Ferro, conductor; Lucia Valentini Terrani, Francisco Araiza, Enzo Dara, Alessandro Corbelli, Vladimiro Ganzarolli; Male Chorus of the Westdeutscher Rundfunk, Cologne; Capella Coloniensis. On original instruments. CBS M2K 39048 [ADD]; two discs.

L'italiana in Algeri. Silvio Varviso, conductor; Teresa Berganza, Luigi Alva, Rolando Panerai, Fernando Corena; Chorus and Orchestra of the Maggio Musicale Fiorentino. London 417 828 2 [ADD]; two discs.

Maometto II. Claudio Scimone, conductor; June Anderson, Margarita Zimmermann, Ernesto Palacio, Samuel Ramey; Ambrosian Opera Chorus; Philharmonia Orchestra. Philips 412 148 2 [DDD]; three discs.

Mosè in Egitto. Bruno Bartoletti, conductor; Boris Christoff, Gabriella Tucci, Franco Tagliavini, Bianca Maria Casoni, Lino Puglisi; Chorus and Orchestra of the Rome Opera. Live performance, 3 April 1971. Giuseppe Di Stefano GDS 21036 [ADD]; two discs.

Mosè in Egitto. Lamberto Gardelli, conductor; Jozsef Gregor, Andras Molnar, Sandor Solyom Nagy, Janos B. Nagy, Attila Fulop, Ferenc Beganyi, Eszter Poka, Magda Kalmar, Julia Hamari; Hungarian State Opera Chorus and Orchestra. Hungaroton HCD 12290 92 2; three discs.

Otello. Fernando Previtali, conductor; Agostino Lazzari, Virginia Zeani, Herbert Handt, Giuseppe Baratti, Franco Ventriglia, Anna Reynolds; Chorus and Orchestra of RAI, Rome. Live performance, June 1960. Great Opera Performances GOP 718 [AAD]; two discs.

La scala di seta. Gabriele Ferro, conductor; Luciana Serra, Cecilia Bartoli, William Matteuzzi, Roberto Coviello, Natale de Carolis, Oslavio di Credico; Orchestra of Teatro Comunale, Bologna. Recorded September 1988. Fonit Cetra RFCD 2003; two discs.

Semiramide. Richard Bonynge, conductor; Joan Sutherland, Marilyn Horne, John Serge, Joseph Rouleau, Spiro Malas; Ambrosian Opera Chorus; London Symphony Orchestra. London 425 481 2 [ADD]; three discs.

Le siège de Corinthe. See *L'assedio di Corinto* and *Maometto II*

Il signor Bruschino. Jacek Kasprzyk, conductor; Warsaw Chamber Opera Orchestra. Pavane ADW 7158; one disc.

Il signor Bruschino. Marcello Viotti, conductor; Patrizia Orciani, Katia Lytting, Luca Canonici, Bruno Praticò, Natale de Carolis, Pietro Spagnoli, Fulvio Massa; I Filarmonici di Torino. Live performance, 1988. Claves CD 50 8904/5; two discs.

Tancredi. Ralf Weikert, conductor; Marilyn Horne, Lella Cuberli, Ernesto Palacio, Nicola Zaccaria; Chorus and Orchestra of La Fenice, Venice. CBS M3K 39073 [DDD]; three discs.

Il turco in Italia. Riccardo Chailly, conductor; Samuel Ramey, Monserrat Caballé, Enzo Dara, Ernesto Palacio, Leo Nucci, Jane Berbié; Ambrosian Opera Chorus; National Philharmonic Orchestra. CBS M2K 37859 [DDD]; two discs.

Il turco in Italia. Gianandrea Gavazzeni, conductor; Maria Callas, Nicolai Gedda, Nicola Rossi-Lemeni, Mariano Stabile, Francesco Calabrese; Jolando Gardina; Chorus and Orchestra of La Scala, Milan. Studio recording, 1954. EMI 7 49344 2 [ADD]; two discs.

Zelmira. Claudio Scimone, conductor; Cecilia Gasdia, Bernarda Fink, William Matteuzzi, Chris Merritt, José Garcia, Boaz Senator, Vernon Midgley, Leslie Fyson; The Ambrosian Singers; I Solisti Veneti. Erato 2292 45419 2 [DDD]; two discs.

Spontini, Gaspare

La vestale. Antonino Votto, conductor; Maria Callas, Franco Corelli, Enzo Sordello, Ebe Stignani; Chorus and Orchestra of La Scala, Milan. Live performance, 7 December 1954. Melodram MEL 26008; two discs.

Verdi, Giuseppe

Aida. Claudio Abbado, conductor; Katia Ricciarelli, Placido Domingo, Elena Obraztsova, Leo Nucci, Ruggero Raimondi, Nicolai Ghiaurov, Lucia Valentini Terrani; Chorus and Orchestra of La Scala, Milan. Deutsche Grammophon 410 092 2 [DDD]; three discs.

Aida. Herbert von Karajan, conductor; Renata Tebaldi, Carlo Bergonzi, Giulietta Simionato, Cornell MacNeil, Fernando Corena; Chorus of the Society of Friends of Music; Vienna Philharmonic. London 414 087 2 [ADD]; three discs.

Aida. Erich Leinsdorf, conductor; Leontyne Price, Placido Domingo, Grace Bumbry, Sherrill Milnes, Ruggero Raimondi, Hans Sotin; John Alldis Choir; London Symphony Orchestra. RCA 61982 RC [ADD]; three discs.

Aida. James Levine, conductor; Aprile Millo, Placido Domingo, Dolora Zajick, James Morris, Samuel Ramey; Metropolitan Opera Chorus and Orchestra. Sony S3K 45973 [DDD]; three discs.

Aida. Lorin Maazel, conductor; Maria Chiara, Luciano Pavarotti, Ghena Dimitrova, Leo Nucci; Chorus and Orchestra of La Scala, Milan. London 417 439 2 [DDD]; three discs.

Aida. Riccardo Muti, conductor; Monserrat Caballé, Placido Domingo, Fiorenza Cossotto, Piero Cappuccilli, Nicolai Ghiaurov; Chorus of the Royal Opera House, Covent Garden; New Philharmonia Orchestra. EMI 7 47271 8 [AAD]; three discs.

Aida. Jonel Perlea, conductor; Zinka Milanov, Jussi Bjoerling, Fedora Barbieri, Leonard Warren, Boris Christoff; Rome Opera Chorus and Orchestra. Recorded 1955. RCA Victor Opera Series 66522 RG [ADD]; two discs.

Alzira. Franco Capuana, conductor; Virginia Zeani, Gianfranco Cecchele, Cornell MacNeil, Carlo Cava; Rome Opera Chorus and Orchestra. Melodram MEL 27013; two discs.

Alzira. Lamberto Gardelli, conductor; Ileana Cotrubas, Francisco Araiza, Renato Bruson; Munich Radio Orchestra. Orfeo 057832; two discs.

Aroldo. Eve Queler, conductor; Monserrat Caballé, Gianfranco Cecchele, Juan Pons, Louis Lebherz; Opera Orchestra of New York. CBS M2K 79328 [ADD]; two discs.

Attila. Lamberto Gardelli, conductor; Ruggero Raimondi, Cristina Deutekom, Carlo Bergonzi, Sherrill Milnes; Ambrosian Singers; Royal Philharmonic Orchestra. Philips 426 115 2; two discs.

Attila. Riccardo Muti, conductor; Samuel Ramey, Cheryl Studer, Neil Shicoff, Giorgio Zancanaro; Chorus and Orchestra of La Scala, Milan. EMI CDS 7 49952 2 [DDD]; two discs.

Un ballo in maschera. Claudio Abbado, conductor; Katia Ricciarelli, Placido Domingo, Edita Gruberova, Elena Obraztsova, Renato Bruson, Ruggero Raimondi; Chorus and Orchestra of La Scala, Milan. Deutsche Grammophon 415 685 2 [ADD]; two discs.

Un ballo in maschera. Erich Leinsdorf, conductor; Leontyne Price, Carlo Bergonzi, Robert Merrill, Shirley Verrett, Reri Grist, Ezio Flagello; RCA Italiana Chorus and Orchestra. RCA Victor Opera Series 66452 RG [ADD]; two discs.

Un ballo in maschera. Sir Georg Solti, conductor; Birgit Nilsson, Carlo Bergonzi, Sylvia Stahlmann, Giulietta Simionato, Cornell MacNeil, Tom Krause, Fernando Corena; Chorus and Orchestra of the Accademia di Santa Cecilia, Rome. Studio recording. London 425 655 2 [ADD]; two discs.

La battaglia di Legnano. Lamberto Gardelli, conductor; Katia Ricciarelli, José Carreras, Matteo Manuguerra, Nicola Ghiuselev, Ann Murray; ORF Symphony Orchestra and Chorus. Philips 422 435 2; two discs.

Il corsaro. Lamberto Gardelli, conductor; José Carreras, Jessye Norman, Monserrat Caballé, Clifford Grant, Gian-Piero Mastromei, John Noble; Ambrosian Singers; New Philharmonia Orchestra. Philips 426 118 2; two discs.

Don Carlo. Carlo Maria Giulini, conductor; Placido Domingo, Monserrat Caballé, Shirley Verrett, Sherrill Milnes, Ruggero Raimondi, Giovanni Foiani, Simon Estes; Chorus and Orchestra of the Royal Opera House, Covent Garden. EMI Angel 7 47701 8 [ADD]; three discs.

Don Carlo. Sir Georg Solti, conductor; Carlo Bergonzi, Renata Tebaldi, Grace Bumbry, Dietrich Fischer-Dieskau, Nicolai Ghiaurov, Martti Talvela; Chorus and Orchestra of the Royal Opera House, Covent Garden. London 421 114 2 [ADD]; three discs.

Don Carlos. Claudio Abbado, conductor; Placido Domingo, Katia Ricciarelli, Lucia Valentini Terrani, Leo Nucci, Ruggero Raimondi, Nicolai Ghiaurov; Chorus and Orchestra of La Scala, Milan. Deutsche Grammophon 415 316 2 [DDD]; four discs.

I due Foscari. Lamberto Gardelli, conductor; José Carreras, Katia Ricciarelli, Elizabeth Connell, Samuel Ramey, Piero Cappuccilli; Chor und Symphonieorchester des Oesterreichischen Rundfunks. Philips 422 426 2; two discs.

Ernani. Riccardo Muti, conductor; Placido Domingo, Mirella Freni, Renato Bruson, Nicolai Ghiaurov; Chorus and Orchestra of La Scala, Milan. Live performance, 1982. EMI CDS 7 47083 8 [DDD]; three discs.

Ernani. Thomas Schippers, conductor; Carlo Bergonzi, Leontyne Price, Mario Sereni; RCA Italiana Opera Chorus and Orchestra. RCA Victor Opera Series 65032 RG [ADD]; two discs.

Falstaff. Leonard Bernstein, conductor; Dietrich Fischer-Dieskau, Ilva Ligabue, Hilde Rössel-Majdan, Graziella Sciutti, Regina Resnik, Juan Oncina; Rolando Panerai; Chorus of the Vienna State Opera; Vienna Philharmonic. Studio recording, 1966. CBS M2K 42535 [ADD]; two discs.

Falstaff. Carlo Maria Giulini, conductor; Renato Bruson, Katia Ricciarelli, Barbara Hendricks, Lucia Valentini Terrani, Brenda Boozer, Dalmacio Gonzales, Leo Nucci; Los Angeles Master Chorale; Los Angeles Philharmonic. Studio recording, 1982. Deutsche Grammophon 410 503 2 [DDD]; two discs.

Falstaff. Sir Georg Solti, conductor; Sir Geraint Evans, Ilva Ligabue, Mirella Freni, Giulietta Simionato, Alfredo Kraus, Robert Merrill; RCA Italiana Opera Chorus and Orchestra. Studio recording, 1964. London 417 168 2 [ADD]; two discs.

Falstaff. Arturo Toscanini, conductor; Giuseppe Valdengo, Herva Nelli, Nan Merriman, Teresa Stich-Randall, Cloe Elmo, Antonio Madasi, Frank Guarrera; Robert Shaw Chorale; NBC Symphony Orchestra. Live NBC broadcast performances of 1 and 8 April 1950. RCA Victor Gold Seal 60251 2 RG "Arturo Toscanini Collection" Vol. 57 [monaural]; two discs.

La forza del destino. Francesco Molinari-Pradelli, conductor; Renata Tebaldi, Giulietta Simionato, Mario del Monaco, Ettore Bastianini, Cesare Siepi, Fernando Corena; Chorus and Orchestra of the Accademia di Santa Cecilia, Rome. London 421 598 2 [ADD]; three discs.

La forza del destino. Riccardo Muti, conductor; Mirella Freni, Placido Domingo, Dolora Zajick, Giorgio Zancanaro, Paul Plishka, Sesto Bruscantini; Chorus and Orchestra of La Scala, Milan. EMI CDS 7 47485 8 [DDD]; three discs.

La forza del destino. Thomas Schippers, conductor; Leontyne Price,

Shirley Verrett, Richard Tucker, Robert Merrill, Giorgio
Tozzi, Ezio Flagello, Piero da Palma; RCA Italiana Opera
Chorus and Orchestra. Studio recording, 1964. RCA 7971 2
RG [ADD]; three discs.

La forza del destino. Giuseppe Sinopoli, conductor; Rosalind
Plowright, Agnes Baltsa, José Carreras, Renato Bruson, Paata
Burchuladze, Juan Pons; Ambrosian Opera Chorus; Philharmonia Orchestra. Deutsche Grammophon 419 203 2 [DDD];
three discs.

Gerusalemme. Gianandrea Gavazzeni, conductor; Leyla Gencer,
Mirella Fiorentini, Giacomo Aragall, Emilio Salvodi, Gian
Giacomo Guelfi, Antonio Zerbini; Chorus and Orchestra of
Teatro La Fenice, Venice. Live performance, 24 September
1963. Melodram MEL 27004; two discs.

Un giorno di regno. Lamberto Gardelli, conductor; Jessye Norman,
Fiorenza Cossotto, José Carreras, Ingvar Wixell, Wladimiro
Ganzarolli; Ambrosian Singers; Royal Philharmonic Orches-
tra. Philips 422 429 2 [ADD]; two discs.

Giovanna d'Arco. James Levine, conductor; Monserrat Caballé,
Placido Domingo, Sherrill Milnes, Keith Erwen, Robert
Lloyd; Ambrosian Opera Chorus; London Symphony Orchestra. Studio recording, 1972. EMI CDMB 63226; two
discs.

Jérusalem. See *Gerusalemme*

Il lombardi alla prima crociata. Lamberto Gardelli, conductor;
Cristina Deutekom, Placido Domingo, Ruggero Raimondi,
Jerome Lo Monaco, Desdemona Malvisi; Ambrosian Singers;
Royal Philharmonic Orchestra. Philips 422 420 2 [ADD]; two
discs.

Luisa Miller. Fausto Cleva, conductor; Anna Moffo, Carlo
Bergonzi, Shirley Verrett, Cornell MacNeil, Giorgio Tozzi,
Ezio Flagello; RCA Italiana Opera Chorus and Orchestra.
RCA Victor Opera Series 66462 RG [ADD]; two discs.

Luisa Miller. Lorin Maazel, conductor; Katia Ricciarelli, Placido
Domingo, Elena Obraztsova, Renato Bruson, Gwynne How-
ell; Chorus and Orchestra of the Royal Opera House, Covent
Garden. Deutsche Grammophon 423 144 2 [ADD]; two discs.

Macbeth. Claudio Abbado, conductor; Piero Cappuccilli, Shirley
Verrett, Placido Domingo, Nicolai Ghiaurov; Chorus and Or-
chestra of La Scala, Milan. Deutsche Grammophon 415 688 2
[ADD]; three discs.

Macbeth. Erich Leinsdorf, conductor; Leonard Warren, Leonie Rysanek, Carlo Bergonzi, Jerome Hines, William Olvis; Metropolitan Opera Chorus and Orchestra. Studio recording, February 1959. RCA Victor Opera Series 45162 RG [ADD]; two discs.

Macbeth. Victor de Sabata, conductor; Maria Callas, Enzo Mascherini, Italo Tajo, Gino Penno; Chorus and Orchestra of La Scala, Milan. Live performance, 7 December 1952. Nuova Era 2202/3 [ADD]; two discs.

I masnadieri. Lamberto Gardelli, conductor; Monserrat Caballé, Carlo Bergonzi, Piero Cappuccilli, Ruggero Raimondi; Ambrosian Singers; New Philharmonia Orchestra. Philips 422 423 2; two discs.

Nabucco. Giuseppe Sinopoli, conductor; Piero Cappuccilli, Ghena Dmitrova, Placido Domingo, Evgeny Nesterenko, Lucia Valentini Terrani; Chor und Orchester der Deutschen Oper Berlin. Deutsche Grammophon 410 512 2 [DDD]; two discs.

Oberto. Lamberto Gardelli, conductor; Carlo Bergonzi, Ghena Dmitrova, Ruza Baldani, Rolando Panerai; Bavarian Radio Chorus; Munich Radio Orchestra. Orfeo CD 105842; two discs.

Otello. Wilhelm Furtwängler, conductor; Ramon Vinay, Dragica Martinis, Paul Schöffler, Anton Dermota; Chorus of the Vienna State Opera; Vienna Philharmonic Orchestra. Live performance, Salzburg 1951. Rodolphe RPC 32561/62; two discs.

Otello. Herbert von Karajan, conductor; Mario del Monaco, Renata Tebaldi, Aldo Protti; Vienna Philharmonic. London 411 618 [ADD]; two discs.

Otello. James Levine, conductor; Placido Domingo, Renata Scotto, Sherrill Milnes; National Philharmonic Chorus and Orchestra. RCA Victor RCD 22951 [ADD]; three discs.

Otello. Tullio Serafin, conductor; Jon Vickers, Leonie Rysanek, Tito Gobbi, Florindo Andreolli; Rome Opera Chorus and Orchestra. Studio recording, 1960. RCA Victor Opera Series 19692 RG [ADD]; two discs.

Rigoletto. Richard Bonynge, conductor; Sherrill Milnes, Joan Sutherland, Luciano Pavarotti, Huguette Tourangeau, Martti Talvela; London Symphony Orchestra. London 414 269 2 [ADD]; two discs.

Rigoletto. Riccardo Chailly, conductor; Leo Nucci, June Anderson, Shirley Verrett, Luciano Pavarotti, Nicolai Ghiaurov; Chorus

and Orchestra of Teatro Comunale, Bologna. London 425 864
2 [DDD]; two discs.

Rigoletto. Carlo Maria Giulini, conductor; Piero Cappuccilli, Ileana
Cotrubas, Placido Domingo, Elena Obraztsova, Nicolai Ghiaurov; Vienna State Opera Chorus; Vienna Philharmonic Orchestra. Deutsche Grammophon 415 288 2 [ADD]; two discs.

Rigoletto. Riccardo Muti, conductor; Giorgio Zancanaro, Daniela
Dessì, Vincenzo La Scola, Martha Senn, Paata Burchuladze;
Chorus and Orchestra of La Scala, Milan. EMI Angel CDS 7
49605 2 [DDD]; two discs.

Rigoletto. Tullio Serafin, conductor; Tito Gobbi, Maria Callas,
Giuseppe di Stefano, Adriana Lazzarini, Nicola Zaccaria; Cho-
rus and Orchestra of La Scala, Milan. Studio recording, 1955.
EMI Angel 47469; two discs.

Rigoletto. Giuseppe Sinopoli, conductor; Renato Bruson, Edita
Gruberova, Brigitte Fassbaender, Neil Shicoff, Robert Lloyd;
Chorus and Orchestra of the Accademia Nazionale di Santa
Cecilia. Philips 412 592 2 [DDD]; two discs.

Rigoletto. Sir Georg Solti, conductor; Robert Merrill, Anna Moffo,
Rosalind Elias, Alfredo Kraus, Ezio Flagello; RCA Italiana
Opera Chorus and Orchestra. RCA Victor Opera Series 65062
RG [ADD]; two discs.

Simon Boccanegra. Claudio Abbado, conductor; Piero Cappuccilli,
Mirella Freni, José Carreras, José van Dam, Nicolai Ghiaurov;
Chorus and Orchestra of La Scala, Milan. Deutsche Gram-
mophon 415 692 2 [ADD]; two discs.

Simon Boccanegra. Gianandrea Gavazzeni, conductor; Piero Cappuccilli, Katia Ricciarelli, Placido Domingo, Ruggero Raimondi; RCA Chorus and Orchestra. RCA RD 70729 [ADD];
two discs.

Simon Boccanegra. Sir Georg Solti, conductor; Leo Nucci, Kiri Te
Kanawa, Giacomo Aragall, Paata Burchuladze, Paolo Coni;
Chorus and Orchestra of La Scala, Milan. London 425 628 2
[DDD]; two discs.

Stiffelio. Lamberto Gardelli, conductor; José Carreras, Sylvia Sass,
Matteo Manuguerra, Wladimiro Ganzarolli; Chorus and Orchestra of the ORF, Vienna. Philips 422 432 2 [ADD]; two
discs.

La traviata. Richard Bonynge, conductor; Joan Sutherland, Luciano Pavarotti, Matteo Manuguerra; National Philharmonic
Orchestra. London 410 154 2 [DDD]; three discs.

La traviata. Carlos Kleiber, conductor; Ileana Cotrubas, Placido Domingo, Sherrill Milnes; Bayerischer Staatsopernchor; Bayerisches Staatsorchester. Deutsche Grammophon 415 132 2 [ADD]; two discs.

La traviata. Georges Prêtre, conductor; Monserrat Caballé, Carlo Bergonzi, Sherrill Milnes; RCA Italiana Opera Chorus and Orchestra. Studio recording, 1967. RCA 61802 RC [ADD]; two discs.

La traviata. Nicola Rescigno, conductor; Maria Callas, Cesare Valletti, Mario Zanasi, Marie Collier; Chorus and Orchestra of the Royal Opera House, Covent Garden. Live performance, 20 June 1958. Melodram MEL 26007; two discs.

Il trovatore. Richard Bonynge, conductor; Luciano Pavarotti, Joan Sutherland, Marilyn Horne, Ingvar Wixell, Nicolai Ghiaurov; London Opera Chorus; National Philharmonic Orchestra. London 417 137 2; two discs.

Il trovatore. Renato Cellini, conductor; Jussi Bjoerling, Zinka Milanov, Fedora Barbieri, Leonard Warren, Nicola Moscona; Robert Shaw Chorale; RCA Victor Orchestra. Studio recording, 1952. RCA Victor Opera Series 66432 RG [ADD]; two discs.

Il trovatore. Carlo Maria Giulini, conductor; Placido Domingo, Rosalind Plowright, Brigitte Fassbaender, Giorgio Zancanaro, Evgeny Nesterenko; Chorus and Orchestra of the Accademia Nazionale di Santa Cecilia. Deutsche Grammophon 423 858 2 [DDD]; two discs.

Il trovatore. Herbert von Karajan, conductor; Giuseppe di Stefano, Maria Callas, Fedora Barbieri, Rolando Panerai; Chorus and Orchestra of La Scala, Milan. Studio recording, 1956. EMI Angel 49347; two discs.

Il trovatore. Zubin Mehta, conductor; Placido Domingo, Leontyne Price, Fiorenza Cossotto, Sherrill Milnes, Bonaldo Giaiotti; Ambrosian Opera Chorus; New Philharmonia Orchestra. RCA 61942 RC [ADD]; two discs.

Il trovatore. Thomas Schippers, conductor; Franco Corelli, Gabriella Tucci, Giulietta Simionato, Robert Merrill; Chorus and Orchestra of the Rome Opera. EMI CMS 7 63640 2 [ADD]; two discs.

I vespri siciliani. James Levine, conductor; Martina Arroyo, Maria Ewing, Placido Domingo, Sherrill Milnes, Ruggero Raimondi, Leo Goeke; John Alldis Choir; New Philharmonia Orchestra.

Studio recording, 1973. RCA Victor 01832 RG [ADD]; three discs.

I vespri siciliani. Riccardo Muti, conductor; Cheryl Studer, Chris Merritt, Giorgio Zancanaro, Ferruccio Furlanetto; Chorus and Orchestra of La Scala, Milan. Live performances, 1989–90. EMI CDS 7 54043 2 [DDD]; three discs.

Wolf-Ferrari, Ermanno

Il segreto di Susanna. John Pritchard, conductor; Renata Scotto, Renato Bruson; Philharmonia Orchestra. CBS MK 36733 [DDD]; one disc.

Zandonai, Riccardo

Francesca da Rimini. Maurizio Arena, conductor; Raina Kabaivan-ska, William Matteuzzi, Matteo Manuguerra, Piero de Palma; Bulgarian Television and Radio Symphony Orchestra and Chorus. RCA RD 71456 [ADD]; two discs.

Francesca da Rimini. Nello Santi, conductor; Ilva Ligabue, Ruggero Bondino, Aldo Protti; Orchestra National. Rodolphe ROD 32492/3; two discs.

APPENDIX

Rossini, ca. 1860. Photo, Mayer & Pierson.

Main Characters

Abigaille (soprano): presumed daughter of Nabucco in Verdi's *Nabucco*.

Adalgisa (mezzo-soprano): Norma's confidante and rival in Bellini's *Norma*.

Adina (soprano): a wealthy young landowner in Donizetti's *L'elisir d'amore*.

Aida (soprano): an Ethiopian slave in Verdi's *Aida*.

Alfio (baritone): the village carter and Lola's husband in Mascagni's *Cavalleria rusticana*.

Alfonso XI (baritone): the King of Castile in Donizetti's *La favorita*.

Alfredo (tenor): Violetta's lover in Verdi's *La traviata*.

Alice (soprano): wife of Ford in Verdi's *Falstaff*.

Almaviva (tenor): a count, in love with Rosina in Rossini's *Il barbiere di Siviglia*.

Alvaro, Don (tenor): a nobleman of part-Inca lineage, in love with Leonora in Verdi's *La forza del destino*.

Amelia (soprano): wife of Anckarström in Verdi's *Un ballo in maschera*.

Amneris (mezzo-soprano): daughter of the King of Egypt in Verdi's *Aida*.

Amonasro (baritone): King of Ethiopia and Aida's father in Verdi's *Aida*.

Anckarström (baritone): husband of Amelia in Verdi's *Un ballo in maschera*.

Angelina (contralto): Cinderella in Rossini's *La Cenerentola*.

Azucena (mezzo-soprano): a gypsy woman in Verdi's *Il trovatore*.

Barnaba (baritone): a spy in Ponchielli's *La Gioconda*.

Basilio (basso buffo): a music master in Rossini's *Il barbiere di Siviglia*.

Belcore (baritone): a sergeant and Nemorino's rival in Donizetti's *L'elisir d'amore*.

Bartolo (basso buffo): Rosina's tutor in Rossini's *Il barbiere di Siviglia*.

Calaf (tenor): the exiled Prince of Tartary, in love with Turandot in Puccini's *Turandot*.

Canio (tenor): husband of Nedda in Leoncavallo's *I pagliacci*.

Carlo, Don (tenor): Spanish infante in Verdi's *Don Carlo*.

Carlo di Vargas, Don (baritone): brother of Leonora in Verdi's *La forza del destino*.

Cavaradossi, Mario (tenor): a painter, in love with Tosca in Puccini's *Tosca*.

Chenier (tenor): poet in Giordano's *Andrea Chenier*.

Cio-Cio-San (soprano): Butterfly in Puccini's *Madama Butterfly*.

Colline (bass): a philosopher in Puccini's *La boheme*.

Desdemona (soprano): wife of Otello in Rossini's and Verdi's *Otello*.

Des Grieux (tenor): in love with Manon in Puccini's *Manon Lescaut*.

Di Luna (baritone): a count, in love with Leonora in Verdi's *Il trovatore*.

Duke of Mantua (tenor): philandering nobleman in Verdi's *Rigoletto*.

Dulcamara (basso buffo): a quack cure-all vendor in Donizetti's *L'elisir d'amore*.

Eboli, Princess (mezzo-soprano): lady-in-waiting to Elisabetta in Verdi's *Don Carlo*.

Edgardo di Ravenswood (tenor): in love with Lucia in Donizetti's *Lucia di Lammermoor*.

Elisabetta (soprano): Princess of Valois and Queen of Spain in Verdi's *Don Carlo*.

Elvino (tenor): a Swiss farmer in Bellini's *La sonnambula*.

Elvira (soprano): daughter of Gualtiero Valton in Bellini's *I puritani*.

Elvira (soprano): a Spanish noblewoman in Verdi's *Ernani*.

Enrico Ashton (baritone): brother of Lucia in Donizetti's *Lucia di Lammermoor*.

Enzo Grimaldo (tenor): a Genoese nobleman, in love with Laura in Ponchielli's *La Gioconda*.

Ernesto (tenor): nephew of Don Pasquale, in love with Norina in Donizetti's *Don Pasquale*.

Falstaff (baritone): impecunious knight in Verdi's *Falstaff*.

Fenton (tenor): in love with Nannetta in Verdi's *Falstaff*.

Fiesco (bass): a Genoese nobleman in Verdi's *Simon Boccanegra*.

Figaro (baritone): town barber and factotum in Rossini's *Il barbiere di Siviglia*.

Filippo II (bass): Philip II, King of Spain, in Verdi's *Don Carlo*.

Fritz Kobus (tenor): rich Alsatian landowner in Mascagni's *L'amico Fritz*.

Ford (baritone): husband of Alice in Verdi's *Falstaff*.

Gennaro (tenor): a Venetian nobleman in Donizetti's *Lucrezia Borgia*.

Gérard (baritone): revolutionary leader and rival of Chénier in Giordano's *Andrea Chénier*.

Germont, Giorgio (baritone): father of Alfredo in Verdi's *La traviata*.

Gilda (soprano): daughter of Rigoletto in Verdi's *Rigoletto*.

Giorgetta (soprano): wife of Michele in Puccini's *Il tabarro*.

Gustavo III (tenor): King of Sweden in Verdi's *Un ballo in maschera*.

Isabella (contralto): a beautiful Italian woman in Rossini's *L'italiana in Algeri*.

Iago (baritone): Otello's ensign in Verdi's *Otello*.

Laura (soprano): Alvise's wife, in love with Enzo in Ponchielli's *La Gioconda*.

Leonora (mezzo-soprano): mistress of the King of Castile in Donizetti's *La favorita*.

Leonora (soprano): a lady-in-waiting to the Princess of Aragon, in love with Manrico in Verdi's *Il trovatore*.

Leonora (soprano): sister of Don Carlo, in love with Alvaro in Verdi's *La forza del destino*.

Lescaut (baritone): brother of Manon in Puccini's *Manon Lescaut*.

Lindoro (tenor): an Italian enslaved by the Mustafà, in love with Isabella in Rossini's *L'italiana in Algeri*.

Lola (mezzo-soprano): wife of Alfio in Mascagni's *Cavalleria rusticana*.

Liu (soprano): a slave girl, in love with Calaf in Puccini's *Turandot*.

Lucia (soprano): Enrico's sister, in love with Edgardo in Donizetti's *Lucia di Lammermoor*.

Lucrezia (soprano): Duchess of Ferrara and mother of Gennaro in Donizetti's *Lucrezia Borgia*.

Luigi (tenor): Giorgetta's lover in Puccini's *Il tabarro*.

Maddalena (mezzo-soprano): Sparafucile's sister in Verdi's *Rigoletto*.

Maddalena de Coigny (soprano): in love with Andrea Chénier in Giordano's *Andrea Chenier*.

Magda (soprano): Rambaldo's mistress in Puccini's *La rondine*.

Malatesta, Dr. (baritone): friend of Don Pasquale in Donizetti's *Don Pasquale*.

Manon (soprano): beautiful young French girl in Puccini's *Manon Lescaut*.

Manrico (tenor): supposed son of Azucena, in love with Leonora in Verdi's *Il trovatore*.

Marcello (baritone): a painter in Puccini's *La boheme*.

Marie (soprano): canteen-keeper and heroine of Donizetti's *La fille du regiment*.

Mefistofele (bass or bass-baritone): prince of darkness in Boito's *Mefistofele*.

Michele (baritone): Giorgetta's husband in Puccini's *Il tabarro*.

Mimi (soprano): a seamstress, in love with Rodolfo in Puccini's *La boheme*.

Minnie (soprano): keeper of the Polka Saloon in Puccini's *La fanciulla del West*.

Monterone (bass): a Mantuan nobleman in Verdi's *Rigoletto*.

Musetta (soprano): Marcello's sweetheart in Puccini's *La boheme*.

Mustafà (basso buffo): Bey of Algiers in Rossini's *L'italiana in Algeri*.

Nannetta (soprano): Ford's daughter in Verdi's *Falstaff*.

Nedda (soprano): Canio's wife in Leoncavallo's *I pagliacci*.

Nemorino (tenor): a young peasant, in love with Adina in Donizetti's *L'elisir d'amore*.

Norina (soprano): a young widow in Donizetti's *Don Pasquale*.

Norma (soprano): high priestess of the Druid temple in Bellini's *Norma*.

Oroveso (bass): high priest of the Druid temple in Bellini's *Norma*.

Oscar (soprano): page boy to Gustavo III in Verdi's *Un ballo in maschera*.

Otello (tenor): Moorish general in the Venetian army in Rossini's and Verdi's *Otello*.

Padre Guardiano (bass): Franciscan monk in Verdi's *La forza del destino*.

Pasquale, Don (bass): a rich, eccentric old bachelor in Donizetti's *Don Pasquale*.

Pinkerton, B. F. (tenor): U.S. Navy lieutenant in Puccini's *Madama Butterfly*.

Pollione (tenor): Roman proconsul and lover of Norma in Bellini's *Norma*.

Preziosilla (mezzo-soprano): a young gypsy in Verdi's *La forza del destino*.

Quickly, Mistress (mezzo-soprano): friend of Alice Ford's in Verdi's *Falstaff*.

Radames (tenor): an Egyptian army captain, in love with Aida in Verdi's *Aida*.

Ramfis (bass): high priest in Verdi's *Aida*.

Renato. See Anckarström

Riccardo. See Gustavo III

Rigoletto (baritone): sarcastic, hunchbacked court jester in Verdi's *Rigoletto*.

Rodolfo (tenor): a poet, in love with Mimi in Puccini's *La bohème*.
Rodrigo (baritone): Marquis of Posa in Verdi's *Don Carlo*.
Rosina (contralto or soprano): Bartolo's ward in Rossini's *Il barbiere di Siviglia*.
Ruggero (tenor): Magda's lover in Puccini's *La rondine*.
Santuzza (soprano): in love with Turiddu in Mascagni's *Cavalleria rusticana*.
Scarpia (baritone): Roman chief of police in Puccini's *Tosca*.
Sharpless (baritone): U.S. consul in Puccini's *Madama Butterfly*.
Silva, Don Ruy Gomez de (bass): grandee of Spain in Verdi's *Ernani*.
Silvio (baritone): Nedda's lover in Leoncavallo's *I pagliacci*.
Simon (baritone): privateer and later Doge of Genoa on Verdi's *Simon Boccanegra*.
Sparafucile (bass): a professional assassin in Verdi's *Rigoletto*.
Spoletta (tenor): a police agent in Puccini's *Tosca*.
Suzel (soprano): a peasant girl in Mascagni's *L'amico Fritz*.
Suzuki (mezzo-soprano): Butterfly's maid in Puccini's *Madama Butterfly*.
Tonio (baritone): an evil, hunchbacked clown in Leoncavallo's *I pagliacci*.
Tonio (tenor): a young Tyrolean, in love with Marie in Donizetti's *La fille du régiment*.
Tosca, Floria (soprano): celebrated singer in Puccini's *Tosca*.
Turandot (soprano): a Peking princess in Puccini's *Turandot*.
Turiddu (tenor): a young soldier, in love with Lola in Mascagni's *Cavalleria rusticana*.
Ulrica (mezzo-soprano): a fortune-teller in Verdi's *Un ballo in maschera*.
Violetta (soprano): a Parisian courtesan in Verdi's *La traviata*.
Zaccaria (bass): a Hebrew prophet in Verdi's *Nabucco*.

Maestro Ruggero Leoncavallo
(1857–1919)

Famous Melodies

Roman numerals indicate the act, arabic numerals indicate the scene or tableau. These are followed by the name of the character who sings the melody. Unless otherwise indicated, these are incipits from arias or ariosos.

"Addio del passato," Verdi, *La traviata* (III), Violetta

"Addio, fiorito asil," Puccini, *Madama Butterfly* (III), Pinkerton

"Ah, che la morte ognora." See Miserere

"Ah, fors'e lui," Verdi, *La traviata* (I), Violetta

"Ah Mathilde, idôle de mon âme," Rossini, *Guillaume Tell* (I), Arnold

"Ah, non credea mirarti," Bellini, *La sonnambula* (II), Amina

"Ah, non giunge," Bellini, *La sonnambula* (II), Amina

"Ah si, ben mio," Verdi, *Il trovatore* (III.2), Manrico

"Ai nostri monti," Verdi, *Il trovatore* (IV.2), Azucena

"Anch'io vorrei dormir." See Lamento di Federico

"Ardon gl'incensi" (Mad Scene), Donizetti, *Lucia di Lammermoor* (III.1), Lucia

"Bella figlia dell'amore," Verdi, *Rigoletto* (III), quartet (Duke, Gilda, Maddalena, Rigoletto)

"Bel raggio lusinghier," Rossini, *Semiramide* (I), Semiramide

"Caro nome," Verdi, *Rigoletto* (I.2), Gilda

"Casta diva," Bellini, *Norma* (I), Norma

"Celeste Aida," Verdi, *Aida* (I.1), Radames

"Chacun le sait, chacun le dit," Donizetti, *La fille du regiment* (I), Marie

"Che gelida manina," Puccini, *La boheme* (I), Rodolfo

"Ch'ella mi creda libero e lontano," Puccini, *La fanciulla del West* (III), Ramerrez [alias Dick Johnson]

"Chi mi frena," Donizetti, *Lucia di Lammermoor* (II), sextet

Chi   mi   fre-na in tal mo- men- to? Chi tron-cò del-l'i-re il cor-   so

"Cielo e mar," Ponchielli, *La Gioconda* (II), Enzo

Cie- lo   e   mar! l'e- te- rea___ ve- lo aplen-de co-me un santo altar

"Com'è gentil," Donizetti, *Don Pasquale* (III), Ernesto

Com' è gen-   til___   la not-te a mez- zo a- pril,___

"Come un bel dì di maggio," Giordano, *Andrea Chenier* (IV), Chenier

Come   un bel dì   di   mag- gio   che con bacio   di ven- to

"Credo," Verdi, *Otello* (II), Iago

Cre   -   do in un Dio cru - del   che m'ha cre - a- to si - mi-le a sè,

"D'amor sull'ali rosee," Verdi, *Il trovatore* (IV.1), Leonora

D'a- mor sull' a - - li ro- se - - - e   van- ne,sos-pir___ do- len - - - te;

"De' miei bollenti spiriti," Verdi, *La traviata* (II.1), Alfredo

De   miei bol- len- ti spi- ri- ti   il gio- va- ni- le ar- do - - re

"Di Provenza, il mar," Verdi, *La traviata* (II.1), Germont

Di Pro-   ven- za il mar, il suol chi dal   cor ti can-cel- lo

"Di quella pira," Verdi, *Il trovatore* (III.2), Manrico

Di quel- la   pi - - - - - ra   l'or- ren- do fo - - - - - co

"Di tanti palpiti," Rossini, *Tancredi* (I.5), Tancredi

Di tan-ti   pal - - pi- ti di - - - - - - tan-te je - - - - - ne

"Dite alla giovine," Verdi, *La traviata* (II.1), Violetta/Germont duet

Di- te al- la   gio - - - vi- ne   si bel- la e pu - - - ra,

"Donna non vidi mai," Puccini, *Manon Lescaut* (I), Des Grieux

Don- na non vi- di ma- i   si- mi-   le a que- sta!

"E lucevan le stelle." See "O dolci baci"

"Era la notte," Verdi, *Otello* (II), Iago

"Eri tu," Verdi, *Un ballo in maschera* (III.1), Anckarström (Renato)

"Ernani! Ernani involami," Verdi, *Ernani* (I.2), Elvira

"E scherzo od e follia," Verdi, *Un ballo in maschera* (I), Gustavo III (Riccardo)

"Guardate, pazzo son," Puccini, *Manon Lescaut* (III), Des Grieux

"Il balen del suo sorriso," Verdi, *Il trovatore* (II.2), Di Luna

"Il lacerato spirito," Verdi, *Simon Boccanegra* (Prologue), Fiesco

"Il mio sangue, la vita darei," Verdi, *Luisa Miller* (I), Miller

Il mio san-gue, la vi-ta da- re- i   per ve-der-lo fe- li-ce,

"In quelle trine morbide," Puccini, *Manon Lescaut* (II), Manon

In quel- le tri- ne _ mor- bi- de   nell'al- co- va do-ra- ta

"La donna e mobile," Verdi, *Rigoletto* (III), Duke of Mantua

La don- na è mo-   bi- le   qual piuma al   ven - - to,

"L'altra notte," Boito, *Mefistofele* (III), Margherita

L al- tra not- te in fon- do al ma- re   il mio bim- bo   han-no git-ta- to

"La mamma morta," Giordano, *Andrea Chénier* (III), Maddalena

La mam- ma mor- ta   m'hanno a la por-ta del-la stan- za mi- a; mo- ri- va

Lamento di Federico ("Anch'io vorrei dormir"), Cilèa, *L'arlesiana* (II), Federico

Anch' i- o vor- re- i   dor- mir   co- sì,____ nel son-no al- men

"La Vergine degli angeli," Verdi, *La forza del destino* (II.2), Leonora

La Ver- gi- ne de- gli an-ge-li   mi co- pra del   suo man- to,

"Largo al factotum," Rossini, *Il barbiere di Siviglia* (I.1), Figaro

"Libiamo, libiamo" (Brindisi), Verdi, *La traviata* (I), Alfredo/Violetta

"L'onore! Ladri!" Verdi, *Falstaff* (I.1), Falstaff

"Ma dall'arido stelo divulsa," Verdi, *Un ballo in maschera* (II), Amelia

"Madre, Madre, pietosa Vergine," Verdi, *La forza del destino* (II.2), Leonora

"Mercè, dilette amiche" (Bolero), Verdi, *I vespri siciliani* (V), Elena

"Mi chiamano Mimi," Puccini, *La boheme* (I), Mimi

"Mira, O Norma," Bellini, *Norma* (II.1), duet Adalgisa/Norma

Miserere: "Ah, che la morte ognora," Verdi, *Il trovatore* (IV.1), Manrico

Miserere: "Quel suon, quelle preci," Verdi, *Il trovatore* (IV.1), Leonora

"Nemico della patria," Giordano, *Andrea Chénier* (III), Gérard

"O cieli azzurri," Verdi, *Aida* (III), Aida

"O dolci baci, languide carezze," Puccini, *Tosca* (III), Cavaradossi

O dol-ci ba-ci, lan-gui-de ca- rez-ze, mentr' io fre-men-te

"O don fatale," Verdi, *Don Carlo* (III.1), Eboli

O don fa- ta- le, o don cru-del che in suo fu- ror___

"O luce di quest'anima," Donizetti, *Linda di Chamounix* (I), Linda

O lu-ce di quest' a --ni - ma de-li-zia a-mo-re e vi - -ta

"O Mimi, tu più non torni," Puccini, *La bohème* (IV), duet Rodolfo/
Marcello

O Mi-mi tu più non tor- ni o gior- ni___ bel- li,

"O mio Fernando," Donizetti, *La favorita* (III), Leonora

O mio Fer-nan - - - -do, del- la ter- ra il tro- no

"O patria mia." See "O cieli azzurri"

"O soave fanciulla," Puccini, *La bohème* (I), duet Rodolfo/Mimi

O so-a-ve fan-ciul- la,___ O dol-ce vi- so

"O terra addio," Verdi, *Aida* (IV.2), duet Radames/Aida

"O tu, Palermo," Verdi, *I vespri siciliani* (II), Procida

"O tu che in seno agli angeli," Verdi, *La forza del destino* (III.1), Alvaro

"Pace, pace, mio Dio," Verdi, *La forza del destino* (IV), Leonora

"Parigi, o cara," Verdi, *La traviata* (III), duet Alfredo/Violetta

"Pari siamo," Verdi, *Rigoletto* (I.2), Rigoletto

"Parmi veder le lagrime," Verdi, *Rigoletto* (II), Duke of Mantua

"Piangea cantando" (Willow Song), Verdi, *Otello* (IV), Desdemona

"Poveri fiori," Cilea, *Adriana Lecouvreur* (IV), Adriana

"Prendi, l'anel ti dono," Bellini, *La sonnambula* (I.1), Elvino

"Pura siccome un angelo," Verdi, *La traviata* (II.1), Germont

"Quand'ero paggio," Verdi, *Falstaff* (II.2), Falstaff

"Quando le sere al placido," Verdi, *Luisa Miller* (II.3), Rodolfo

"Quanto e bella," Donizetti, *L'elisir d'amore* (I), Nemorino

"Quel suon, quelle preci." See Miserere

"Questa o quella," Verdi, *Rigoletto* (I.1), Duke of Mantua

"Qui la voce" (Mad Scene), Bellini, *I puritani* (II.1), Elvira

"Recondita armonia," Puccini, *Tosca* (I), Cavaradossi

"Regnava nel silenzio," Donizetti, *Lucia di Lammermoor* (I.2), Lucia

"Ritorna vincitor," Verdi, *Aida* (I.1), Aida

"Sempre libera" (cabaletta of "Ah, fors'è lui"), Verdi, *La traviata* (I), Violetta

Sem- pre li- be- ra____ deg- g'i- o fol- leg- gia- re

"Senza mamma," Puccini, *Suor Angelica*, Suor Angelica

Sen- za mam- ma, o bim- bo, tu sei mor- to Le tue lab- bra

"Si, fui soldato," Giordano, *Andrea Chenier* (III), Chénier

Si, fui sol- da- to e glo-rioso af- fron- ta- to

"Si pel ciel," Verdi, *Otello* (II), duet Otello/Iago

Si pel ciel mar- mo- reo giu- ro! Per le at-tor- te fol- go- ri!

"Sola, perduta, abbandonata," Puccini, *Manon Lescaut* (IV), Manon

So- la, per- du-ta, ab- ban- do- na- ta,____ per- du- ta,

"Solenne in quest'ora," Verdi, *La forza del destino* (III.2), duet Alvaro/Carlo

So- len- ne in que- st'o-ra giu- rar- mi do- ve- te

"Son lo spirito che nega," Boito, *Mefistofele* (I), Mefistofele

"Son vergin vezzosa," Bellini, *I puritani* (I.3), Elvira

"Spirto gentil," Donizetti, *La favorita* (IV), Fernando

"Stride la vampa," Verdi, *Il trovatore* (II.1), Azucena

"Suicidio!" Ponchielli, *La Gioconda* (IV), Gioconda

"Suoni la tromba," Bellini, *I puritani* (II.1), duet Riccardo/Giorgio

"Tacea la notte placida," Verdi, *Il trovatore* (I.2), Leonora

"Tu che le vanita," Verdi, *Don Carlo* (IV), Elisabetta

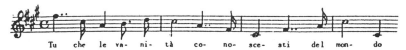

"Tutte le feste," Verdi, *Rigoletto* (II), Gilda

"Udite! udite! o rustici," Donizetti, *L'elisir d'amore* (I), Dulcamara

"Un bel dì, vedremo," Puccini, *Madama Butterfly* (II), Butterfly

"Una furtiva lagrima," Donizetti, *L'elisir d'amore* (II), Nemorino

"Una voce poco fa," Rossini, *Il barbiere di Siviglia* (I.2), Rosina

"Un dì all'azzurro spazio," Giordano, *Andrea Chénier* (I), Chenier

"Un dì felice," Verdi, *La traviata* (I), duet Alfredo/Violetta

Un dì fe-li- ce, e- te- re- a, mi ba- le- na-ste in-nan - - - - - te

"Va pensiero," Verdi, *Nabucco* (III.2), chorus of Hebrew slaves

Va pen- sie- ro sull' a- li do- ra - - - - - te:

"Vecchia zimarra," Puccini, *La boheme* (IV), Colline

Vec-chia zi- mar- ra, sen- ti, io re-sto al pian,tu a- scen- de-re il

"Verranno a te sull'aure," Donizetti, *Lucia di Lammermoor* (I.2), duet Edgardo/Lucia

Ver- ran- no a te sul l'a- u- re i miei so- spi-ri ar-den - - ti,

"Vesti la giubba," Leoncavallo, *I pagliacci* (I), Canio

Ve- sti la giub- ba e la fac- cia in fa- ri- na

"Vi ravviso," Bellini, *La sonnambula* (I.1), Rodolfo

Vi rav- vi- so O luoghi a- me - - - - - ni in cui lie- ti,

"Vissi d'arte," Puccini, *Tosca* (II), Tosca

Vis- si d'ar- te, vis- si d'a- mo- re, non fe-ci mai ma- le

"Voce di donna," Ponchielli, *La Gioconda* (I), La Cieca

Celebrated Singers

Albani, Emma (1847–1930)

Canadian soprano (née Marie Louise Cecilia Lajeunesse) who sang Oscar (*Un ballo in maschera*) in Messina in 1870, then in London and Paris in 1872. In 1878 she married Ernest Gye, the impresario of Covent Garden, and appeared almost every season thereafter in that house.

Alboni, Marietta (1826–1894)

Italian contralto who studied in Bologna and debuted there in 1842 in Pacini's *Saffo*. She created several Rossini roles and sang until her 1872 farewell performance at Paris's Théâtre-Italien.

Ancona, Mario (1860–1931)

Baritone who made his debut in Trieste in 1889 in Massenet's *Le roi de Lahore*. Active until 1916, he sang numerous roles by Verdi (Don Carlo in *Ernani*, Rigoletto, Amonasro, Iago, Rodrigo) and Puccini (Lescaut and Marcello).

Andrade, Francisco (1859–1921)

Portuguese baritone who studied in Milan and debuted as Amonasro in San Remo in 1881. He appeared in many European countries, particularly in Germany.

Anselmi, Giuseppe (1876–1929)

Italian tenor, violinist, and composer, particularly active after 1904. He debuted in 1896 as Turiddu in Athens and sang Cavaradossi, Maurizio, Edgardo, and Rodolfo.

Artot, Désirée (1835–1907)

Belgian mezzo-soprano, a student of Pauline Viardot-Garcia. She became established in Italy beginning in 1859 and later added soprano roles to her repertoire.

Barbieri-Nini, Marianna (1818–1887)

Italian soprano who made her debut in 1840 at La Scala in Donizetti's *Belisario* and sang many of that composer's roles before becoming famous in Verdi's works (as Lady Macbeth, Lucrezia in *I due Foscari*, Gulnara in *Il corsaro*). She retired from the stage in 1856.

Battistini, Mattia (1856–1928)

This Italian baritone sang for fifty years following his 1878 debut at Teatro Argentina in Rome. His success earned him the nicknames "Il re dei baritoni" and "La gloria d'Italia." His voice's wide range is captured in over one hundred recordings made between 1903 and 1924.

Bellincioni, Gemma (1864–1950)

Italian soprano who made her debut in Naples in 1879 and lived, from 1886 to 1897, with the famous tenor Roberto Stagno. An extraordinary actress, she was especially suited to verismo; she was the first Santuzza (*Cavalleria rusticana*, 1890) and the first Fedora (1898). She made fourteen recordings between 1903 and 1905.

Bonci, Alessandro (1870–1940)

Italian tenor who debuted in Parma in 1896, as Fenton. A rival of Caruso, his voice was lighter and had more agility; Rossini, Donizetti, and early Verdi suited him particularly well. He sang until the 1920s.

Boninsegna, Celestina (1877–1947)

Italian soprano who sang Norina at the age of fifteen in Reggio Emilia. Her rich voice was well suited to Verdi parts like Aïda, Amelia, and Leonora.

Borghi, Adelaide (1829–1901)

Mezzo-soprano whose 1843 debut took place in Urbino in *Il giuramento*. She was a protégée of G. Braga and retired from the stage in 1875.

Borghi-Mamo, Erminia (1855–1941)

Italian soprano, daughter of Adelaide Borghi. She made her debut in Nice in 1873, and two years later was Margherita in the revised version of Boito's *Mefistofele* in Bologna. She left the stage at age thirty-eight.

Bosio, Angiolina (1830–1859)

Soprano, debuted in Milan as Lucrezia in *I due Foscari* at the age of sixteen. After singing in Paris, New York, and London, she died suddenly in St. Petersburg at the age of twenty-eight.

Brambilla, Marietta (1807–1875)

Contralto who made her debut in London as Arsace in *Semiramide*. She played numerous trouser roles: Adriano in Meyerbeer's *Il crociato*, Romeo in Zingarelli's *Giulietta e Romeo*, Pippo in *La gazza ladra*. Donizetti wrote the parts of Orsini (*Lucrezia Borgia*, 1833) and Pierotto (*Linda di Chamounix*, 1842) for her. She retired from the stage in 1848.

Brambilla, Teresa (1813–1895)

Soprano, sister of Marietta Brambilla. She debuted in 1831 and was the first Gilda (1851).

Brambilla, Teresina (1845–1921)

Dramatic soprano, niece of Marietta and Teresa Brambilla. She made her debut in Odessa in 1863 and married Ponchielli in 1874. A famous Gioconda, she retired in 1889.

Caruso, Enrico (1873–1921)

Italian tenor who debuted in Naples in 1894 and made his first sensation three years later in *La Gioconda*. He was the first Maurizio (*Adriana Lecouvreur*, 1902) and the first Loris (*Fedora*, 1898). He sang on the stage until 1920. His impeccable intonation, admirable breath control, and the brilliance of his high register, combined with a great warmth of expression, justify his fame, documented in many books and even films (*Enrico Caruso: Leggenda di una voce*, *The Great Caruso*).

Colbran, Isabella (1785–1845)

Spanish contralto who began singing in Paris in 1801 and appeared in public for the first time in Italy in 1807. She created the roles of Elisabetta (1815), Desdemona (1816), and Semiramide (1823) in operas by Rossini, whom she married in 1822. They were legally separated in 1837.

Cotogni, Antonio (1831–1918)

After singing in churches, this Italian dramatic baritone earned fame in the opera house in 1852. He sang in more than 150 works, including many nineteenth-century Italian scores for which his aristocratic and velvety tone was so well suited. One of his greatest successes was as Rodrigo in *Don Carlo*.

Cruvelli, Sophie (1826–1907)

German soprano (née Jeanne Sophie Charlotte Crüwell) who debuted in Venice as Odabella (*Attila*) in 1847 and who was well suited temperamentally to play Verdi heroines. She created the character of Hélène in the Paris premiere of *Les vêpres siciliennes* (1855) and retired the following year, after her marriage to Baron Vigier.

Delle Sedie, Enrico (1822–1907)

Italian baritone who debuted in San Casciano in *Nabucco* in 1851 and earned success in Paris in *Un ballo in maschera* in 1861. His vocal limitations caused him to be nicknamed "Il baritono senza voce." He was a professor at the Paris Conservatory from 1867 to 1871 and acquired a well-deserved reputation as a teacher.

De Luca, Giuseppe (1876–1950)

This Italian baritone, whose diction was exceptionally clear, debuted in Piacenza in 1897 as Valentin and participated in the premieres of many operas, including *Adriana Lecouvreur* (1902), *Siberia* (1903), and *Madama Butterfly* (1904). He made numerous recordings.

De Lucia, Fernando (1860–1925)

Italian tenor whose first public appearance took place in 1885 at Teatro San Carlo in Naples. He became celebrated for his many verismo roles and created the title role of *L'amico Fritz* in 1891. He also took part in the premieres of Mascagni's *I Rantzau* (1892) and *Iris* (1898). He retired from the stage in 1917 and left some four hundred recordings.

De Marchi, Emilio (1861–1917)

Italian tenor who made his debut at Milan's Teatro dal Verme in 1886 and first appeared at La Scala in 1898. He created the role of Cavaradossi in *Tosca* (1900) and repeated it for his 1902 Metropolitan Opera debut.

Donzelli, Domenico (1790–1873)

Italian tenor who first appeared on the opera stage at the age of eighteen. He was the first Torvaldo in Rossini's *Torvaldo e Dorliska* (1815) and the first Pollione, at La Scala in 1831. He interpreted numerous Donizetti roles and achieved an outstanding success in Mercadante's *Il bravo* (1839) before retiring from the stage in 1844.

Fancelli, Giuseppe (1833–1888)

Success came to this Italian tenor at La Scala in 1866, but despite the promise of his rich voice, his career fell short. Insufficient musical training and his shortcomings as an actor held him back.

Ferrani, Cesira (1863–1943)

Italian soprano whose debut took place in Turin in 1887 in the role of Micaela. In 1893 she was Puccini's first Manon, and in 1896, his first Mimi. She was also the first Italian Mélisande in 1908, the year before her retirement.

Figner, Medea (1859–1952)

Italian mezzo-soprano (née Zoraide Amedea Mei) and later soprano, who debuted as Azucena while still in her teens. She married the Russian tenor Nicolai Figner and settled in St. Petersburg in the late 1880s. In 1930 she emigrated to France.

Frezzolini, Erminia (1818–1884)

Daughter of the basso buffo Giuseppe Frezzolini, this Italian soprano debuted in Florence in 1838 in *Beatrice di Tenda*. She was the first Viclinda (*I lombardi alla prima crociata*, 1843) and also took part in the premiere of *Giovanna d'Arco* (1845). Verdi is said to have admired her so much that he removed his hat whenever he uttered her name. From 1841 to 1845, she was married to the tenor Antonio Poggi; she later remarried and ended her career in Paris, where she became a voice teacher.

Gardoni, Italo (1821–1882)

Italian tenor whose 1840 debut took place in Viadana in *Roberto Devereux*. He sang extensively in London and was particularly distinguished for his Rossini roles.

Graziani, Francesco (1828–1901)

Italian baritone whose 1851 debut took place in Ascoli Pisceno in *Gemma di Vergy*. He appeared extensively in Paris (1853–61) and London (after 1855); he sang until 1880, achieving his greatest success in Verdi roles. According to some, he had the most beautiful baritone voice of the nineteenth century, though little acting ability.

Graziani, Lodovico (1820–1885)

Brother of Francesco Graziani, this Italian tenor made his debut in Bologna in 1845. He was the first Alfredo in *La traviata* (1853) and took part in the 1865 Italian premiere of Meyerbeer's *L'africana* in Bologna.

Grisi, Giuditta (1805–1840)

Italian mezzo-soprano who debuted in Vienna in 1826 as Falliero in Rossini's *Bianca e Falliero*. She excelled in the music of Bellini, who expressed a special affection for her, and retired from the stage in 1838.

Grisi, Giulia (1811–1869)

Sister of Giuditta Grisi, this Italian soprano debuted in Bologna in 1828. She was the first Adalgisa in *Norma* (1831) and appeared extensively abroad, notably in Paris (beginning in 1832) and London (after 1834). She retired in 1861.

Malibran, Maria (1808–1836)

Daughter of Manuel Garcia, one of the most famous tenors of

the time, this dramatic soprano made her 1825 debut in London as Rosina in *Il barbiere di Siviglia*. From 1828 to 1832, she was applauded in Paris for her Rossini roles, and she subsequently sang in Bologna, Naples, and Milan.

Marchisio, Barbara (1833–1919)

Italian contralto who debuted in Vicenza as Adalgisa in 1856. She sang until 1876. Toti Dal Monte was her pupil.

Marchisio, Carlotta (1835–1872)

Sister of Barbara Marchisio, this Italian soprano debuted in Madrid as Norma in 1856. She often sang with her sister.

Mario, Giovanni Matteo, Cavaliere de Candia (1810–1883)

Italian tenor who debuted at the Paris Opéra in 1838 in the title role of *Robert le diable*. In London the next year, he was Gennaro to Giulia Grisi's Lucrezia, and the two remained intimate for twenty-two years thereafter. Mario, as he was professionally known, sang mainly in Paris and London. His stage appearances ended in 1873.

Masini, Angelo (1844–1926)

Italian tenor with a tremendously agile voice who debuted in Finale Emilia as Pollione in 1867. He turned down the role of Fenton in the first *Falstaff* but sang many other different parts, from Rossini to Wagner. He ended his career in Paris in 1905 and made more than twenty recordings in the 1920s.

Mei-Figner, Medea. See Figner, Medea

Mongini, Pietro (1830–1874)

Italian tenor who made his stage debut in 1853 and was the first Radames in *Aida* (Cairo, 1871).

Moriani, Napoleone (1808–1878)

The "tenor of the beautiful death scene" debuted in Paris in 1833 and excelled in Donizetti roles. He left the stage in 1851.

Nantier-Didiée, Constance (1831–1867)

French mezzo-soprano, a pupil of Duprez, whose 1850 debut took place in Turin in Mercadante's *Vestale*. She created the role of Preziosilla in *La forza del destino* (1862).

Naudin, Emilio (1823–1890)

Son of a French painter, this Italian tenor made his 1843 debut in Cremona in Pacini's *Saffo*. He achieved his greatest success in the roles of Edgardo (*Lucia*) and the Duke of Mantua (*Rigoletto*). After singing extensively in London and Paris, he retired in 1885.

Navarrini, Francesco (1855–1923)

Italian bass who debuted in Treviso as Alfonso in *Lucrezia Borgia*. In 1887 he was the first Lodovico in Verdi's *Otello*. Among his favorite roles were Silva (in *Ernani*) and Alvise (*La Gioconda*).

Nicolini, Ernesto (1834–1898)

French tenor (né Ernest Nicolas) who debuted at the Paris Opera-Comique in 1857 and first appeared at La Scala two years later, in *La traviata*. He was Rodrigo in Rossini's *Otello* and was admired for his acting ability. He married Patti in 1886, the year he ended his operatic career.

Nourrit, Adolphe (1802–1839)

French tenor and gifted actor who debuted in Paris in 1821. Some of the roles he created there were Néocles (*Le siège de Corinthe*, 1826), Robert le diable (1831), and Arnold (*Guillaume Tell*, 1829). He went to Italy in 1837 to work with Donizetti. He sang in Naples in Mercadante's *Giuramento* and a few months later committed suicide.

Novello, Clara (1818–1908)

British soprano who made her 1841 debut in Italy, in *Semiramide*. She sang extensively in England until 1861.

Pacini, Giuseppe (1862–1910)

Italian baritone who made his debut in Florence in 1887. He

achieved great success when he created the role of Douglas in Mascagni's *Guglielmo Ratcliff* at La Scala in 1895. He also sang Barnaba, Di Luna, Amonasro, Enrico, and Tonio (*Pagliacci*).

Pancani, Emilio (1830–1898)

Italian tenor who debuted in Florence as a member of the chorus. He was noticed for his solo abilities in 1851 and in 1856 achieved fame as Rossini's Otello in Milan. He was also a distinguished Manrico.

Pandolfini, Francesco (1838–1916)

Italian baritone who made his debut in Pisa in 1859 and was particularly noted for his Verdi roles.

Pantaleoni, Romilda (1847–1917)

Italian soprano enthusiastically applauded at her debut in Carcano in 1856. She had great success three years later in the role of Margherita in *Mefistofele* and created the role of Desdemona in Verdi's *Otello* at La Scala in 1887. Conductor Franco Faccio was her lover.

Pasqua, Giuseppina (1855–1930)

Italian mezzo-soprano who made her stage debut at the age of fourteen. She created the role of Dame Quickly in *Falstaff* and earned praise for her Eboli, Azucena, and Amneris.

Pasta, Giuditta (1797–1865)

Italian soprano who made her debut in Milan in 1815. She sang extensively abroad, notably the roles of Anna Bolena and Amina (*La sonnambula*), which she created. She was also the first Norma (1831) and the first Beatrice di Tenda (1833). Considered the finest soprano in Europe, she had a genuine influence on Bellini's vocal style.

Patierno, Antonio (1839–1908)

Italian tenor, popular between 1870 and 1886. He was one of the last tenors to have a work like Donizetti's *Belisario* in his repertoire.

Patierno, Filippo (1835–1877)

Brother of Antonio Patierno, this Italian tenor became known in the early 1860s and achieved great success in *Aida*.

Patti, Adelina (1843–1919)

Italian soprano born in Madrid and brought up in New York, she made her debut as Lucia at New York's Academy of Music in 1859. She made a sensation in *La traviata* at La Scala in 1877 and continued to sing in benefit concerts as late as 1914. Her voice, pure and flexible, was considered the most beautiful since the era of Angelica Catalani.

Penco, Rosina (1823–1894)

Italian soprano who made her debut in the late 1840s. She acquired fame at the premiere of *Il trovatore* (1853) and notably appeared in *Lucrezia Borgia*, *Poliuto*, *Norma*, and *Un ballo in maschera*.

Persiani, Fanny (1812–1867)

Italian soprano (nee Tacchinardi) who achieved recognition in Livorno in 1832. In 1835, *Lucia di Lammermoor* was composed for her; she was the idol of Paris in the 1840s. Her blond hair made her look like a Raphael Madonna; she had a crystal-clear voice of moderate size. In 1830 she married the composer Giuseppe Persiani.

Piccolomini, Marietta (1834–1899)

Beautiful Italian dramatic soprano whose career was launched in Florence in 1852 (*Lucrezia Borgia*). She sang in England from 1856 until she retired in 1863.

Pini-Corsi, Antonio (1858–1918)

Italian baritone whose career began in Cremona in 1878 as Dandini in *La Cenerentola*. While he specialized at first in works by Rossini and Donizetti, he also created the role of Ford in Verdi's *Falstaff* (1893) and Schaunard in Puccini's *Bohème* (1896).

Pozzoni, Antonietta (1846–1914)

Starting out as a soprano, she debuted at La Scala in *Faust* in

1865 and created the role of Aida in 1871. From 1881, she sang mezzo roles, including Azucena. She retired in 1887.

Ronconi, Giorgio (1810–1890)

Italian baritone, a favorite of Donizetti, who debuted in Pavia in 1831 and was the first Nabucco at La Scala (1842). He sang extensively in England as well. While his range was somewhat limited, he possessed great dramatic flair.

Rubini, Giovanni Battista (1794–1854)

The "king of Italian tenors" debuted in Pavia in 1814 and led a glorious career in Italy until the late 1820s in a variety of works, creating the tenor leads in many Bellini and Donizetti operas. In 1825 he had a great success in Paris at the Théâtre-Italien. He retired in 1845.

Sammarco, Mario (1868–1930)

Italian baritone whose debut took place in Palermo in 1888. He first appeared at La Scala in 1896 and created the role of Gérard in *Andrea Chénier*. He also sang in Russia, South America, and the United States. After 1919, he devoted his time to teaching.

Sasse, Marie (1838–1907)

Belgian soprano who made her debut at the Paris Théâtre-Lyrique in 1859. Known professionally as Marie Sax in the early 1860s, she was applauded in Italy in 1869. She created the role of Elisabeth de Valois in *Don Carlos* (1867), but later Verdi declined to offer her the role of Amneris.

Scalchi, Sofia (1850–1922)

Italian mezzo-soprano who debuted in Mantua in 1866. She was successful as Pierotto (*Linda di Chamounix*), Orsini (*Lucrezia Borgia*), Arsace (*Semiramide*), Maddalena (*Rigoletto*), Ulrica, and Azucena.

Scotti, Antonio (1866–1936)

Italian baritone who debuted in Naples in 1889 and became

famous in England and America for his roles in *I pagliacci*, *Tosca*, *La bohème*, and *Madama Butterfly*.

Shaw, Mary (1814–1876)

British contralto (née Postans) who debuted at La Scala in *Oberto* in 1839. Her subsequent career was carried out for the most part in England.

Singer, Teresina (1850–1928)

Moravian soprano who traveled to Italy in 1873. She was a noted Aida at La Scala and, beginning in 1889, sang mezzo roles.

Stehle, Adelina (1865–1945)

Bohemian soprano whose Italian debut took place in 1881. After 1888 she became famous for the roles she created in *La Wally*, *I pagliacci*, and *Falstaff* (Nannetta). She also appeared memorably with her husband, the tenor Edoardo Garbin, in *La boheme* and *Fedora*.

Stoltz, Rosine (1815–1903)

French mezzo-soprano (née Victoire Noël) who sang mostly in Paris. She created the role of Léonore in *La favorite* (1840).

Stolz, Teresa (1834–1902)

Bohemian soprano whose first Italian appearances occurred in 1863. She was the first Elisabetta in the Italian premiere of *Don Carlo* (1867) and the first Aida on Italian soil (1872). Intimately involved with the conductor Mariani until 1871, she was to become the inseparable companion of Verdi after the death of his wife Giuseppina Strepponi.

Storchio, Rosina (1876–1945)

Italian soprano who debuted in Milan in 1892 and first sang at La Scala in 1895. She had great success in the roles of Nedda and Mimi. Her relatively light voice lent itself perfectly to Puccini and Massenet.

Strepponi, Giuseppina (1815–1897)

Italian soprano who debuted in Trieste in 1835. She sang the leading soprano part in Verdi's *Oberto* (1839) and created Abigaille in his *Nabucco* (1842). After her liaison with the tenor Moriani, she retired from the stage in 1846 and married Verdi in 1859.

Tamagno, Francesco (1850–1905)

Italian tenor who began his career in 1870 and first sang at La Scala in 1877. He created the role of Azael in Ponchielli's *Il figliuol prodigo* and was Verdi's first Otello. He was considered the greatest *tenore di forza* of his day.

Tamberlick, Enrico (1829–1889)

The debut of this Italian tenor took place in 1841 in *I Capuleti e i Montecchi* (Rome). He created the role of Alvaro in *La forza del destino* and became especially famous for his appearances in *Otello* (Rossini), *Poliuto*, *Norma*, and *Il trovatore*. His voice had incomparable presence and a beautiful high C.

Tamburini, Antonio (1800–1876)

Italian baritone who debuted in his own country in 1818 but left the peninsula in 1832 to appear mainly in France and England. He became most popular in *Marino Faliero*, *I puritani*, and *Don Pasquale*.

Varesi, Felice (1813–1889)

Italian baritone who made his debut in Varese in 1834 and created the roles of Macbeth, Rigoletto, and Germont.

Celebrated Conductors

Campanini, Cleofonte (1860–1919)

This violinist began his conducting career directing *Carmen* at Parma's Teatro Regio in 1882. He conducted the premieres of *Adriana Lecouvreur* (1902), *Siberia* (1903), and *Madama Butterfly* (1904). For the centenary of Verdi's birth, he mounted a cycle of the composer's operas in Parma.

Faccio, Franco (1840–1891)

Friend of Boito, he was also a pianist and composer of operas: *I profughi fiamminghi* (Milan premiere, 1863), *Amleto* (Genoa premiere, 1865). He led the Italian premiere of *Aida* (1872), the first *Gioconda* (1876), the revised version of *Simon Boccanegra* (1881), and the premiere of Verdi's *Otello* (1887). The first great modern opera conductor, he appeared with the orchestra of La Scala at the Paris International Exhibition of 1878.

Mancinelli, Luigi (1848–1921)

This cellist and composer first conducted in Perugia in 1874. From there he went on to Rome's Teatro Apollo (1874–81), Bayreuth (1889), and New York (1893). Boito considered this Wagnerite the ideal conductor for his *Mefistofele*.

Mariani, Angelo (1821–1873)

This composer and violinist, who replaced the traditional bow with the conductor's baton, made his conducting debut in Messina in 1844. He directed *I due Foscari* in Milan in 1846 and Genoa's San Felice orchestra in 1852; he directed in Bologna beginning in 1860. He conducted the Italian premieres of *Lohengrin* (1871) and *Tannhäuser* (1872). The first modern conductor, he was closely associated with Verdi until 1869.

Mascheroni, Edoardo (1859–1941)

He made his debut in Brescia in 1880 and later conducted at Rome's Teatro Apollo (1885–92) and La Scala. He conducted the premieres of *La Wally* (1892) and *Falstaff* (1893). Verdi called him "the third author of *Falstaff*." He retired in 1925.

Mugnone, Leopoldo (1858–1941)

Conductor at Teatro Costanzi in Rome beginning in 1888, he conducted the premieres of *Cavalleria rusticana* (1890) and *Tosca* (1900). He began directing at La Scala in 1891. Sir Thomas Beecham considered him the best Italian opera conductor of his day.

Polacco, Giorgio (1875–1960)

He debuted in London in 1893 and led the premiere of *Zazà* (1900) in Milan.

Pome, Alessandro (1851–1934)

He made his debut in 1874 and led the premiere of *Manon Lescaut* (1893) at Teatro Regio in Turin.

Toscanini, Arturo (1867–1957)

This cellist made his unscheduled debut in 1886 as a substitute conductor and from then on had great success on the podium. The premieres he directed include *I pagliacci* (1892) in Milan and *La bohème* (1896) in Turin. He conducted the orchestra of La Scala from 1898 to 1902.

Principal Librettists

Tottola, Andrea Leone (d. 1831)

For Rossini: *Mose in Egitto, Ermione, Eduardo e Cristina, La donna del lago, Zelmira.*
For Donizetti: *La zingara, Il fortunato inganno, Alfredo il Grande, Il castello di Kenilworth, Imelda de'Lambertazzi.*
For Bellini: *Adelson e Salvini.*
For Pacini: *Alessandro nelle Indie, L'ultimo giorno di Pompei.*

Rossi, Gaetano (1774–1855)

For Rossini: *La cambiale di matrimonio, La scala di seta, Tancredi, Semiramide.*
For Donizetti: *Maria Padilla, Linda di Chamounix.*
For Mercadante: *Il giuramento, Il bravo.*

Romani, Felice (1788–1865)

For Rossini: *Il turco in Italia, Aureliano in Palmira, Bianca e Falliero.*
For Bellini: *Bianca e Fernando, Il pirata, La straniera, Zaira, I Capuleti e i Montecchi, La sonnambula, Norma, Beatrice di Tenda.*
For Donizetti: *Lucrezia Borgia, L'elisir d'amore.*

Cammarano, Salvatore (1801–1852)

For Donizetti: *Lucia di Lammermoor, L'assedio di Calais, Belisario, Roberto Devereux, Maria de Rudenz, Poliuto, Maria di Rohan.*
For Verdi: *Alzira, La battaglia di Legnano, Luisa Miller, Il trovatore* (with E. Bardare).

Piave, Francesco Maria (1810–1876)

For Verdi: *Ernani, I due Foscari, Macbeth, Il corsaro, Rigoletto, La traviata, Simon Boccanegra* (first version), *La forza del destino.*

Solera, Temistocle (1815–1878)

For Verdi: *Oberto, Nabucco, I lombardi alla prima crociata, Giovanna d'Arco, Attila.*

Ghislanzoni, Antonio (1824–1893)

For Verdi: *La forza del destino* (1869 reworking), *Aida*.

Boito, Arrigo (1842–1918)

For himself: *Mefistofele*, *Nerone*.
For Ponchielli: *La Gioconda*.
For Verdi: *Simon Boccanegra* (second version), *Otello*, *Falstaff*.

Illica, Luigi (1857–1919)

For Catalani: *La Wally*.
For Giordano: *Andrea Chénier*.
For Mascagni: *Iris*.
For Puccini (with G. Giacosa): *Manon Lescaut*, *La bohème*, *Tosca*,
   Madama Butterfly.

Giuseppe Verdi (1813–1901).
Caricature by Gédéon.

"Il gran vegliardo,"
Verdi ca. 1900.
Photo, D. R.

NOTE ON ITALIAN PRONUNCIATION

a	"ah" as in mama
e	"eh" as in red
i	"ee" as in ski
o	"oh" as in open
u	"oo" as in soon
ci	"chee" as in Medici
ce	"cheh" as in chess
chi	"kee" as in chianti
che	"keh" as in kettle
gi	"gee" as in Gina
ge	"jeh" as in jelly
gh	(before e and i) "gh" as in go
gl	(before e and i, except at the beginning of a word, when it is pronounced as it is spelled) the "lli" in million
gn	"nya" as in lasagna
sc	(before e and i) "shh" as in luscious
r	rolled at the tip of the tongue
z	pronounced "ts" as in pizza or "dz" as in lends

There are no letters J, K, W, X, and Y; diphthongs; or nasals. H is always silent. The primary stress is most often on the next-to-last syllable of a word. When it does fall on the last syllable, it is indicated by a grave accent: Zazà, metà, papà.

Giuseppe Verdi.
Caricature by Dalsani.

GLOSSARY

aria (fem.; plural, *arie*): an extended vocal solo in opera generally
    providing a moment of intense lyricism.

arioso: a vocal passage that is more melodic than recitative and less
    lyrical than an aria.

basso cantante: a term still used in the nineteenth century for bari-
    tone.

bel canto: literally, "beautiful singing"; a style of singing character-
    ized by vocal flexibility and virtuosity, practiced in the seven-
    teenth and eighteenth centuries. It reached its peak in Naples
    at the time of Alessandro Scarlatti and the castratos. Gluck was
    one of the first to react against the style, which rapidly declined
    after 1850. In the late nineteenth century it was used to de-
    scribe the style of those singers who still practiced the eight-
    eenth-century techniques and remained unaffected by the
    verismo trend.

bozzetto: sketch.

cabaletta: the short, brilliant concluding movement of an extended
    aria or duet, often repeated, and usually occurring after a
    slower cavatina.

canto fiorito: a florid style of singing; melody adorned with *fioriture*,
    or ornaments.

canto spianato: calm, sustained singing; lyrical expression without
    many ornaments, cultivated by Bellini.

cavatina: the diminutive of *cavata*, a short *arioso* occurring after a recitative in the eighteenth century, this was usually a short entrance solo, less animated and simpler in form than a formal aria, e.g., "Una voce poco fa" in *Il barbiere di Siviglia*.

comprimario: a singer of a secondary role in an opera, e.g., Wurm or Federica in *Luisa Miller*.

contralto: the lowest female voice, generally encompassing a range from G to E″.

cupa (*voce*): deep, dark voice.

falsettista. See *tenorino*

farsa: farce.

filo di voce: sung in one breath, very softly.

libretto: the printed book of the words or text of an opera.

loggione: large balcony; the upper gallery of an Italian opera house.

maestro al cembalo: the name for the musician who conducted from the harpsichord, accompanying the recitatives in opera from the baroque era until the early nineteenth century.

melodramma: a drama which is sung throughout, i.e., opera.

mezzo-soprano: female vocal range lying between soprano and contralto, normally extending from A to A″.

opera buffa: a comic opera, generally sung throughout.

opera semi-seria: an opera whose subject is less dramatic than an *opera seria*.

palchettisti: holders of boxes (*palchi*) in Italian opera houses.

pezzo chiuso: a "closed piece," structurally still in A-B-A form; arias that can be easily sung out of context.

platea: orchestra-level seating in an Italian opera house.

prima donna: leading female role.

primo uomo: leading male role.

recitativo: recitative.

recitativo secco: dry recitative, accompanied by keyboard and often close to speech.

scapigliatura, scapigliati: the "disheveled ones"; avant-garde literary circle and its adherents that flourished in Milan during the second half of the nineteenth century.

scenografia: staging.

scritturato: engaged or commissioned by contract.

tenorino: "little tenor"; light, clear-toned tenor, singing frequently in falsetto, hence the alternate term, *falsettista*. In the seventeenth and eighteenth centuries, these singers were also called *alti naturali* (natural altos) to distinguish them from castratos.

voce di petto: chest voice.

INDEX OF
MUSICAL EXAMPLES

Arranged alphabetically according to composer and opera, and then according to position within the work. Roman numerals indicate the act in which the excerpt appears.

Mme Héricléa-Darclée as Mascagni's Iris
(Felicetti plate, Rome). In *Le Théâtre* 15,
1899, 21.

INDEX OF OPERAS

The titles of works are followed by an English translation (when deemed appropriate) and the name of the composer.

INDEX OF NAMES

The statue of Puccini in Torre del Lago.

	1790	1800	1810	1820	1830	1840

Rossini (1792–1868) ——————— 1810 —— 1829 ———————

Mercadante (1795–1870) ——————— 1819 ————————————

Pacini (1796–1867) ——————— 1813 ————————————

Donizetti (1797–1848) ——————— 1818 —— 1843 —

Bellini (1801–1835) ——————— 1825 — 1835

Verdi (1813–1901) ——————— 1839 ■

Pedrotti (1817–1893) ——————— 1840 ■

Ponchielli (1834–1886) ———

Boito (1842–1918) —

Catalani (1854–1893)

Smareglia (1854–1929)

Puccini (1858–1924)

Leoncavallo (1858–1919)

Mascagni (1863–1945)

Cilèa (1866–1950)

Giordano (1867–1948)